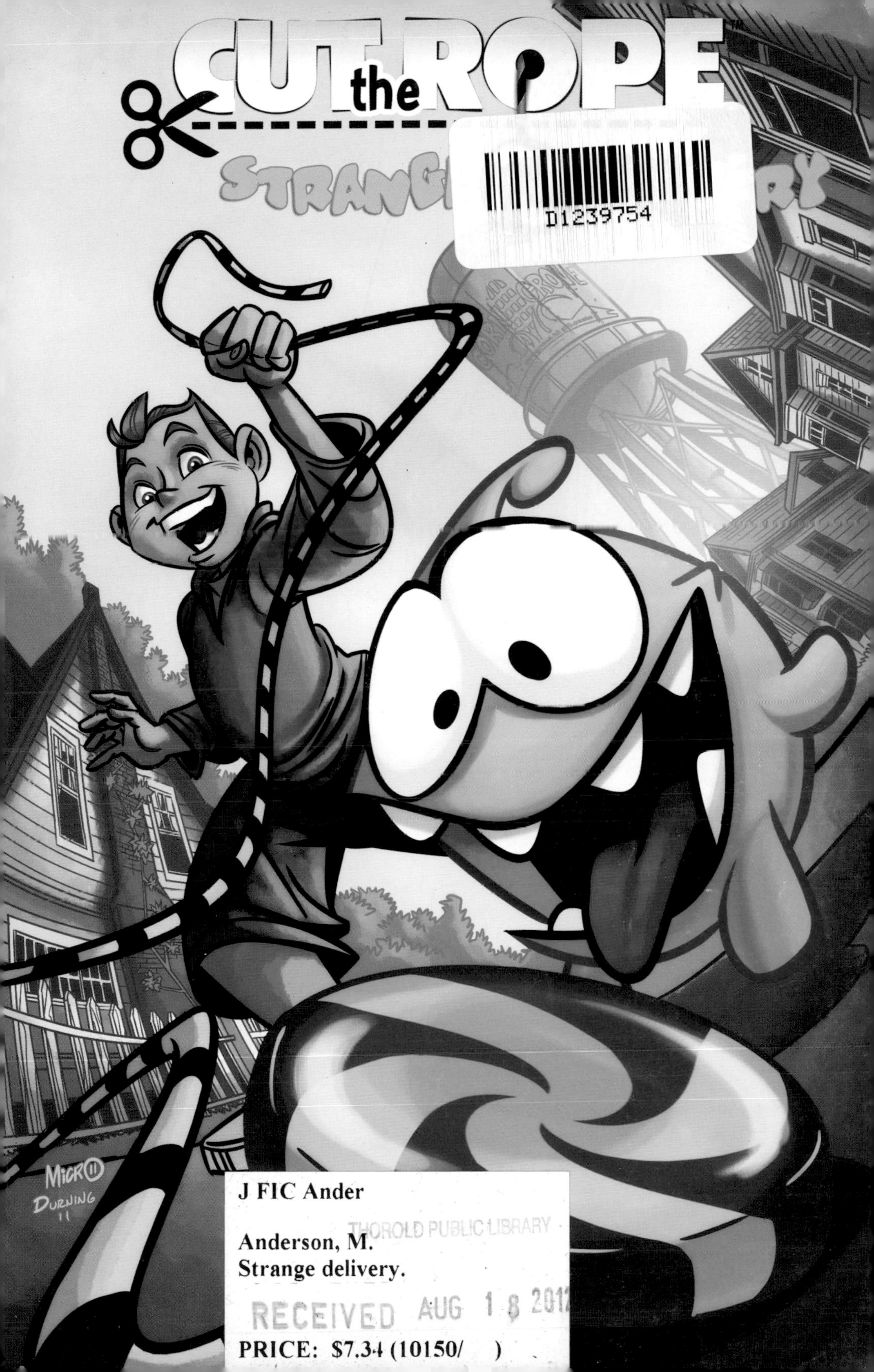
CUT the ROPE™
MICRO 11
DURNING 11

CUT the ROPE

FOR APE ENTERTAINMENT

David Hedgecock
CEO | Partner
DHedgecock@Ape-Entertainment.com

Brent E. Erwin
COO | Partner
BErwin@Ape-Entertainment.com

Aaron Sparrow
Editor
ASparrow@Ape-Entertainment.com

Weldon Adams
Editor
WAdams@Ape-Entertainment.com

Kevin Freeman
Editor | Special Projects
KFreeman@Ape-Entertainment.com

Ryan Davis
Graphic Design
RDavis@Ape-Entertainment.com

Company Information:
Ape Entertainment
P.O. Box 212344
Chula Vista, CA 91921

For Advertising contact:
The Bonfire Agency
Ed Cato
ed.cato@bonfireagency.com
917.595.4107

APE DIGITAL COMIC SITE:
Apecomics.com
Apecmx.com

TWITTER:
Twitter.com/ApeComics
Twitter.com/cut_the_rope

FACEBOOK:
Facebook.com/pages/ApeEntertainment
Facebook.com/cuttherope

YOUTUBE:
Youtube.com/user/ApeComics

Download the Cut The Rope
Comics App now and get each
issue as it becomes available
on your favorite iOS device!

Let us know what you think!
OmNom@Ape-Entertainment.com

STRANGE DELIVERY

WRITTEN BY:
MATT ANDERSON

ART BY:
RICARDO GARCIA AND
ANTONIO ALFARO

COLORS BY:
TIM DURNING

LETTERS BY:
DERON BENNETT

EDITS BY:
DAVID HEDGECOCK

COVER BY:
JAMES NELMS

ADDITIONAL DESIGN BY: DAVID HEDGECOCK AND BRENT
ERWIN

SPECIAL THANKS TO:
SEMYON VOINOV AND THE ENTIRE ZEPTOLAB TEAM!

zeptolab

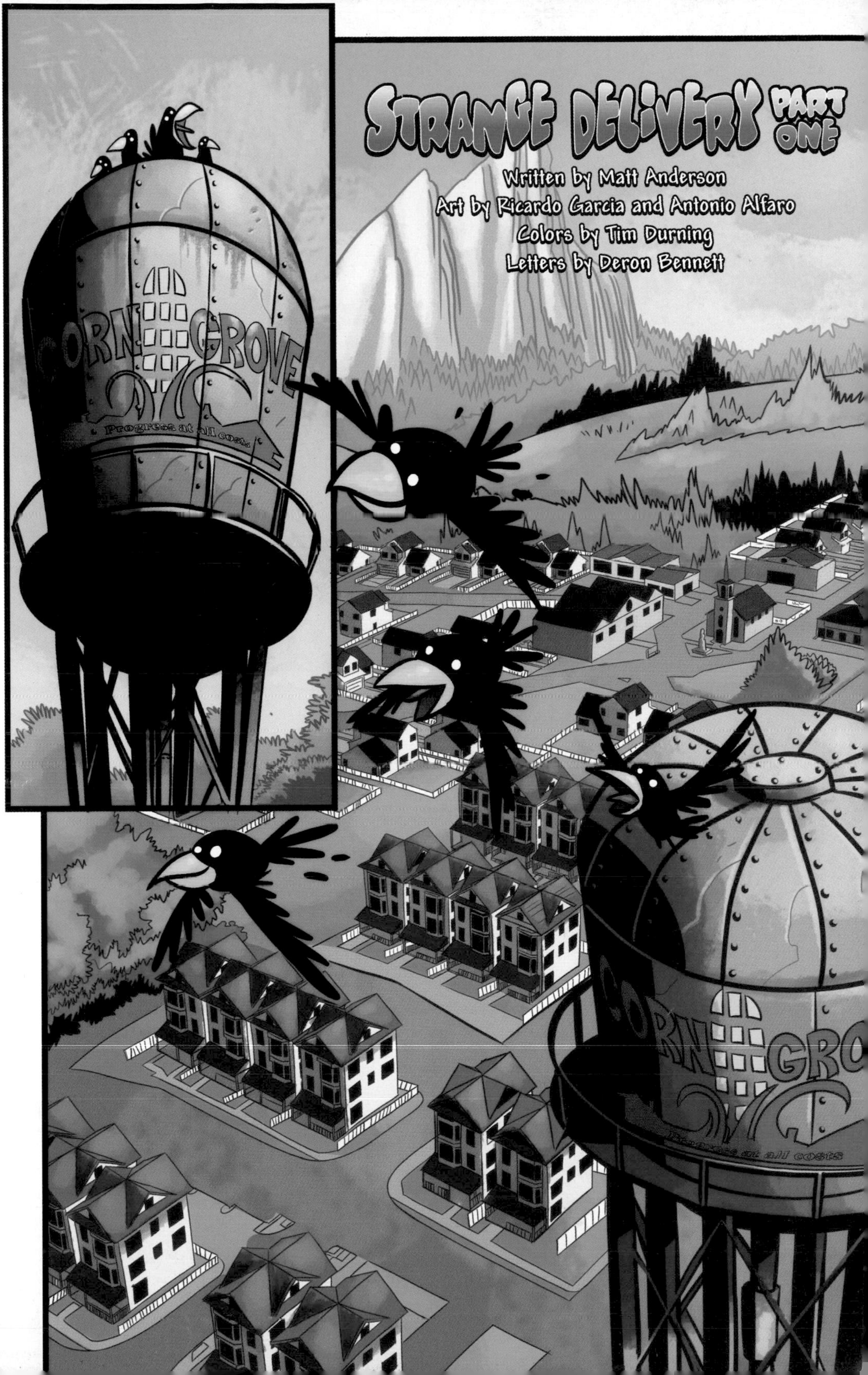
STRANGE DELIVERY PART ONE
Written by Matt Anderson
Art by Ricardo Garcia and Antonio Alfaro
Colors by Tim Durning
Letters by Deron Bennett
CORN GROVE
Progress at all costs
CORN GRO
Progress at all costs

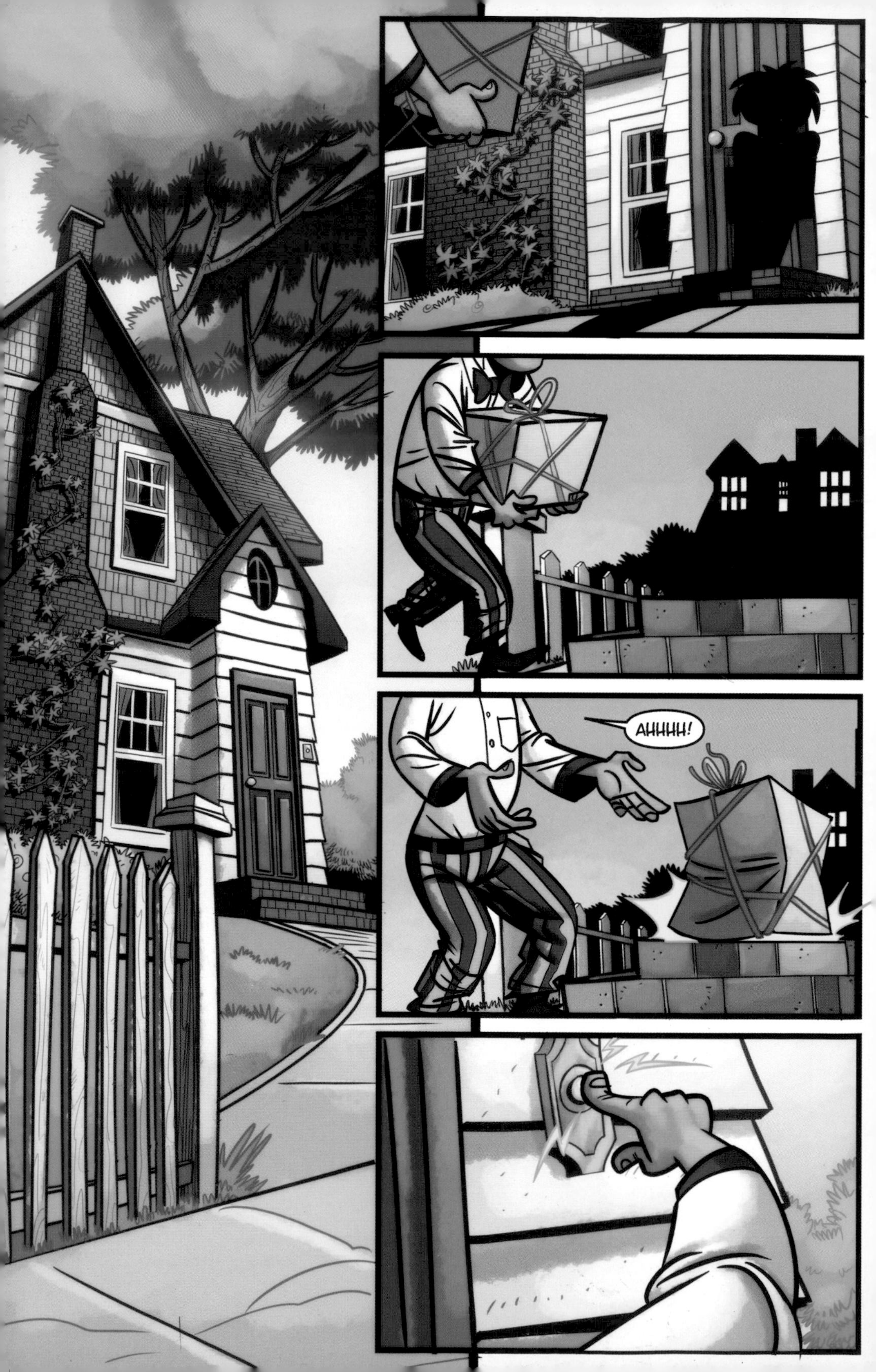
AHHHH!

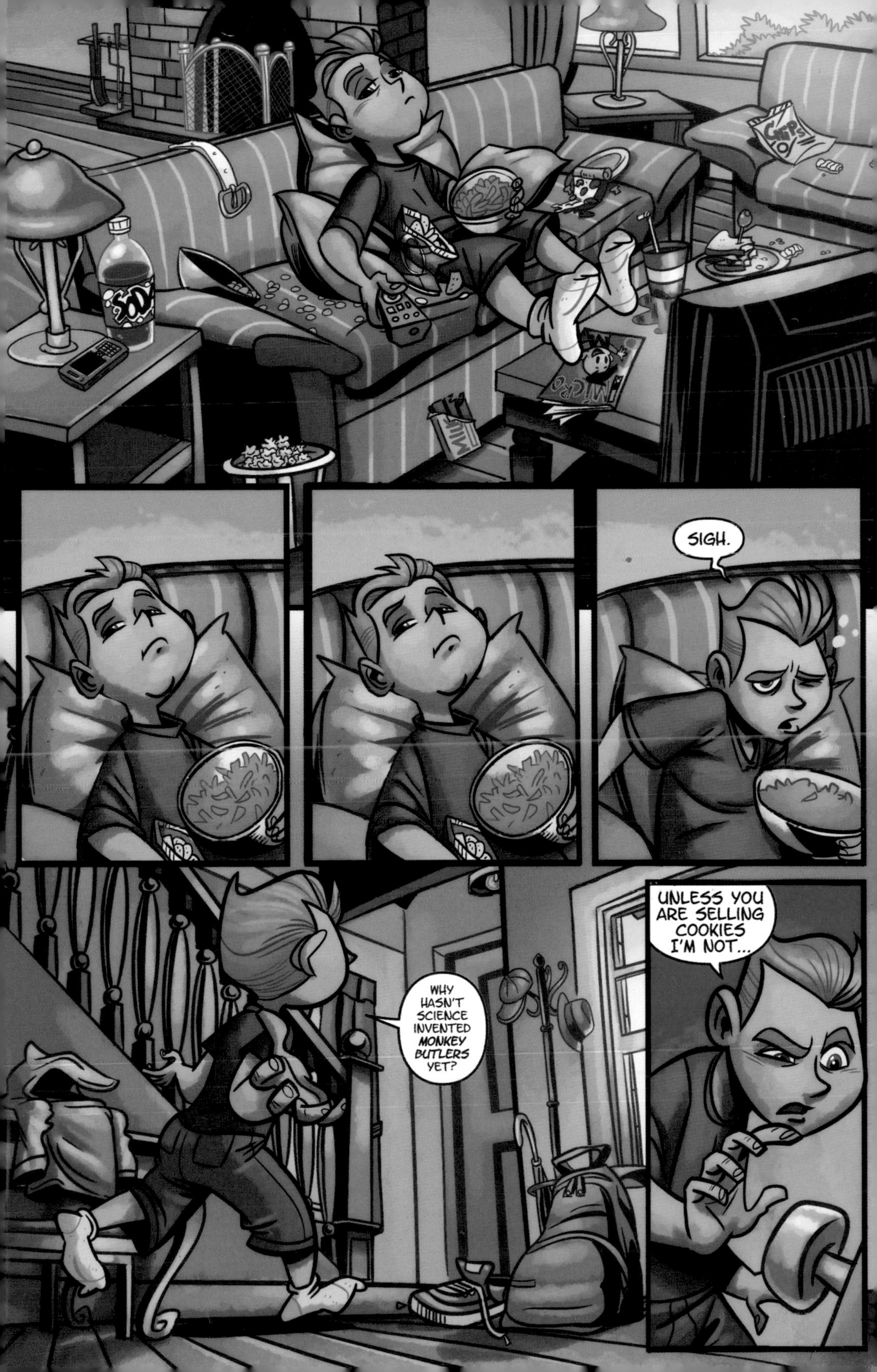
SODA
CHIPS
MILK
SIGH.
WHY HASN'T SCIENCE INVENTED MONKEY BUTLERS YET?
UNLESS YOU ARE SELLING COOKIES I'M NOT...

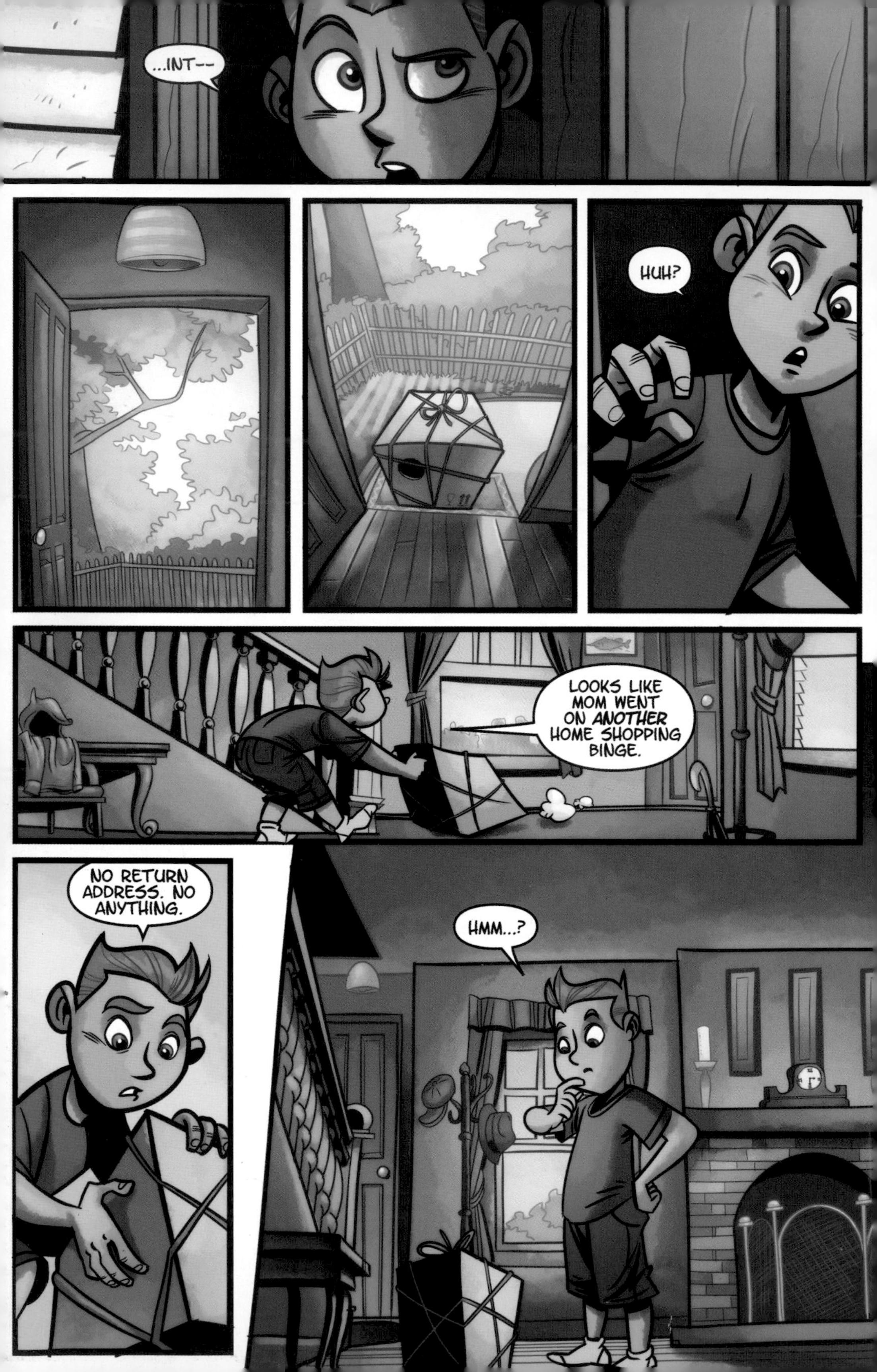
...INT--
HUH?
LOOKS LIKE MOM WENT ON ANOTHER HOME SHOPPING BINGE.
NO RETURN ADDRESS. NO ANYTHING.
HMM...?

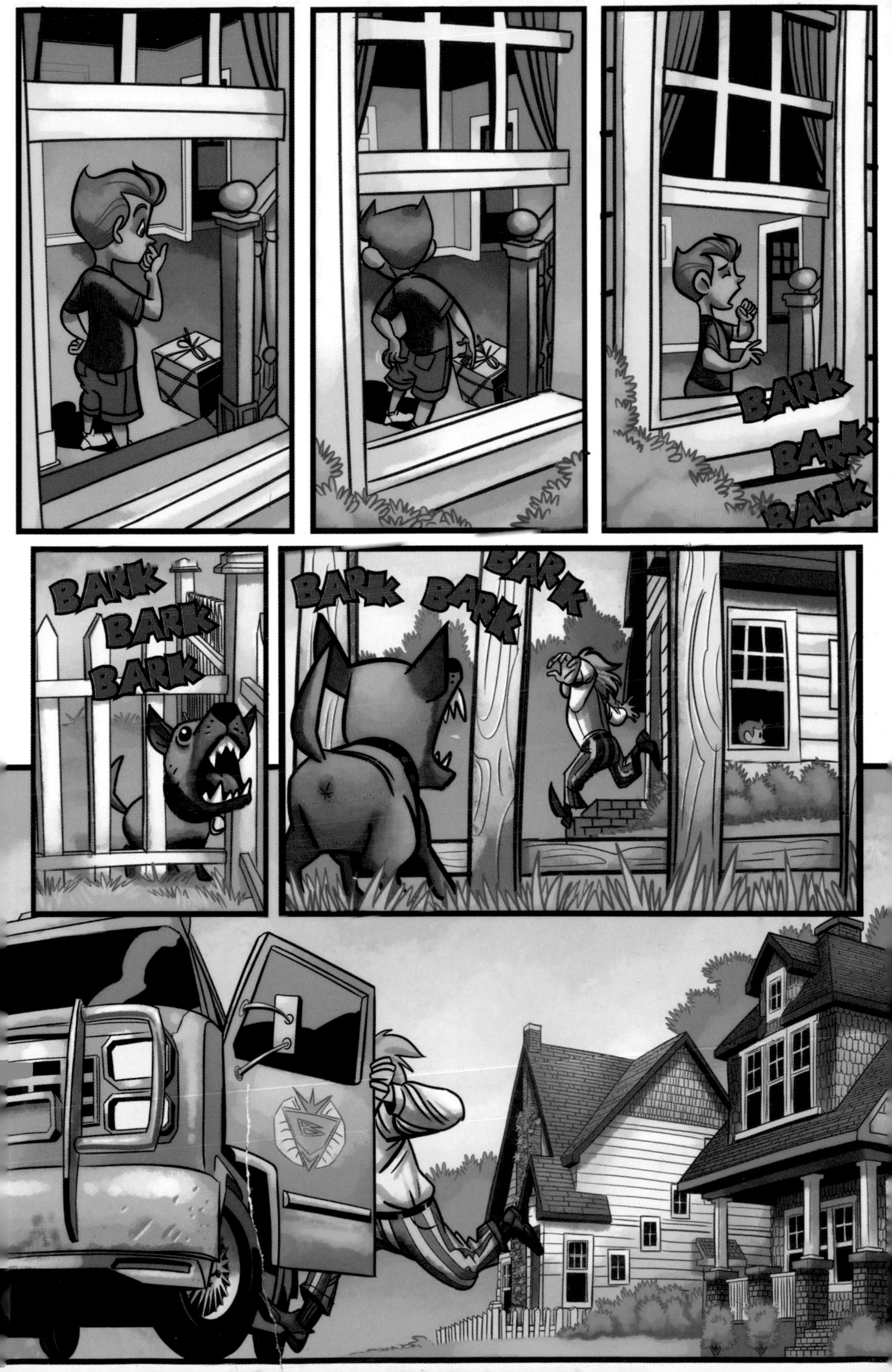
BARK
BARK
BARK
BARK
BARK
BARK
BARK
BARK
BARK

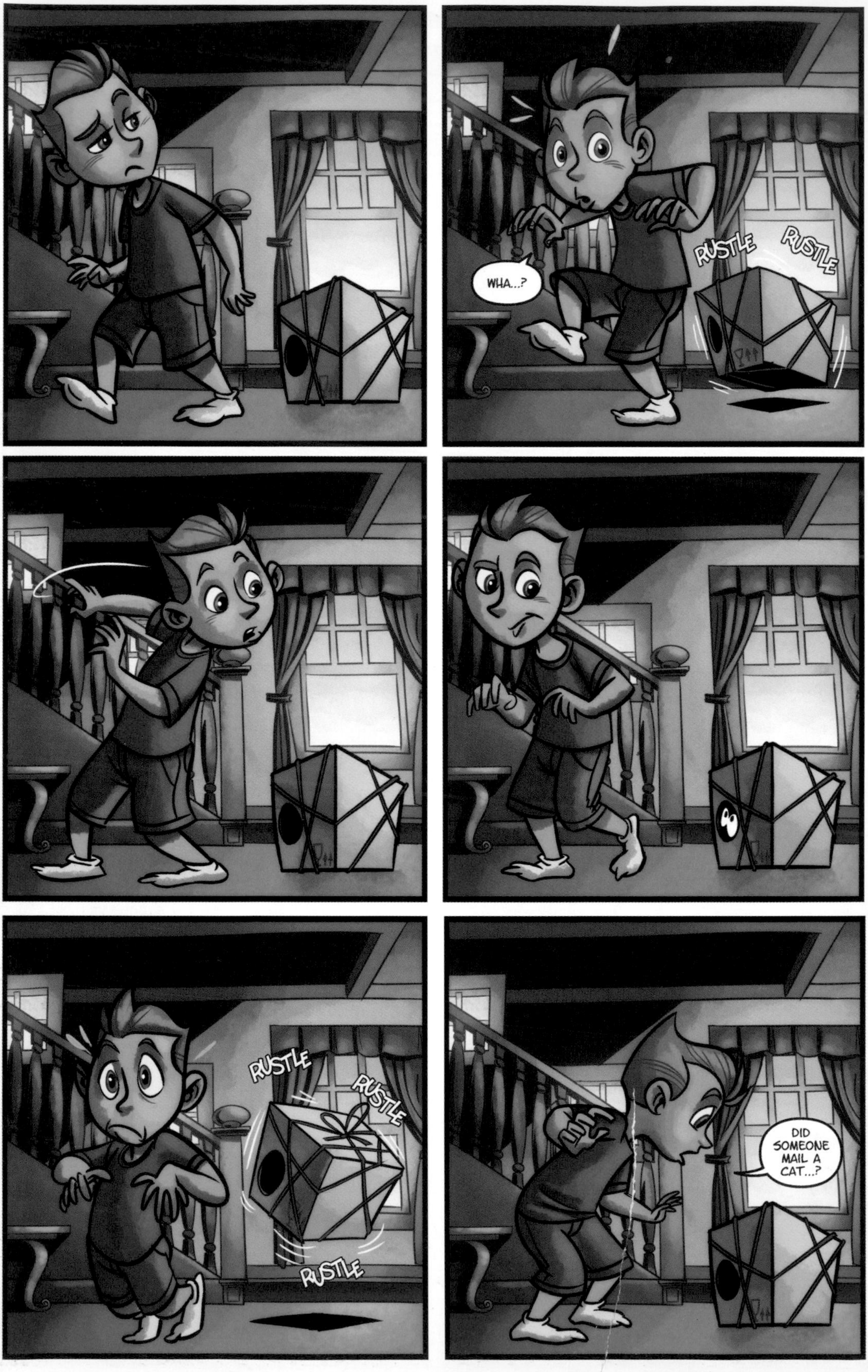
WHA...?
RUSTLE
RUSTLE
RUSTLE
RUSTLE
RUSTLE
DID SOMEONE MAIL A CAT...?

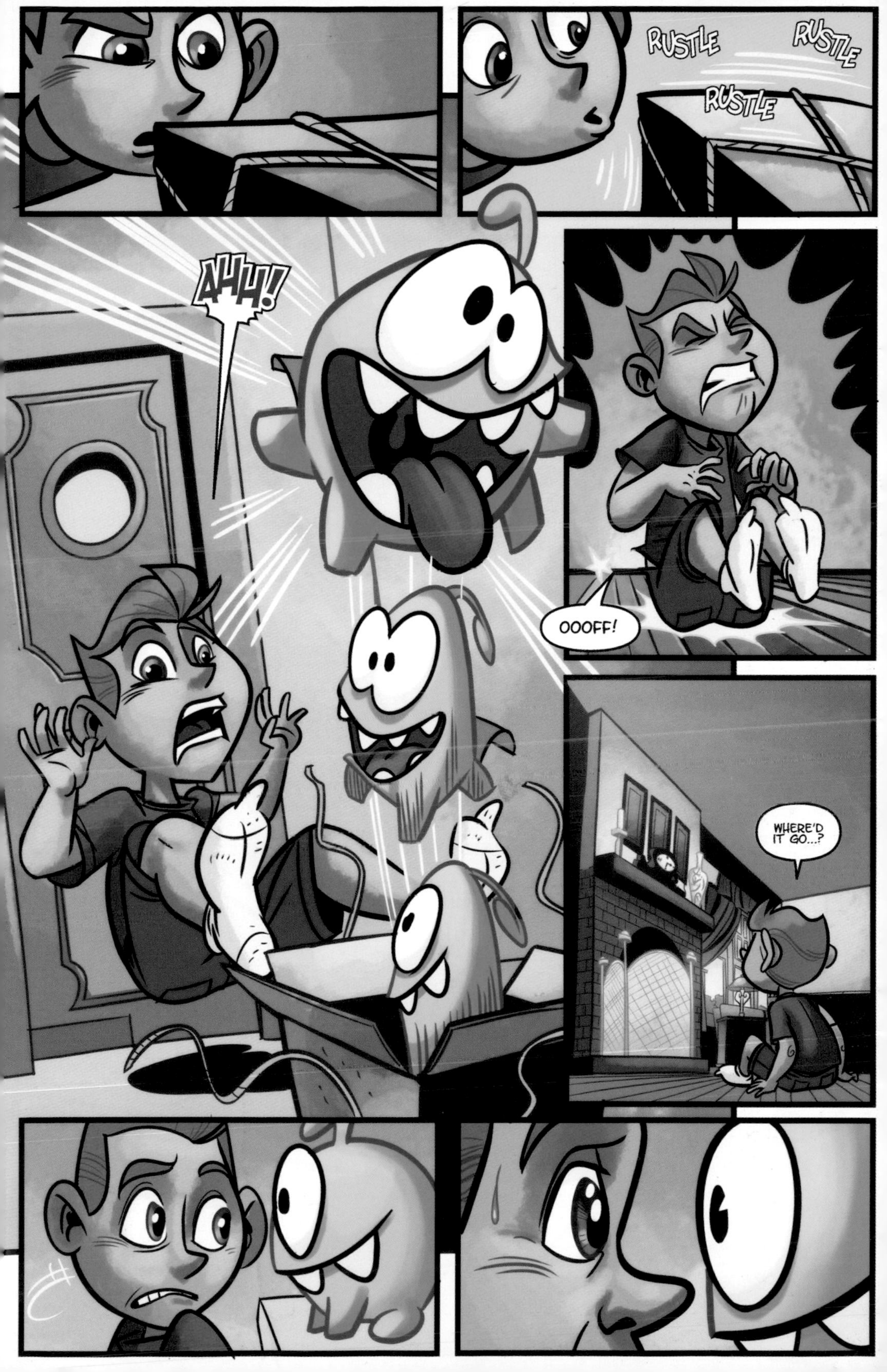
RUSTLE
RUSTLE
RUSTLE
AHH!
OOOFF!
WHERE'D IT GO...?

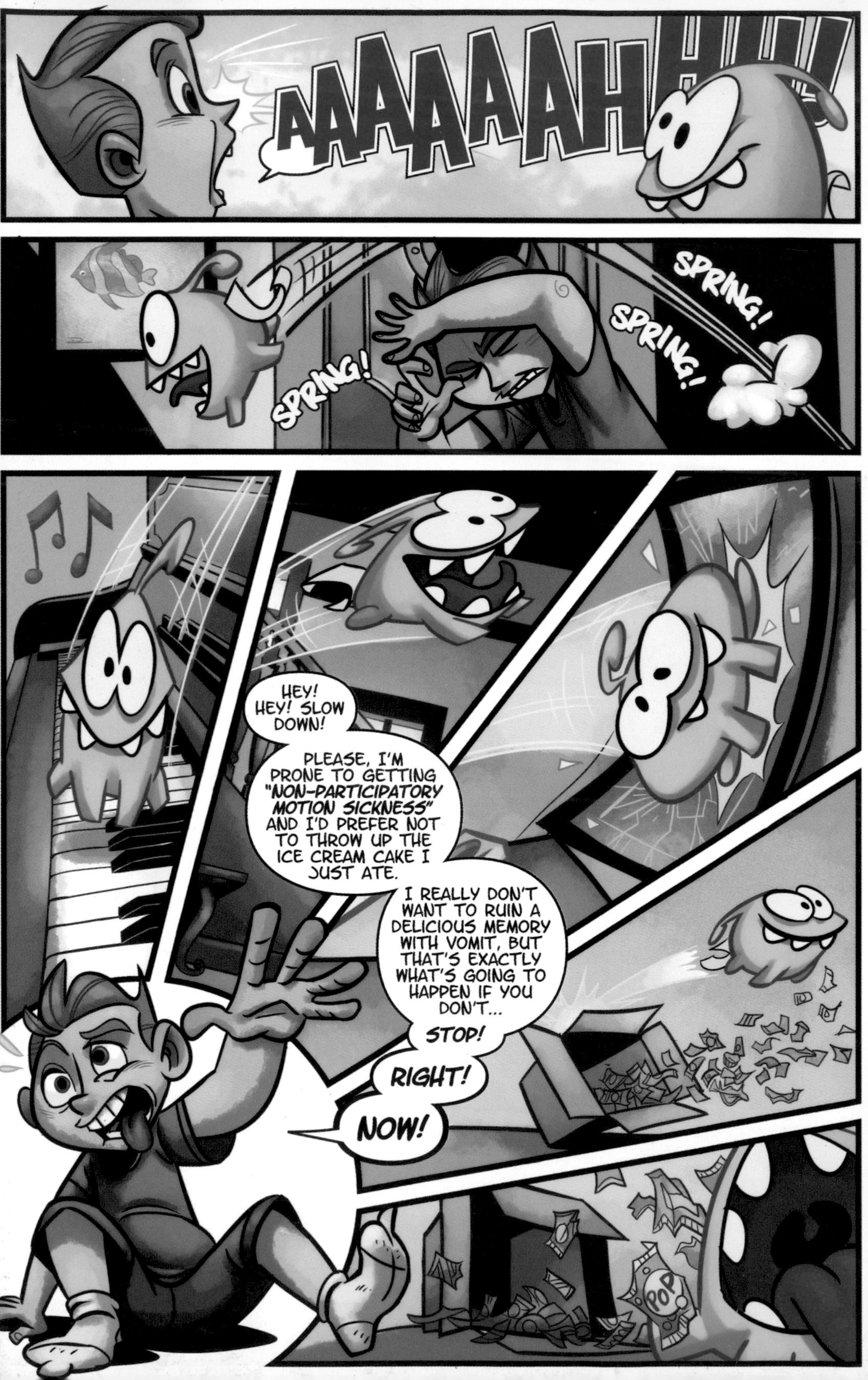
AAAAAAAHHH!
SPRING!
SPRING!
SPRING!
HEY! HEY! SLOW DOWN!
PLEASE, I'M PRONE TO GETTING "NON-PARTICIPATORY MOTION SICKNESS" AND I'D PREFER NOT TO THROW UP THE ICE CREAM CAKE I JUST ATE.
I REALLY DON'T WANT TO RUIN A DELICIOUS MEMORY WITH VOMIT, BUT THAT'S EXACTLY WHAT'S GOING TO HAPPEN IF YOU DON'T...
STOP!
RIGHT!
NOW!
POP

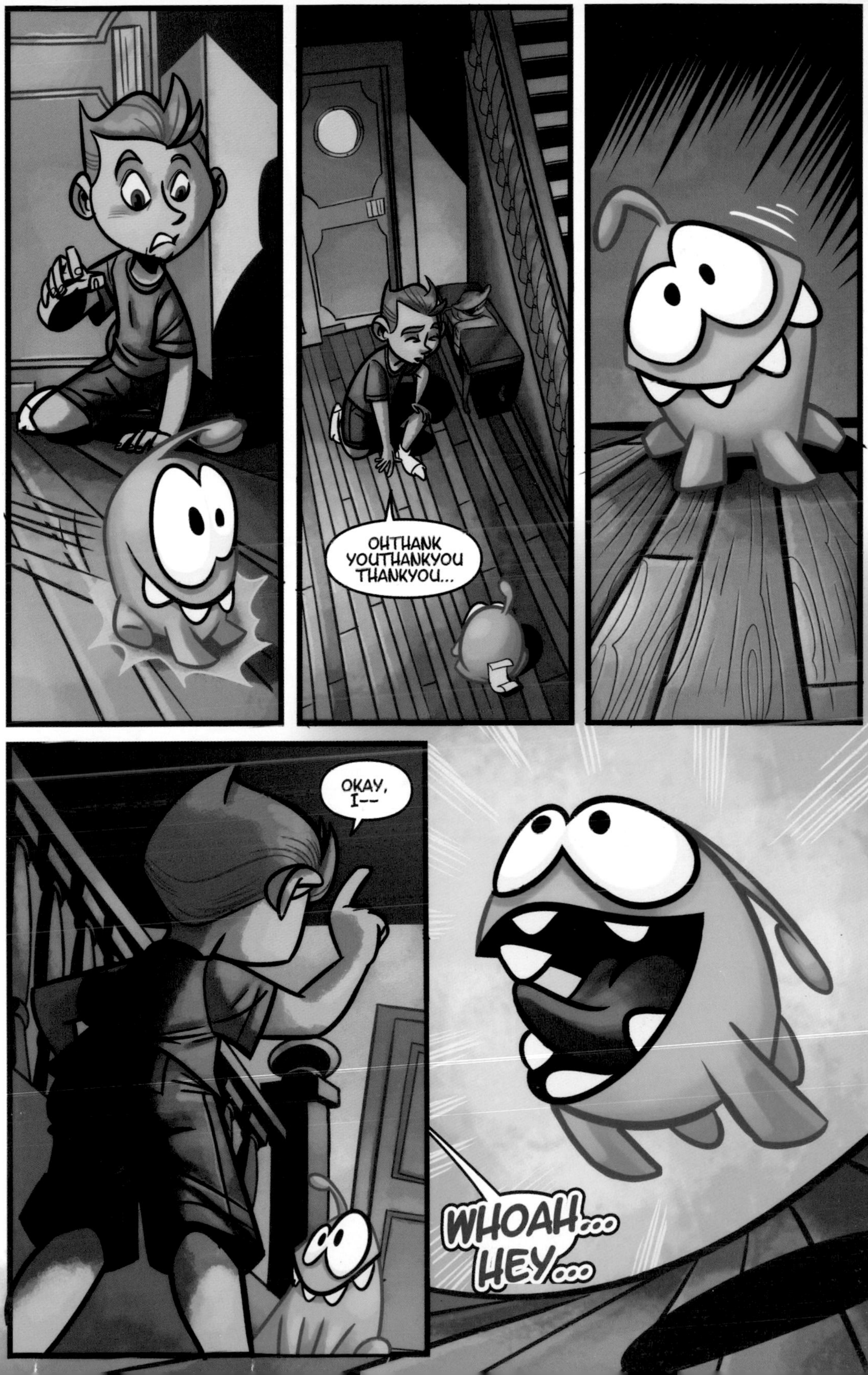
OHTHANK YOUTHANKYOU THANKYOU...
OKAY, I--
WHOAH... HEY...

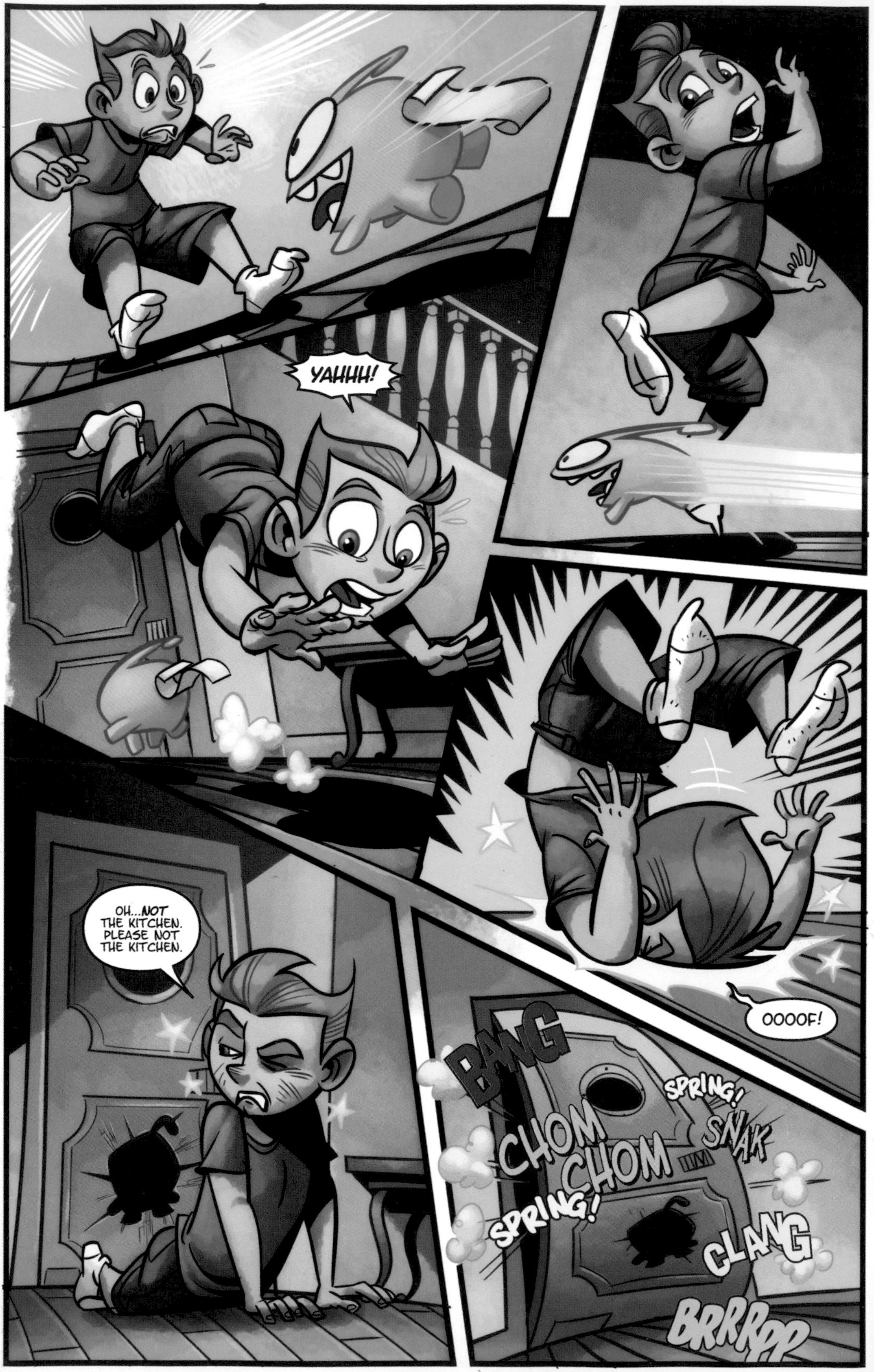

YAHHH!
OOOOF!
OH...NOT THE KITCHEN. PLEASE NOT THE KITCHEN.
BANG
CHOM
CHOM
SPRING!
SNAK
SPRING!
CLANG
BRRRPP

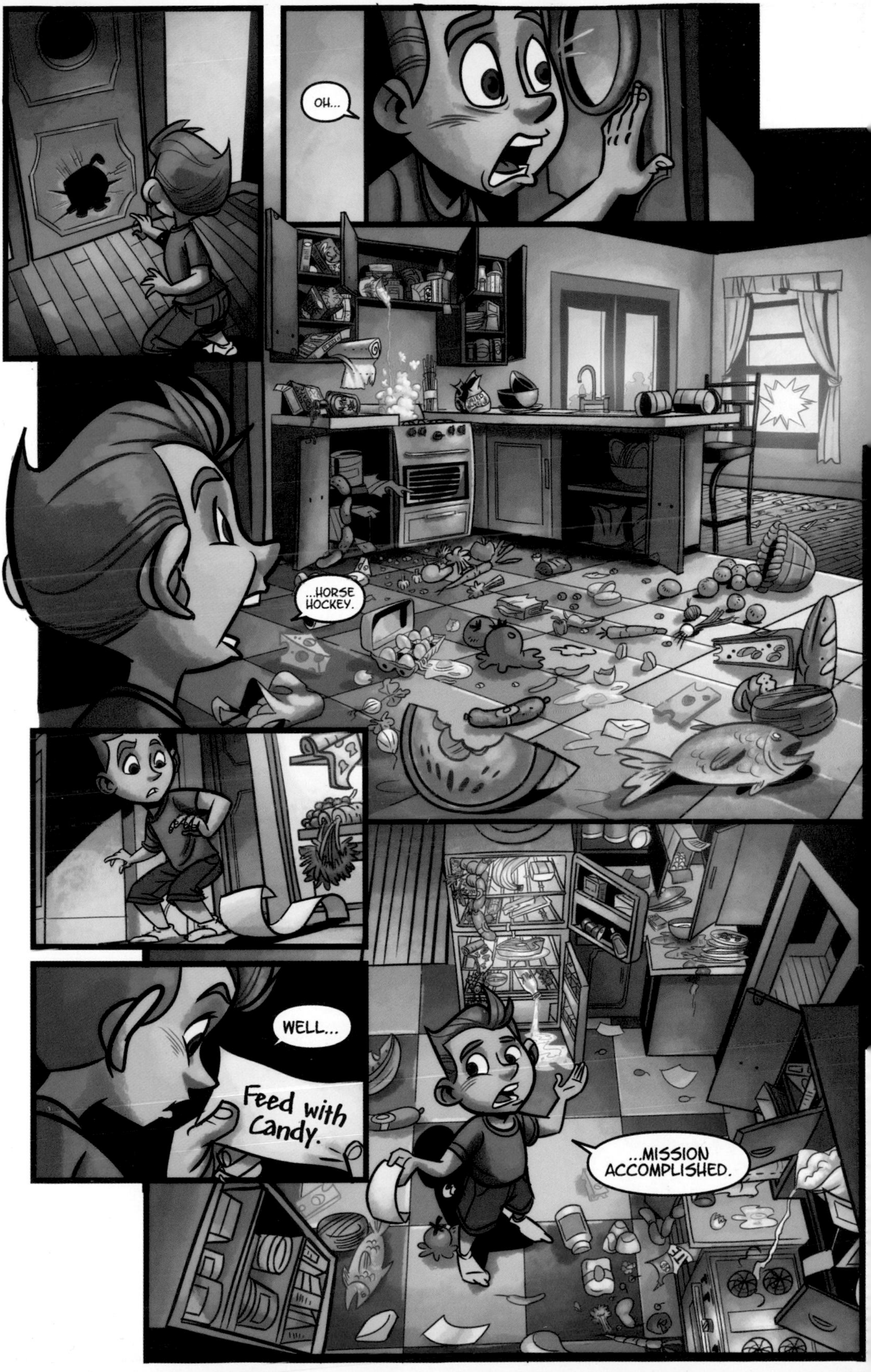
OH...
...HORSE HOCKEY.
WELL...
Feed with Candy.
...MISSION ACCOMPLISHED.

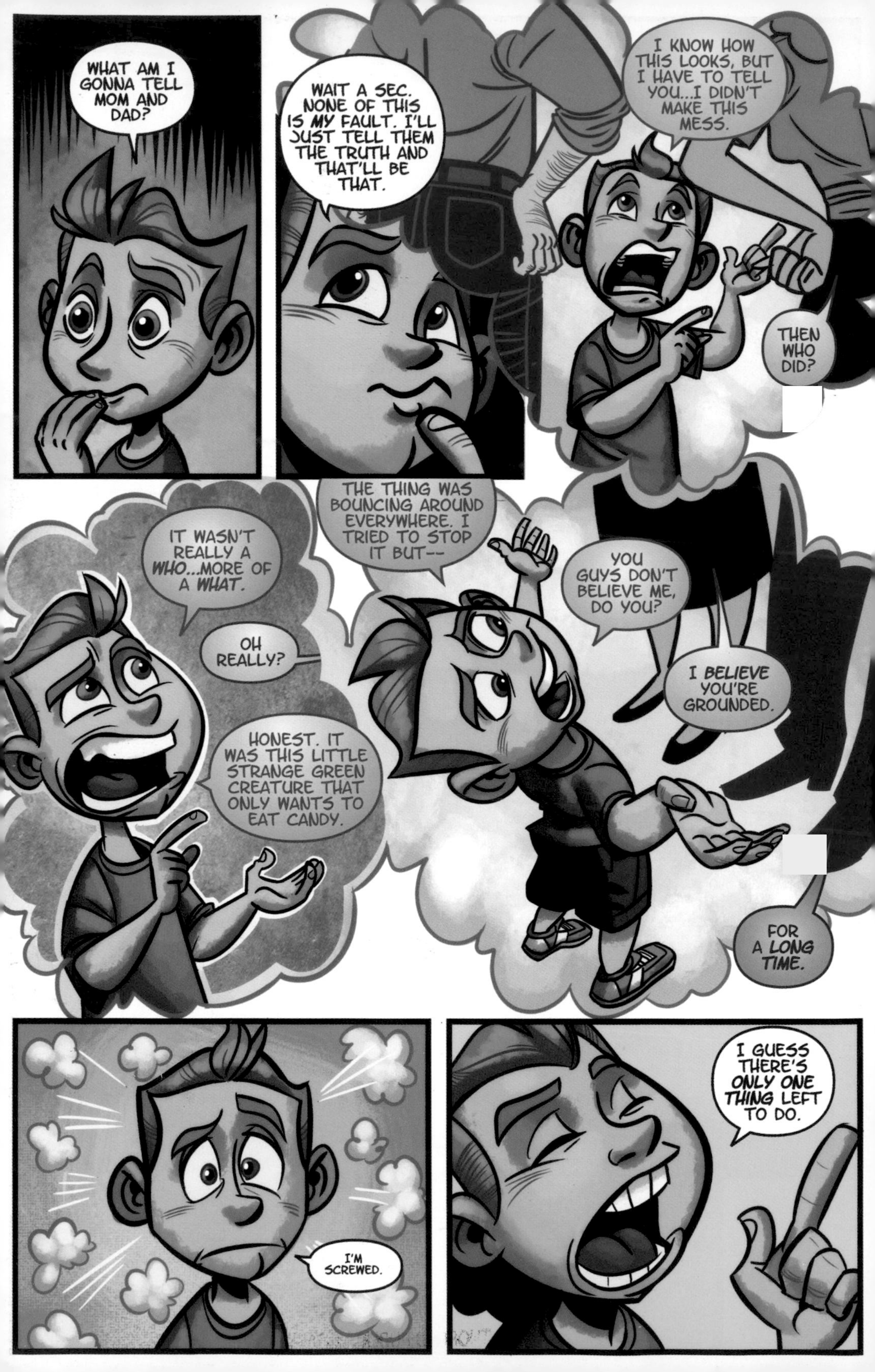
WHAT AM I GONNA TELL MOM AND DAD?
WAIT A SEC. NONE OF THIS IS MY FAULT. I'LL JUST TELL THEM THE TRUTH AND THAT'LL BE THAT.
I KNOW HOW THIS LOOKS, BUT I HAVE TO TELL YOU...I DIDN'T MAKE THIS MESS.
THEN WHO DID?
IT WASN'T REALLY A WHO...MORE OF A WHAT.
OH REALLY?
HONEST. IT WAS THIS LITTLE STRANGE GREEN CREATURE THAT ONLY WANTS TO EAT CANDY.
THE THING WAS BOUNCING AROUND EVERYWHERE. I TRIED TO STOP IT BUT--
YOU GUYS DON'T BELIEVE ME, DO YOU?
I BELIEVE YOU'RE GROUNDED.
FOR A LONG TIME.
I'M SCREWED.
I GUESS THERE'S ONLY ONE THING LEFT TO DO.

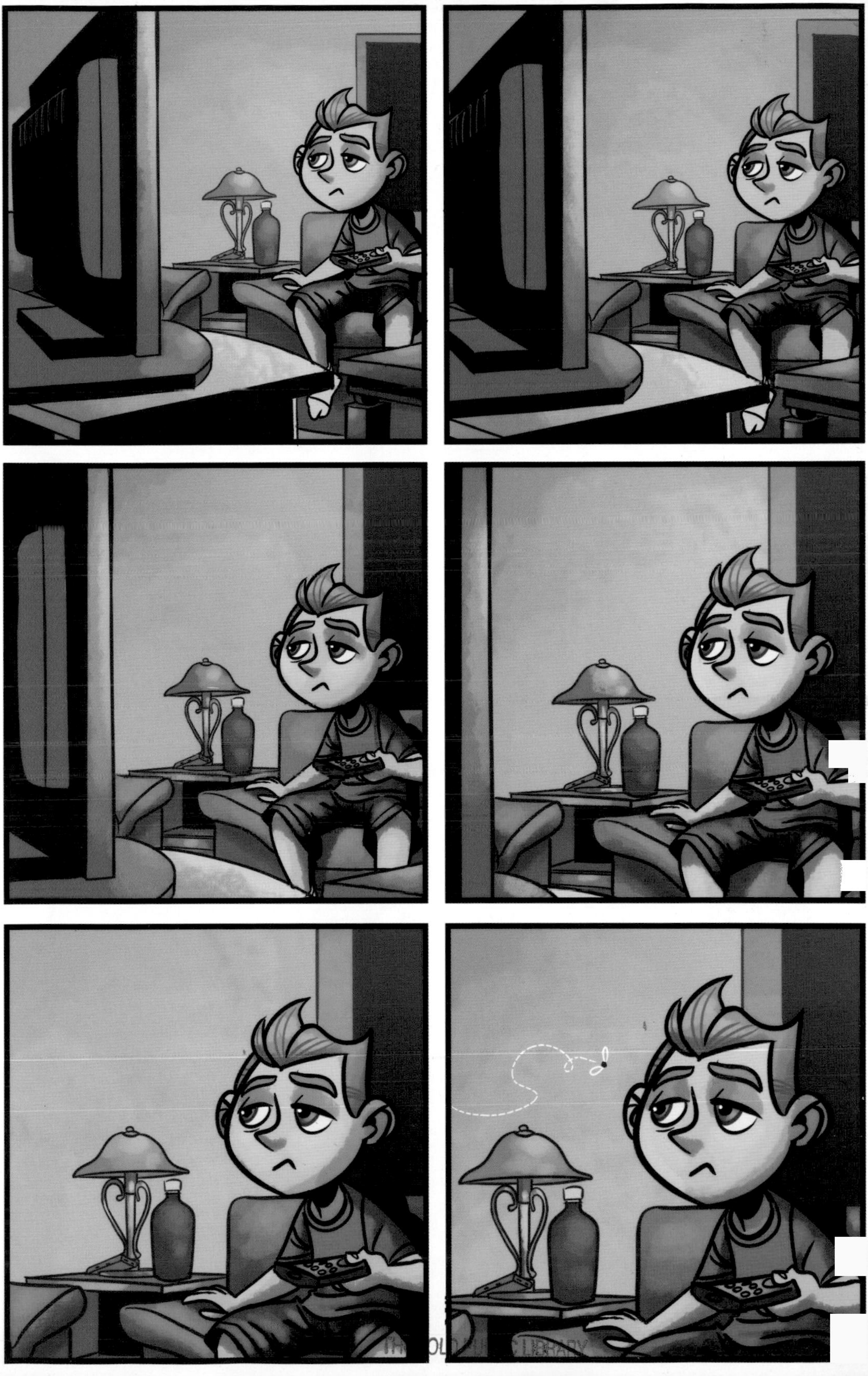

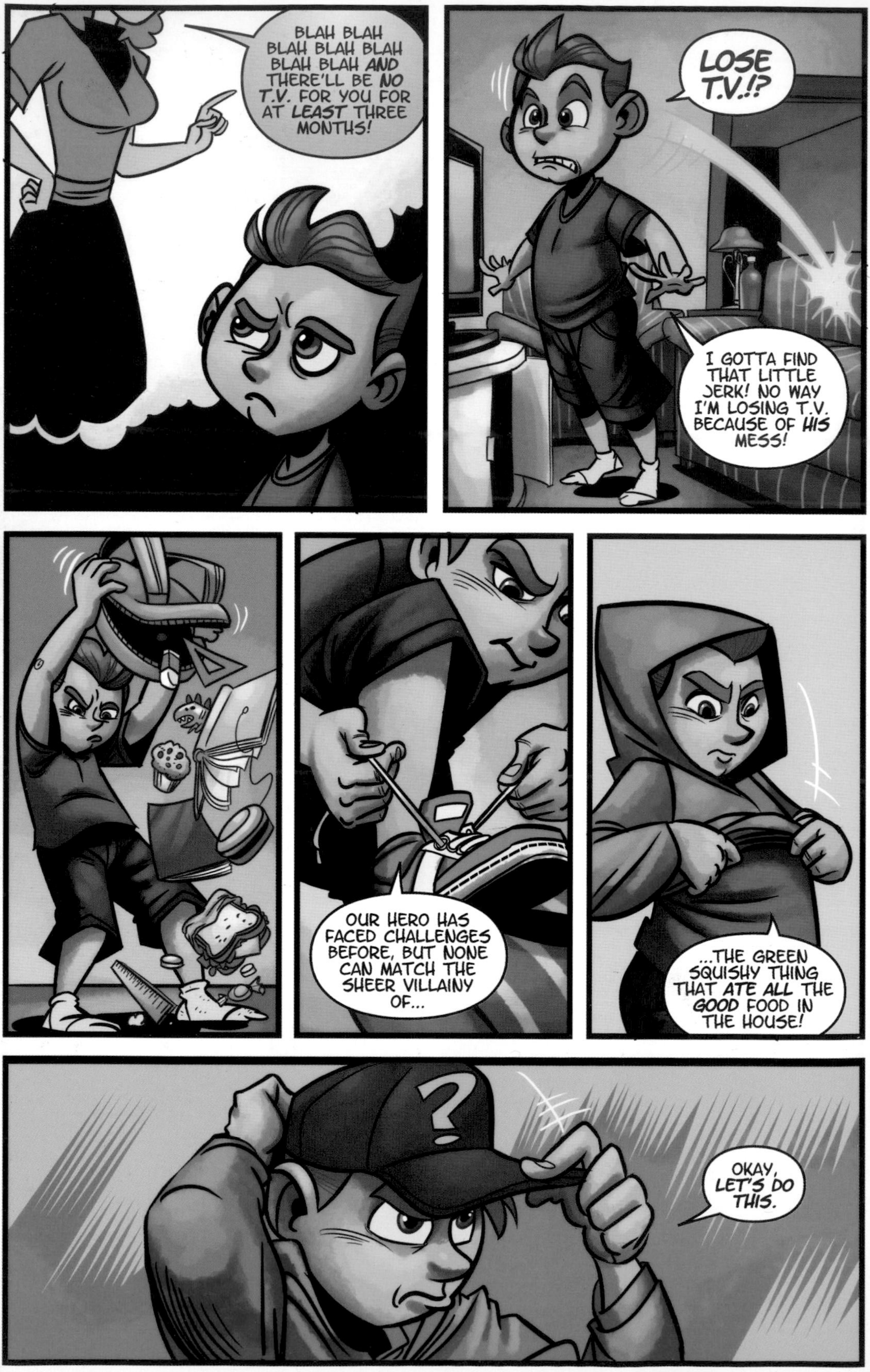

BLAH BLAH BLAH BLAH BLAH BLAH BLAH AND THERE'LL BE NO T.V. FOR YOU FOR AT LEAST THREE MONTHS!
LOSE T.V.!?
I GOTTA FIND THAT LITTLE JERK! NO WAY I'M LOSING T.V. BECAUSE OF HIS MESS!
OUR HERO HAS FACED CHALLENGES BEFORE, BUT NONE CAN MATCH THE SHEER VILLAINY OF...
...THE GREEN SQUISHY THING THAT ATE ALL THE GOOD FOOD IN THE HOUSE!
OKAY, LET'S DO THIS.

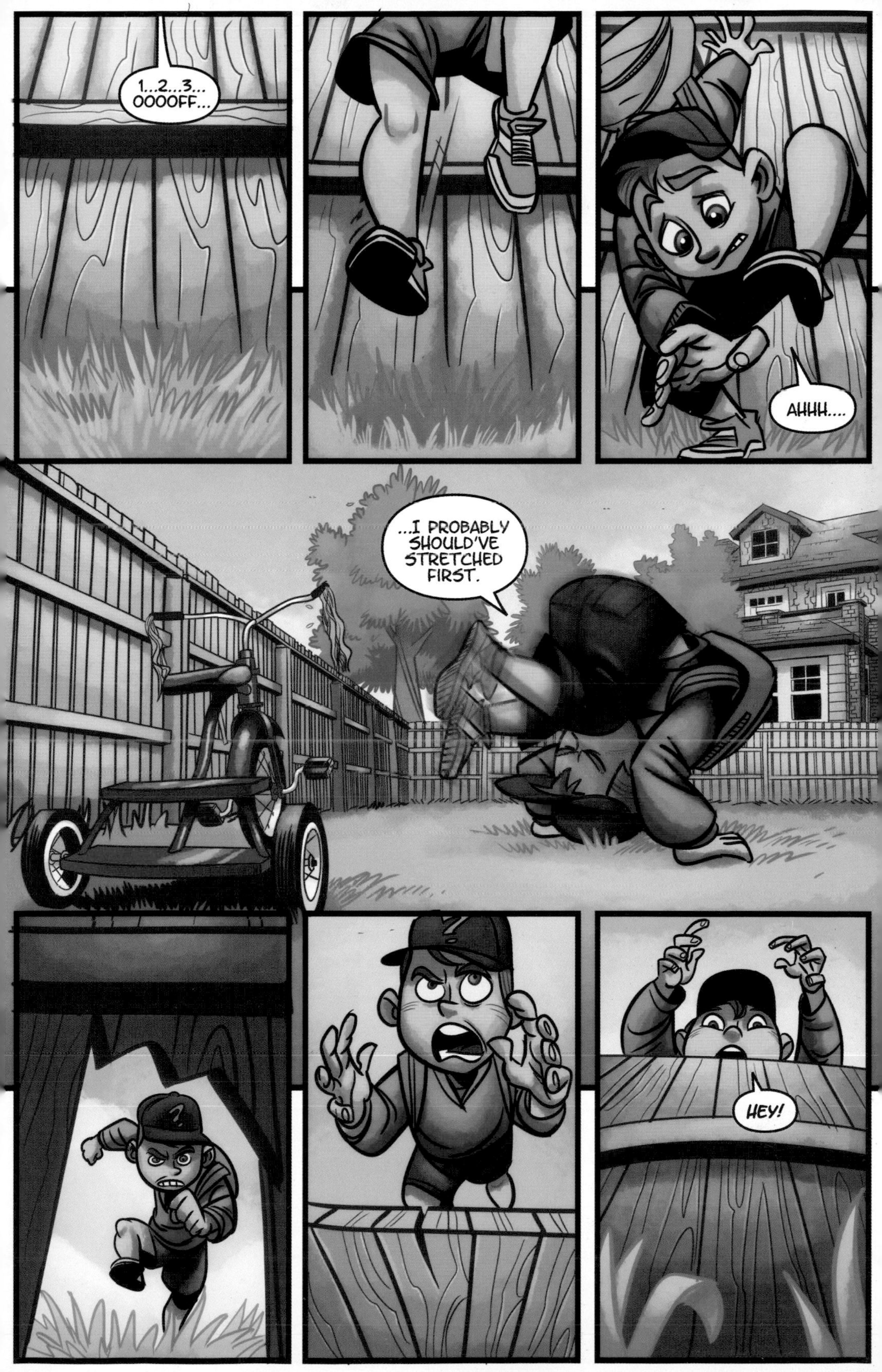
1...2...3...
OOOOFF...
AHHH....
...I PROBABLY SHOULD'VE STRETCHED FIRST.
HEY!

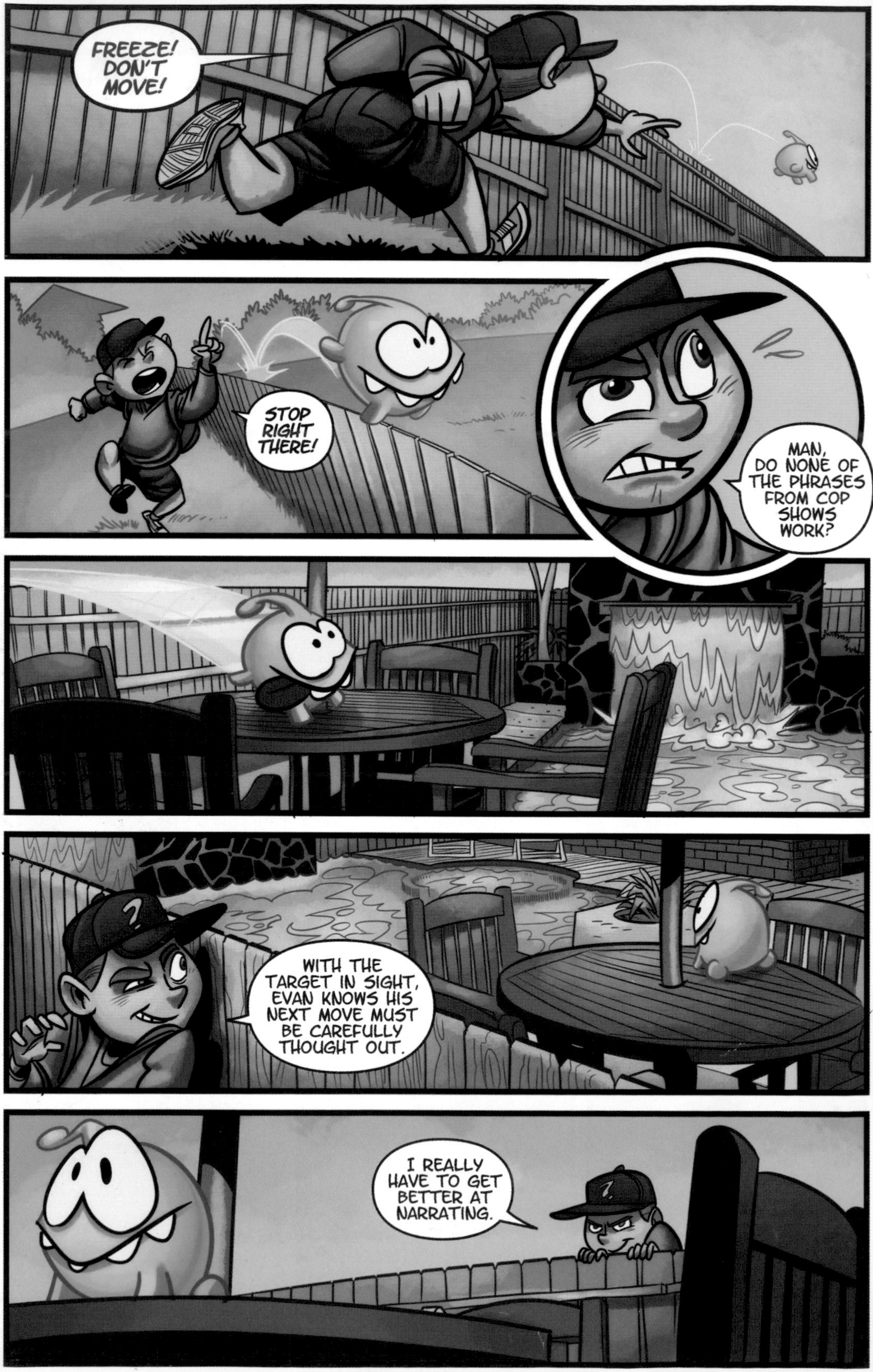
FREEZE! DON'T MOVE!
STOP RIGHT THERE!
MAN, DO NONE OF THE PHRASES FROM COP SHOWS WORK?
WITH THE TARGET IN SIGHT, EVAN KNOWS HIS NEXT MOVE MUST BE CAREFULLY THOUGHT OUT.
I REALLY HAVE TO GET BETTER AT NARRATING.

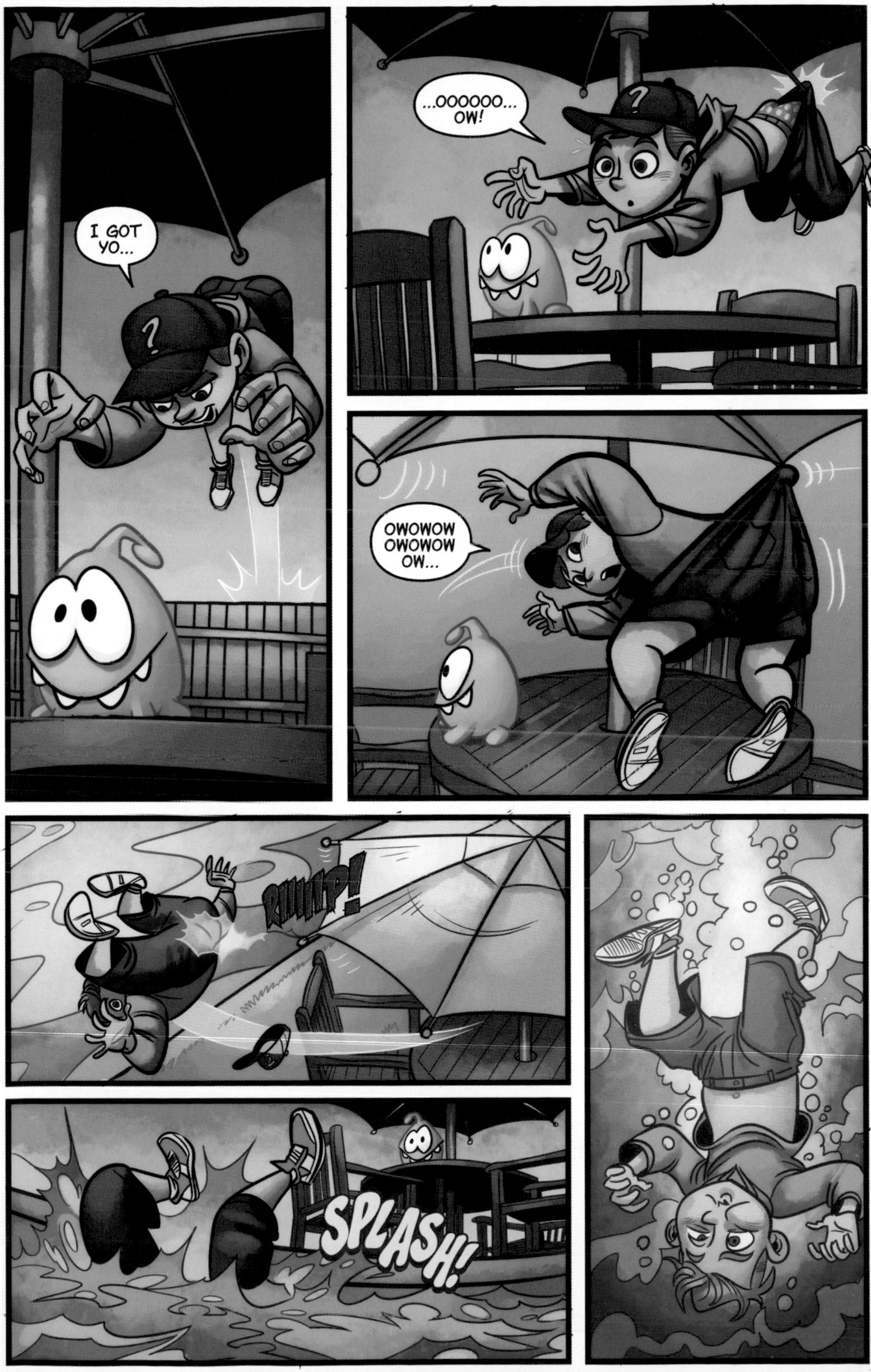
I GOT YO...
...OOOOOO... OW!
OWOWOW OWOWOW OW...
RIIIIIIP!
SPLASH!

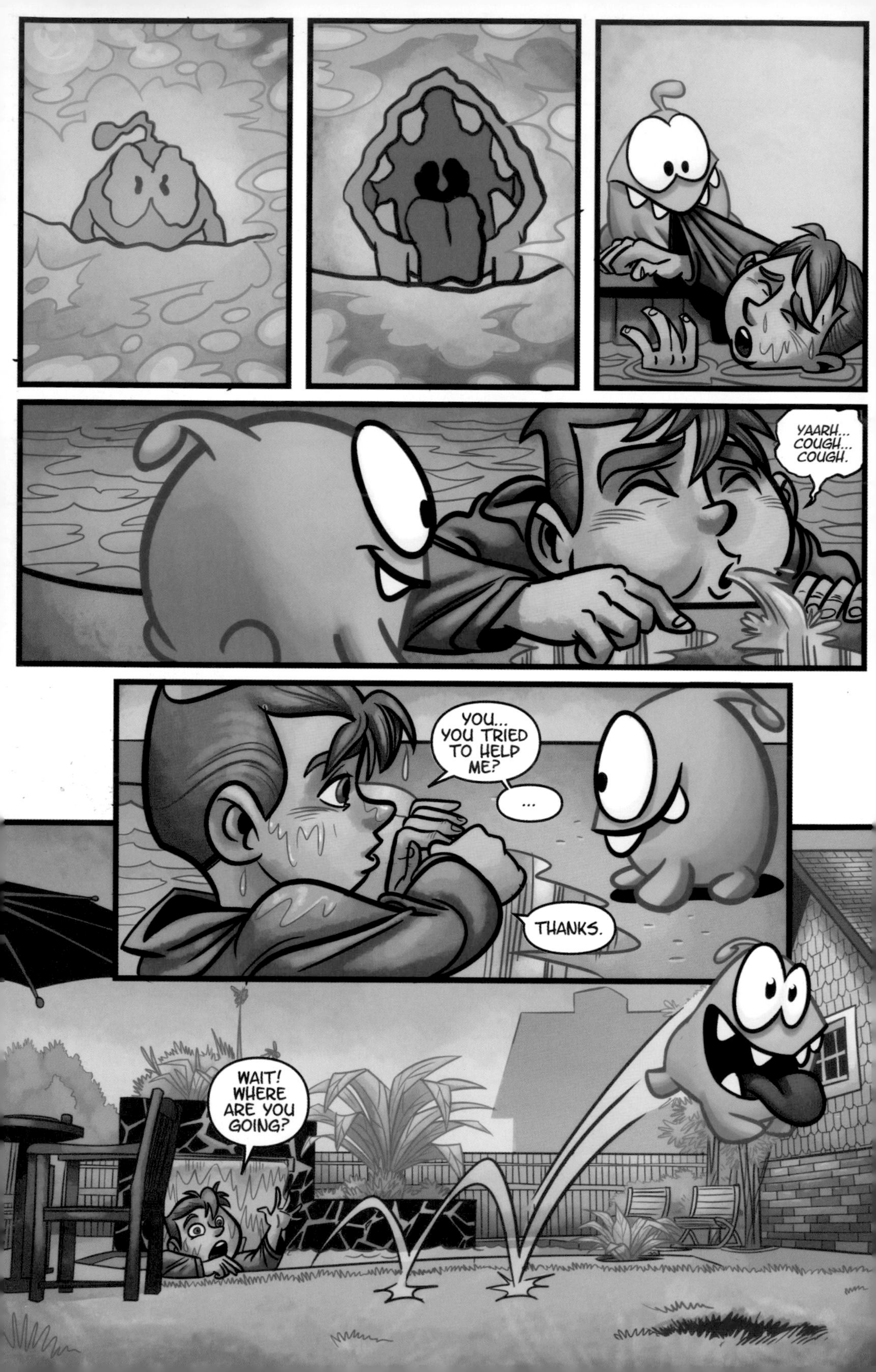
YAARH... COUGH... COUGH.
YOU... YOU TRIED TO HELP ME?
...
THANKS.
WAIT! WHERE ARE YOU GOING?

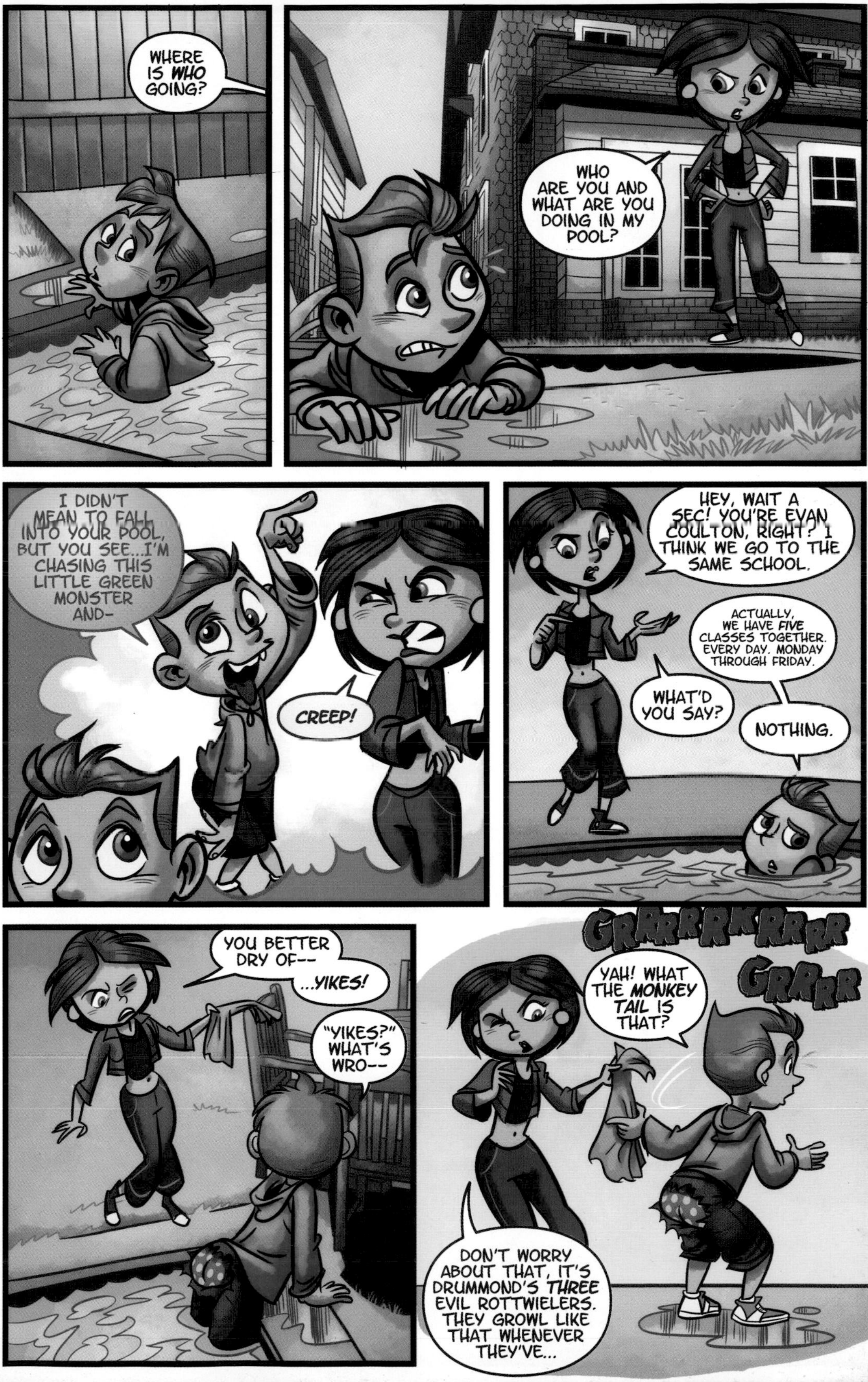

WHERE IS WHO GOING?
WHO ARE YOU AND WHAT ARE YOU DOING IN MY POOL?
I DIDN'T MEAN TO FALL INTO YOUR POOL, BUT YOU SEE...I'M CHASING THIS LITTLE GREEN MONSTER AND-
CREEP!
HEY, WAIT A SEC! YOU'RE EVAN COULTON, RIGHT? I THINK WE GO TO THE SAME SCHOOL.
ACTUALLY, WE HAVE FIVE CLASSES TOGETHER. EVERY DAY. MONDAY THROUGH FRIDAY.
WHAT'D YOU SAY?
NOTHING.
YOU BETTER DRY OF--
...YIKES!
"YIKES?" WHAT'S WRO--
GRRRRRKRRRR
GRRRR
YAH! WHAT THE MONKEY TAIL IS THAT?
DON'T WORRY ABOUT THAT, IT'S DRUMMOND'S THREE EVIL ROTTWIELERS. THEY GROWL LIKE THAT WHENEVER THEY'VE...

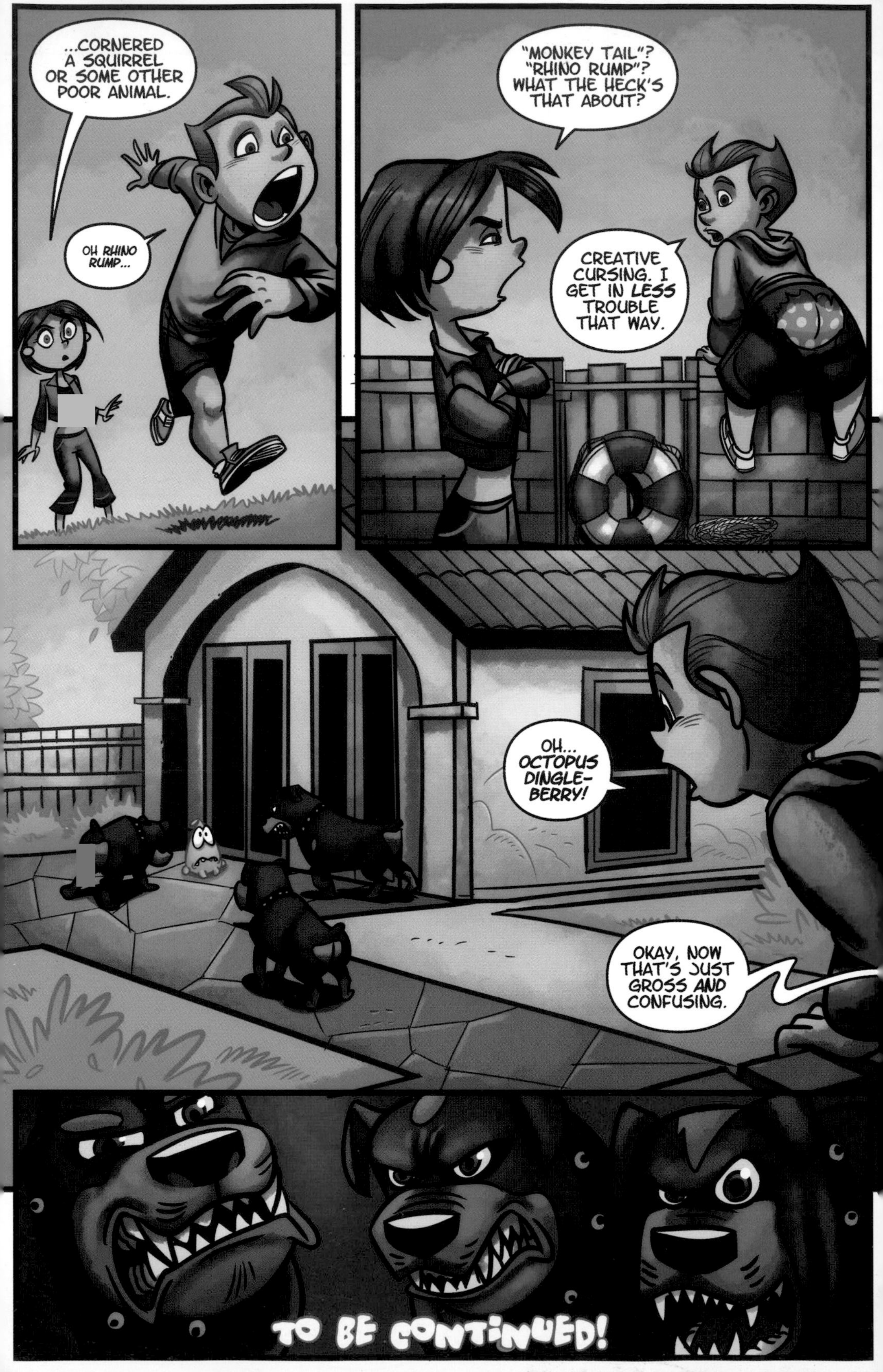

...CORNERED A SQUIRREL OR SOME OTHER POOR ANIMAL.
OH RHINO RUMP...
"MONKEY TAIL"? "RHINO RUMP"? WHAT THE HECK'S THAT ABOUT?
CREATIVE CURSING. I GET IN LESS TROUBLE THAT WAY.
OH... OCTOPUS DINGLE-BERRY!
OKAY, NOW THAT'S JUST GROSS AND CONFUSING.
TO BE CONTINUED!

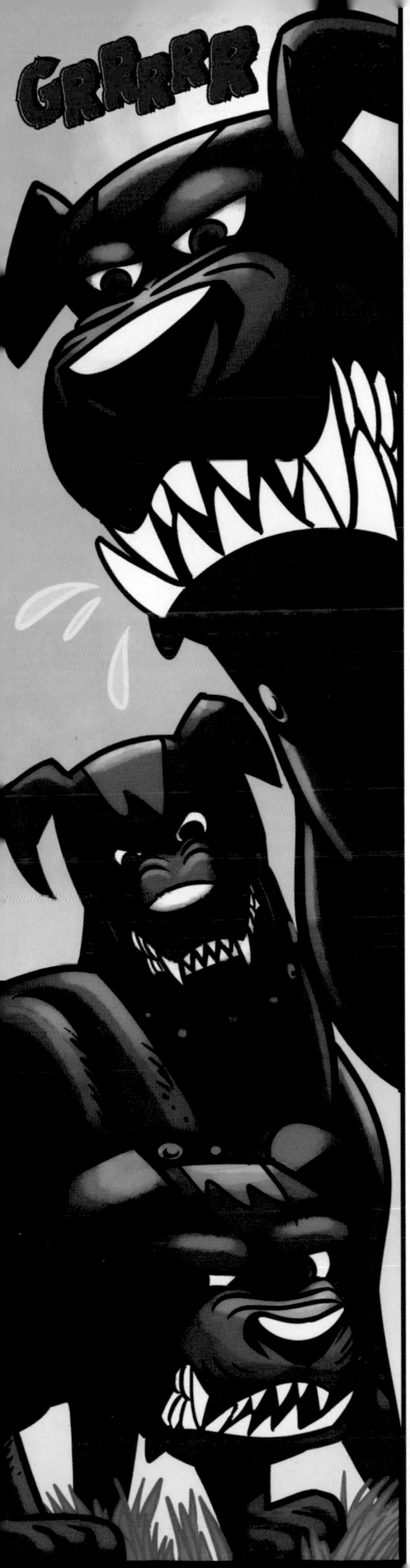
GRRRRR

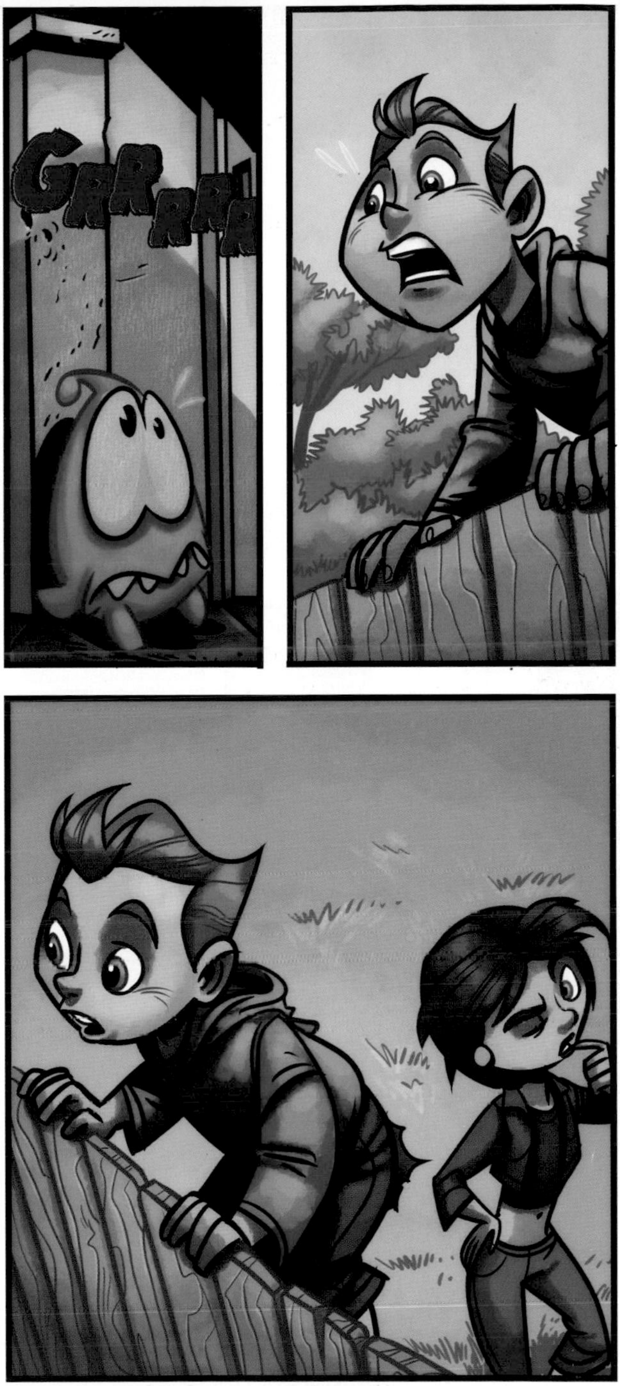
GRRRRR

STRANGE DELIVERY PART TWO

Written by Matt Anderson
Art by Ricardo Garcia and Antonio Alfaro
Colors by Tim Durning
Letters by Deron Bennett

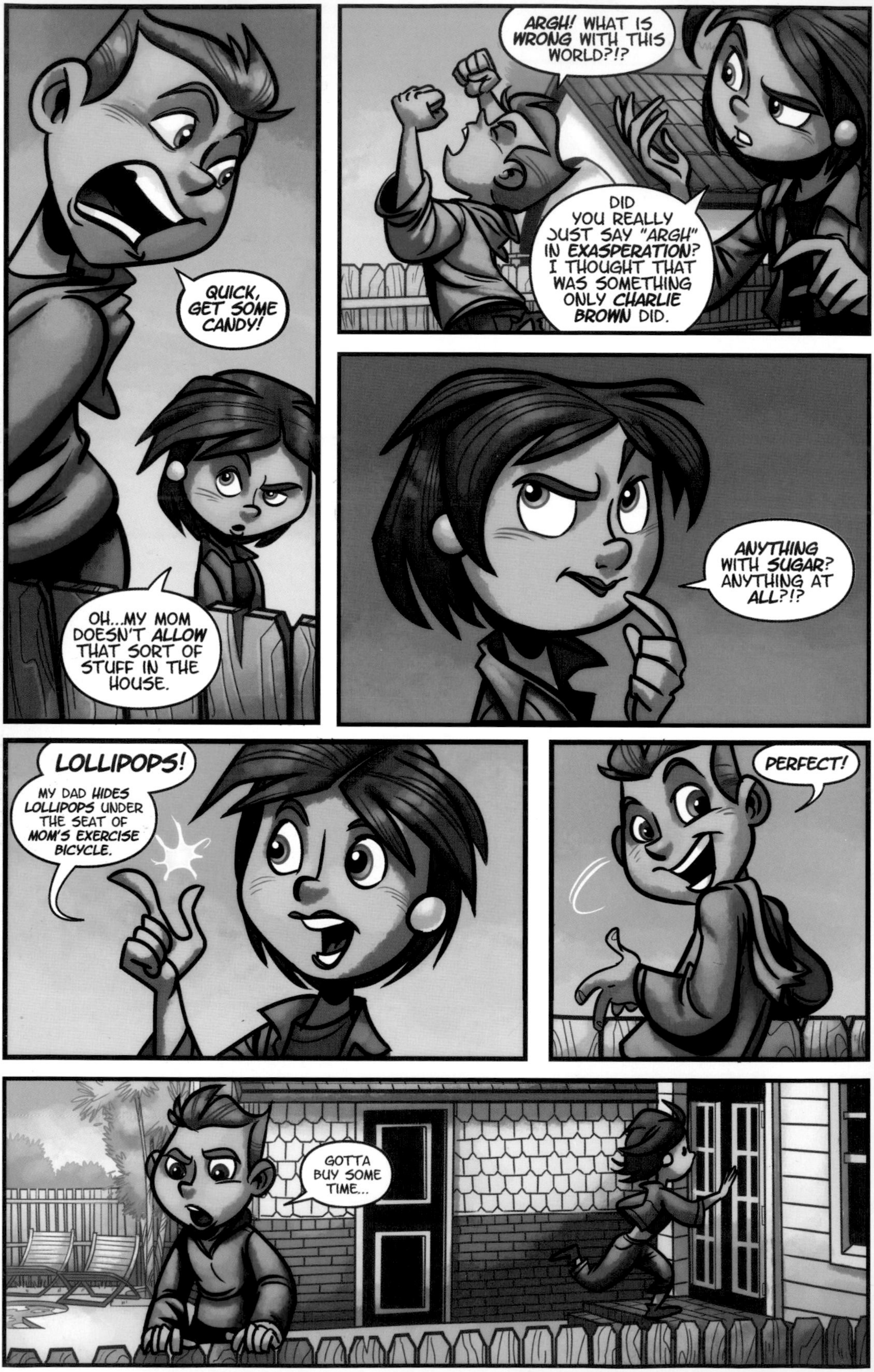
QUICK, GET SOME CANDY!
OH...MY MOM DOESN'T ALLOW THAT SORT OF STUFF IN THE HOUSE.
ARGH! WHAT IS WRONG WITH THIS WORLD?!?
DID YOU REALLY JUST SAY "ARGH" IN EXASPERATION? I THOUGHT THAT WAS SOMETHING ONLY CHARLIE BROWN DID.
ANYTHING WITH SUGAR? ANYTHING AT ALL?!?
LOLLIPOPS!
MY DAD HIDES LOLLIPOPS UNDER THE SEAT OF MOM'S EXERCISE BICYCLE.
PERFECT!
GOTTA BUY SOME TIME...

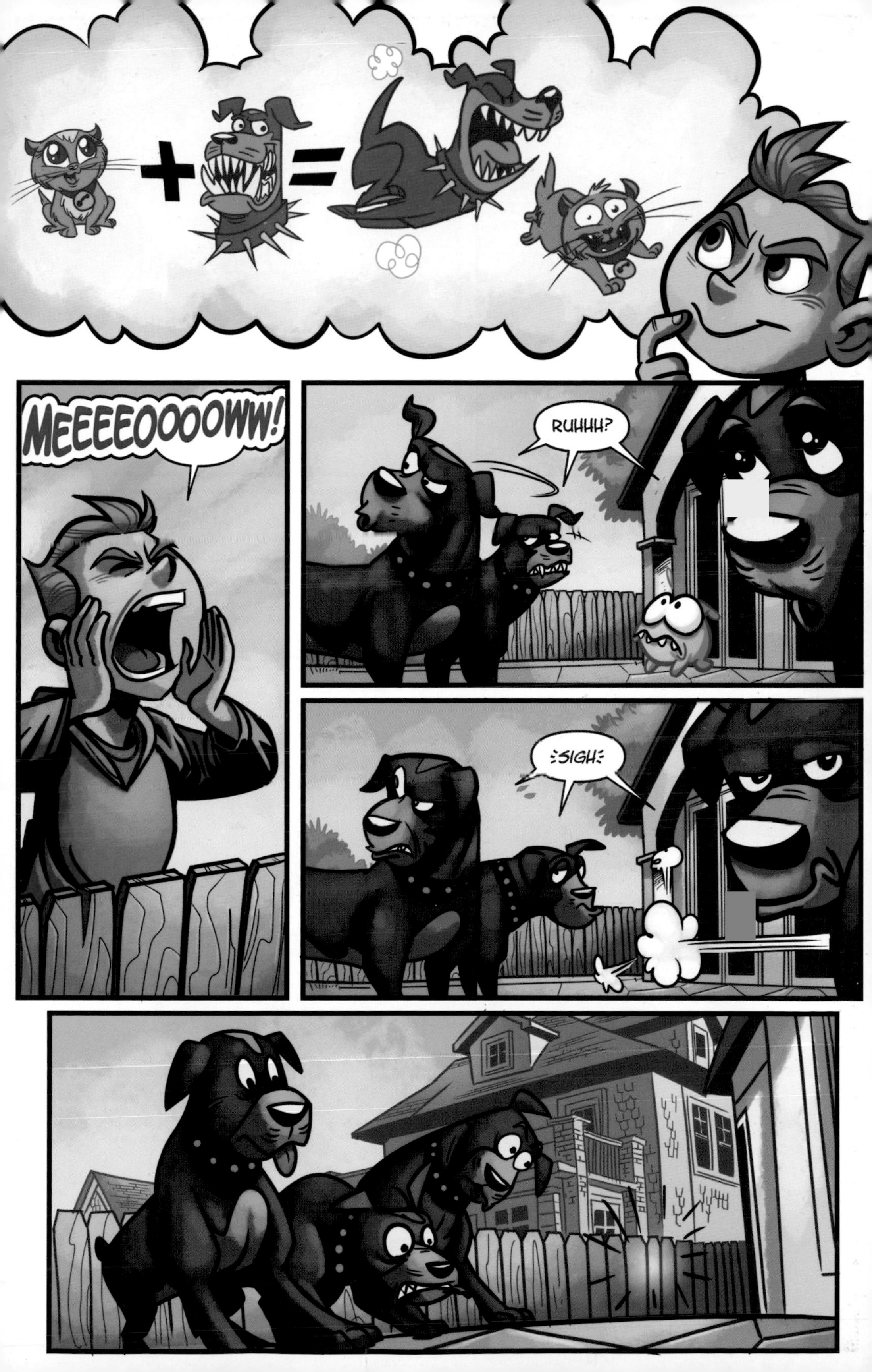
MEEEEOOOOWW!
RUHHH?
SIGH

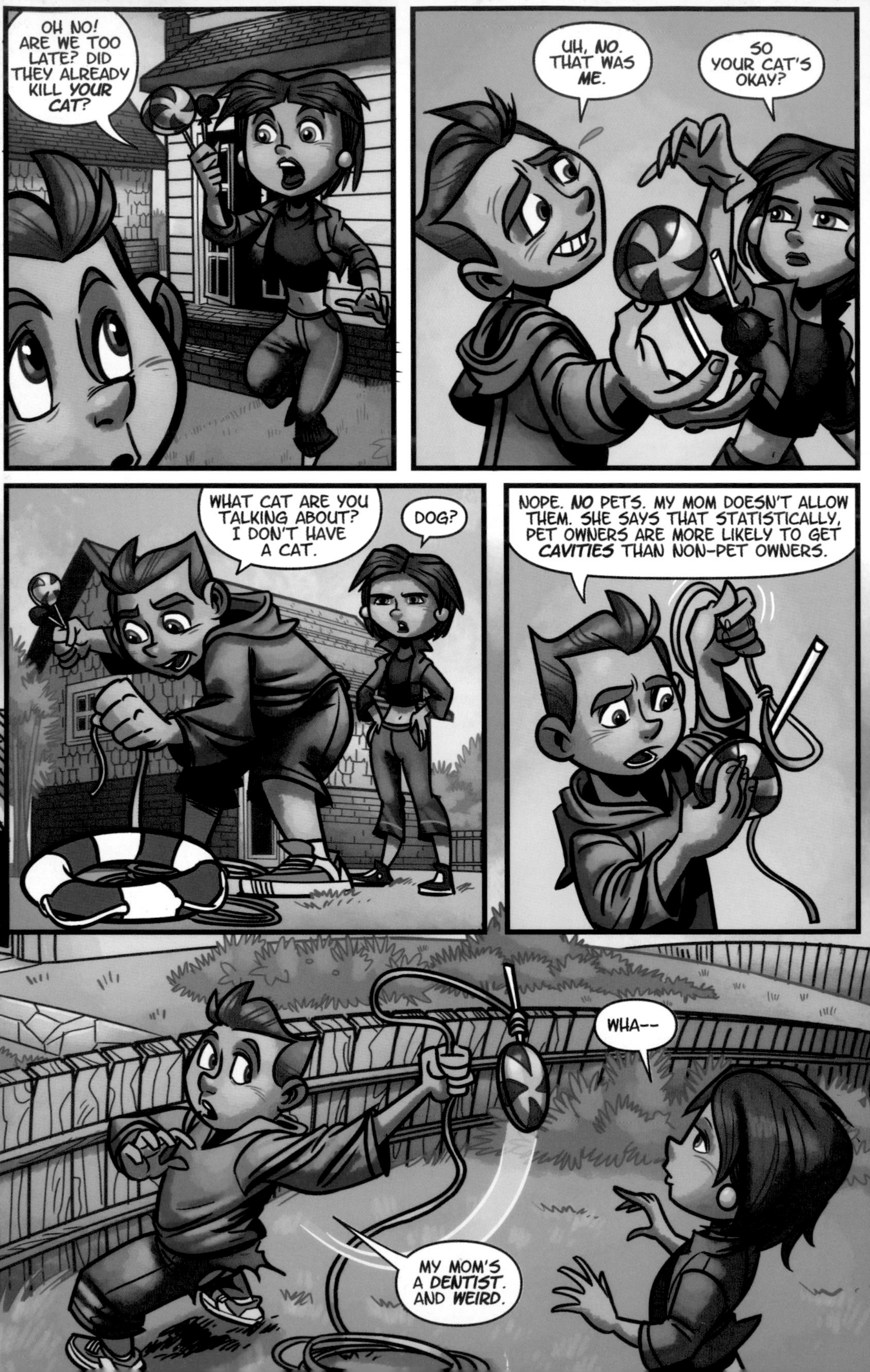
OH NO! ARE WE TOO LATE? DID THEY ALREADY KILL YOUR CAT?
UH, NO. THAT WAS ME.
SO YOUR CAT'S OKAY?
WHAT CAT ARE YOU TALKING ABOUT? I DON'T HAVE A CAT.
DOG?
NOPE. NO PETS. MY MOM DOESN'T ALLOW THEM. SHE SAYS THAT STATISTICALLY, PET OWNERS ARE MORE LIKELY TO GET CAVITIES THAN NON-PET OWNERS.
WHA--
MY MOM'S A DENTIST. AND WEIRD.

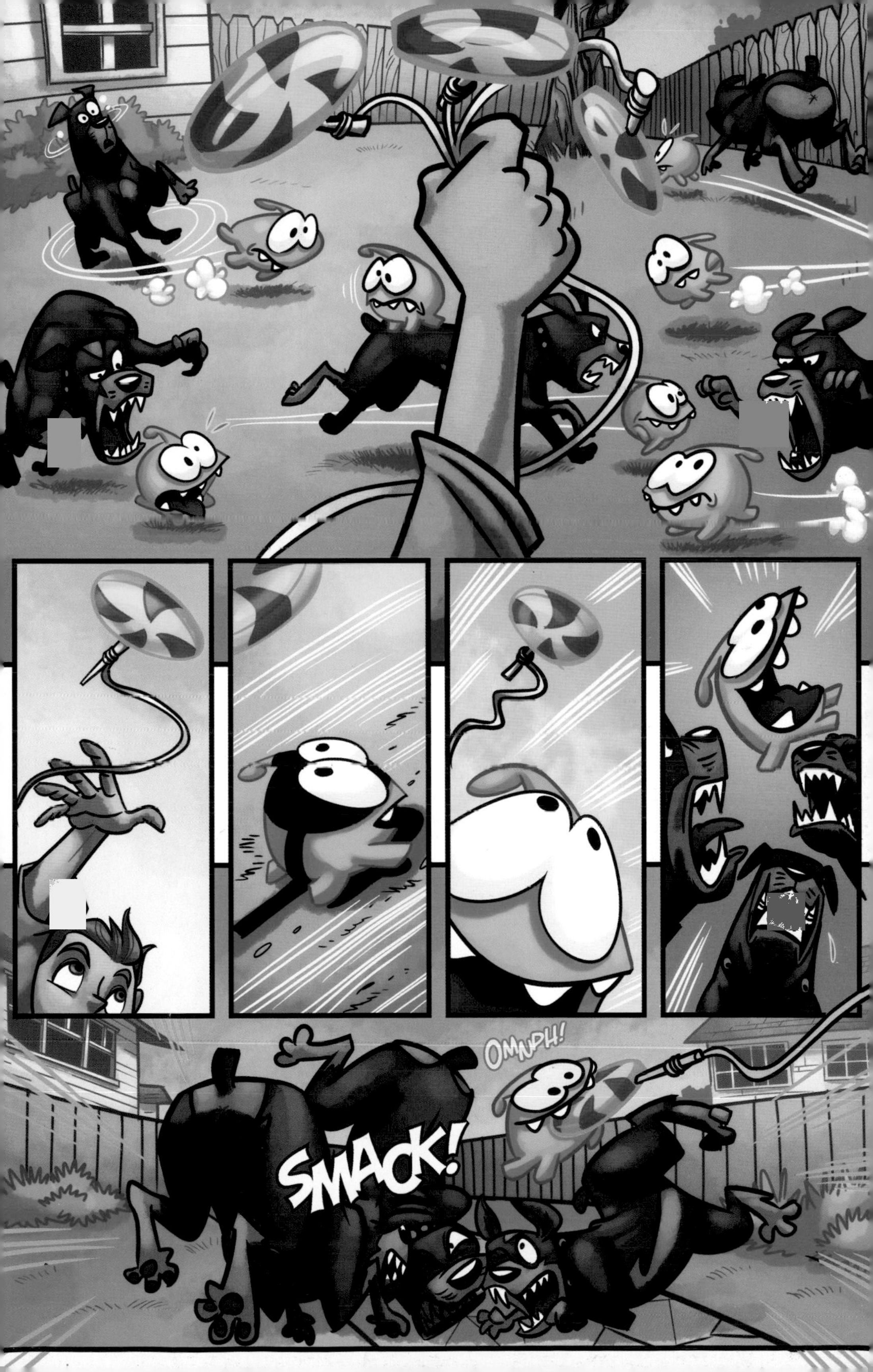
OMNPH!
SMACK!

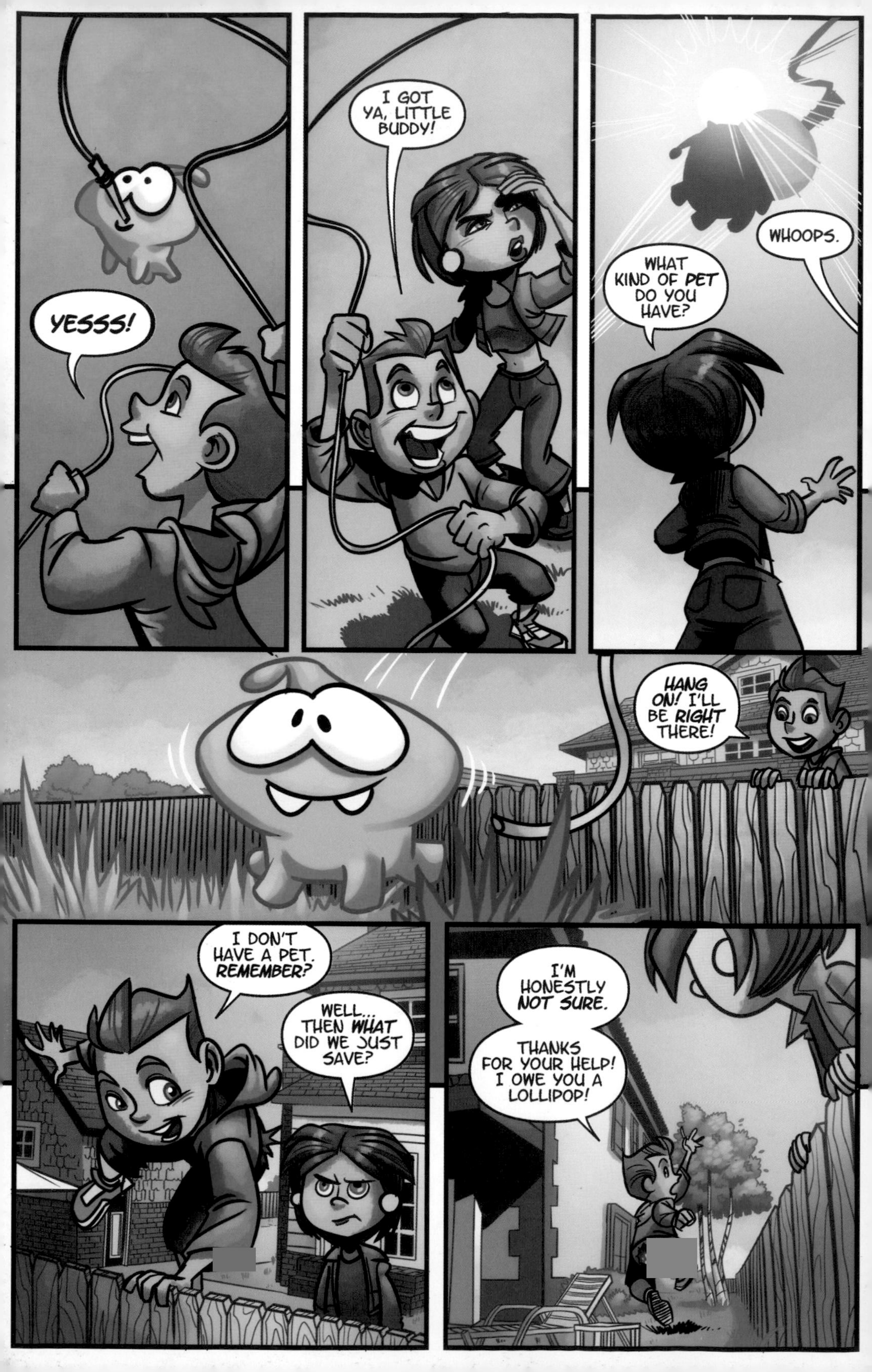
YESSS!
I GOT YA, LITTLE BUDDY!
WHAT KIND OF PET DO YOU HAVE?
WHOOPS.
HANG ON! I'LL BE RIGHT THERE!
I DON'T HAVE A PET. REMEMBER?
WELL... THEN WHAT DID WE JUST SAVE?
I'M HONESTLY NOT SURE.
THANKS FOR YOUR HELP! I OWE YOU A LOLLIPOP!

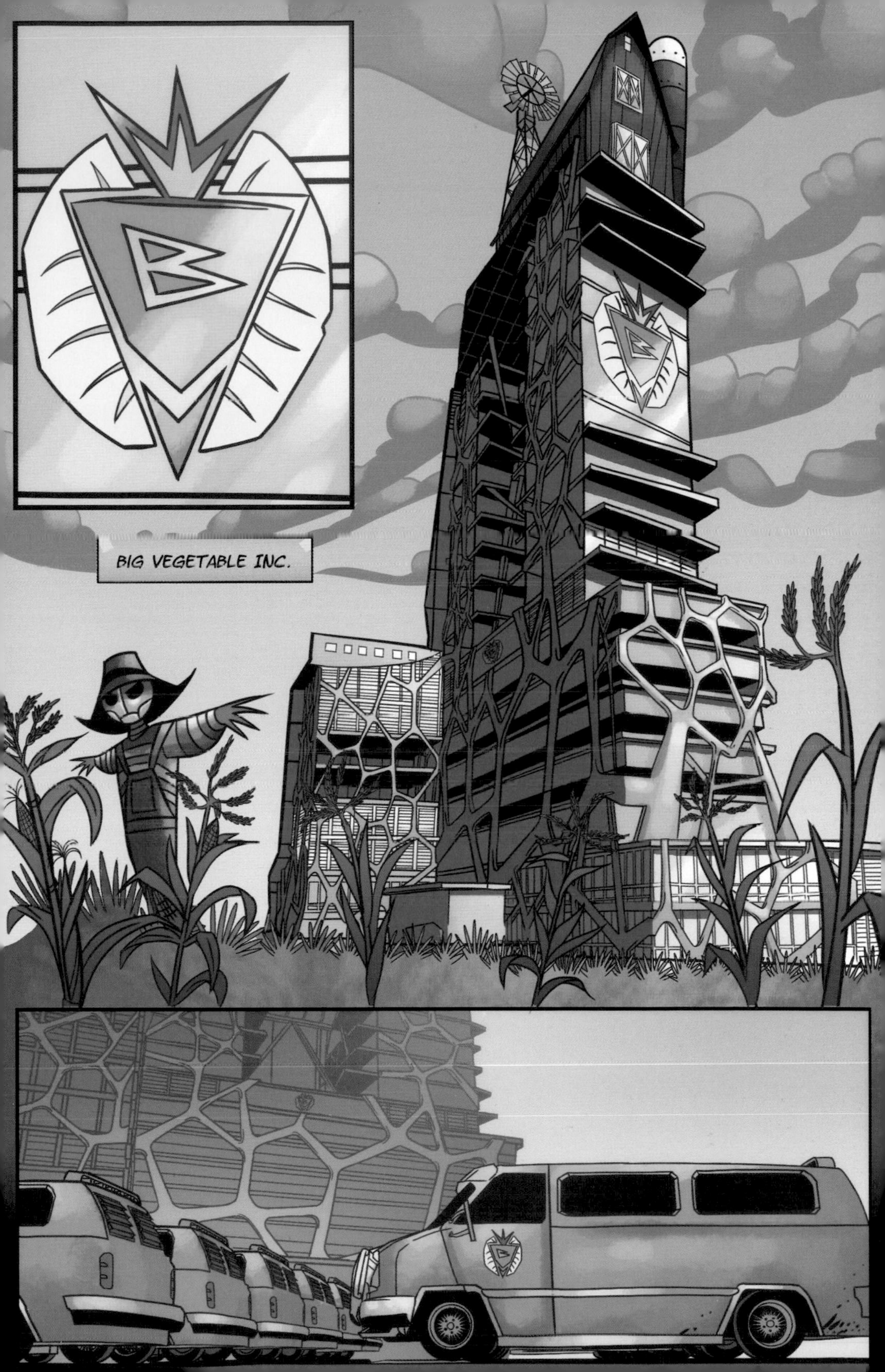
BIG VEGETABLE INC.

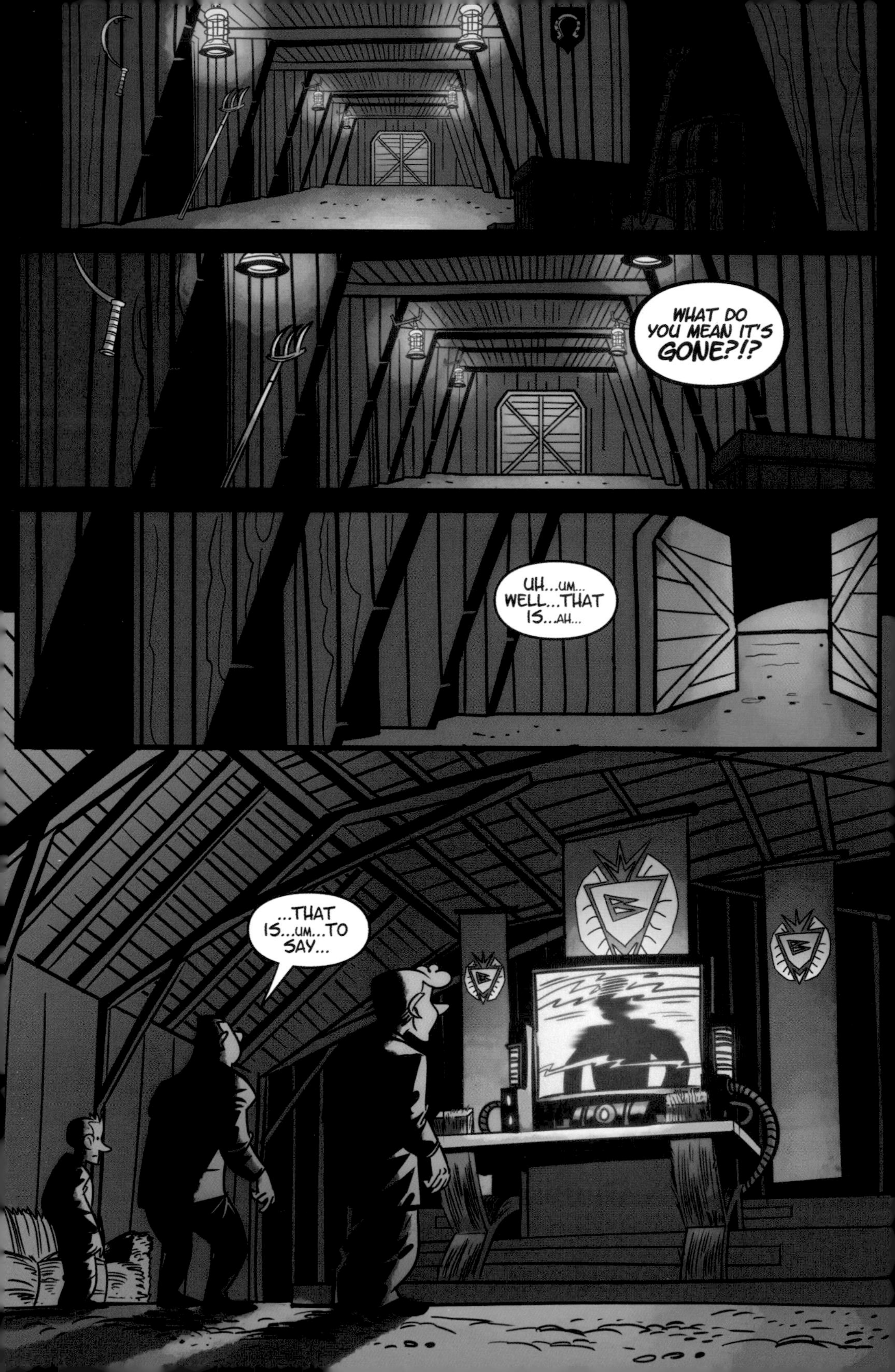
WHAT DO YOU MEAN IT'S GONE?!?
UH...UM... WELL...THAT IS...AH...
...THAT IS...UM...TO SAY...

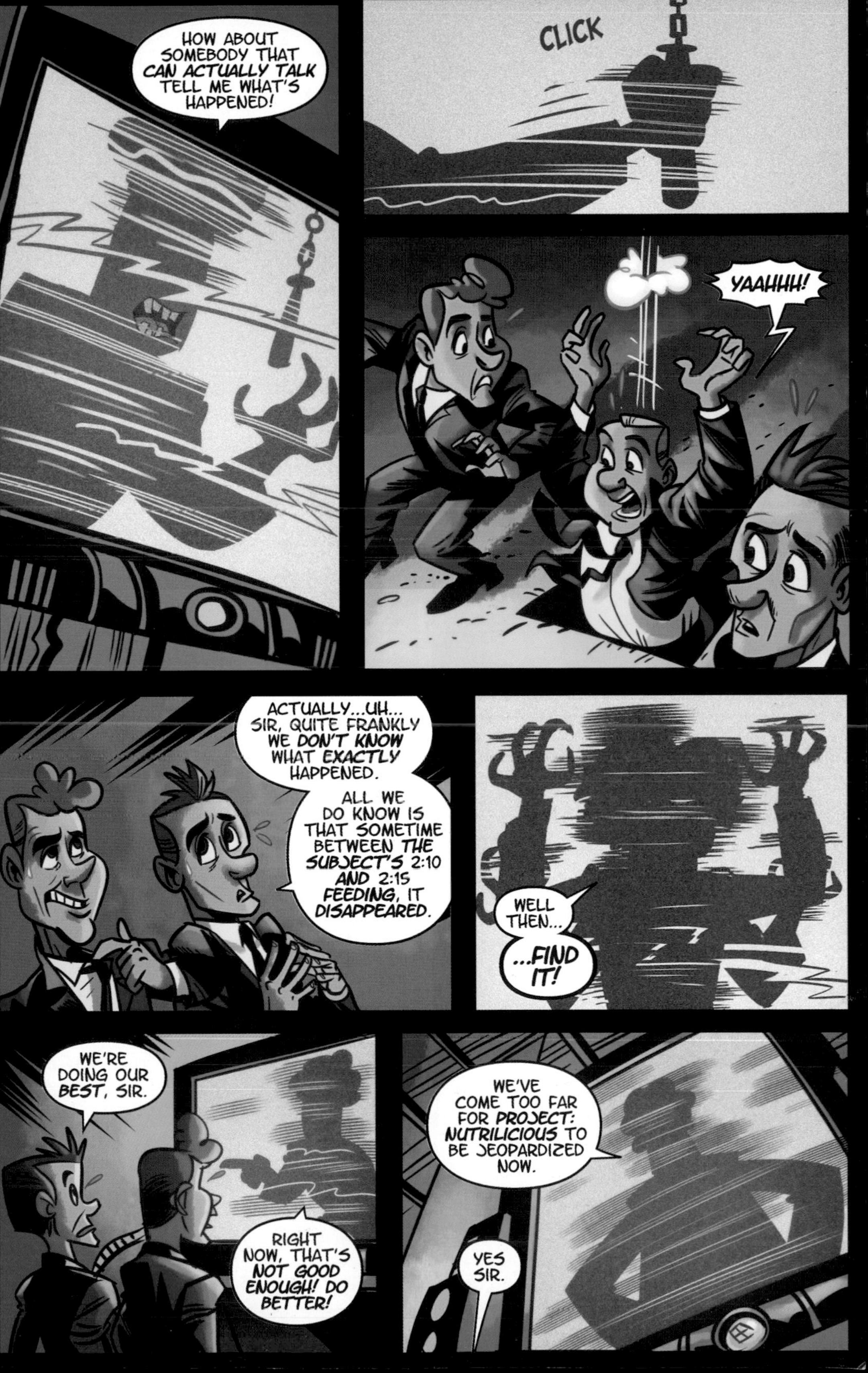
HOW ABOUT SOMEBODY THAT CAN ACTUALLY TALK TELL ME WHAT'S HAPPENED!
CLICK
YAAHHH!
ACTUALLY...UH... SIR, QUITE FRANKLY WE DON'T KNOW WHAT EXACTLY HAPPENED.
ALL WE DO KNOW IS THAT SOMETIME BETWEEN THE SUBJECT'S 2:10 AND 2:15 FEEDING, IT DISAPPEARED.
WELL THEN...
...FIND IT!
WE'RE DOING OUR BEST, SIR.
RIGHT NOW, THAT'S NOT GOOD ENOUGH! DO BETTER!
WE'VE COME TOO FAR FOR PROJECT: NUTRILICIOUS TO BE JEOPARDIZED NOW.
YES SIR.

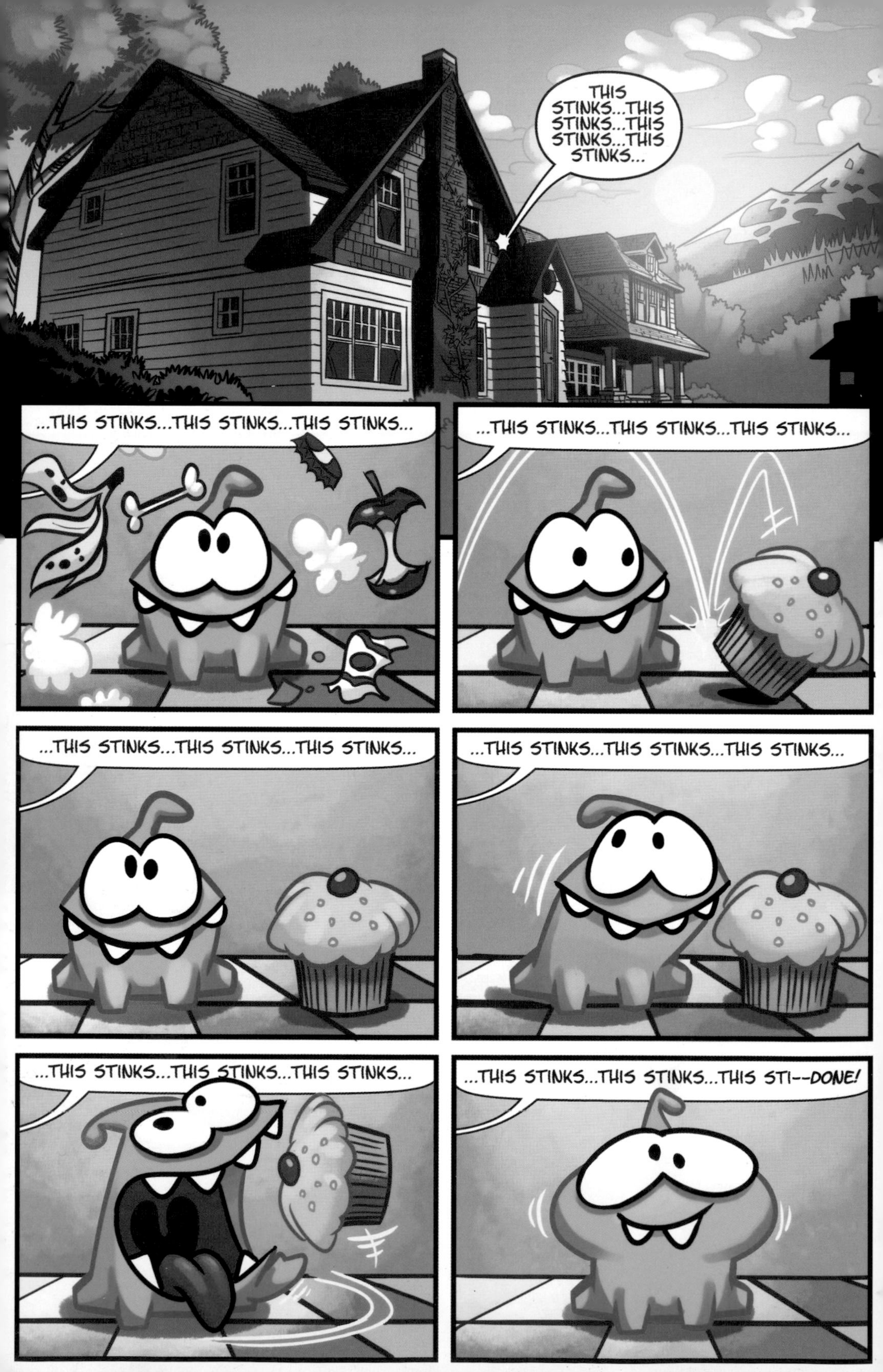
THIS STINKS...THIS STINKS...THIS STINKS...THIS STINKS...
...THIS STINKS...THIS STINKS...THIS STINKS...
...THIS STINKS...THIS STINKS...THIS STINKS...
...THIS STINKS...THIS STINKS...THIS STINKS...
...THIS STINKS...THIS STINKS...THIS STINKS...
...THIS STINKS...THIS STINKS...THIS STINKS...
...THIS STINKS...THIS STINKS...THIS STI--DONE!

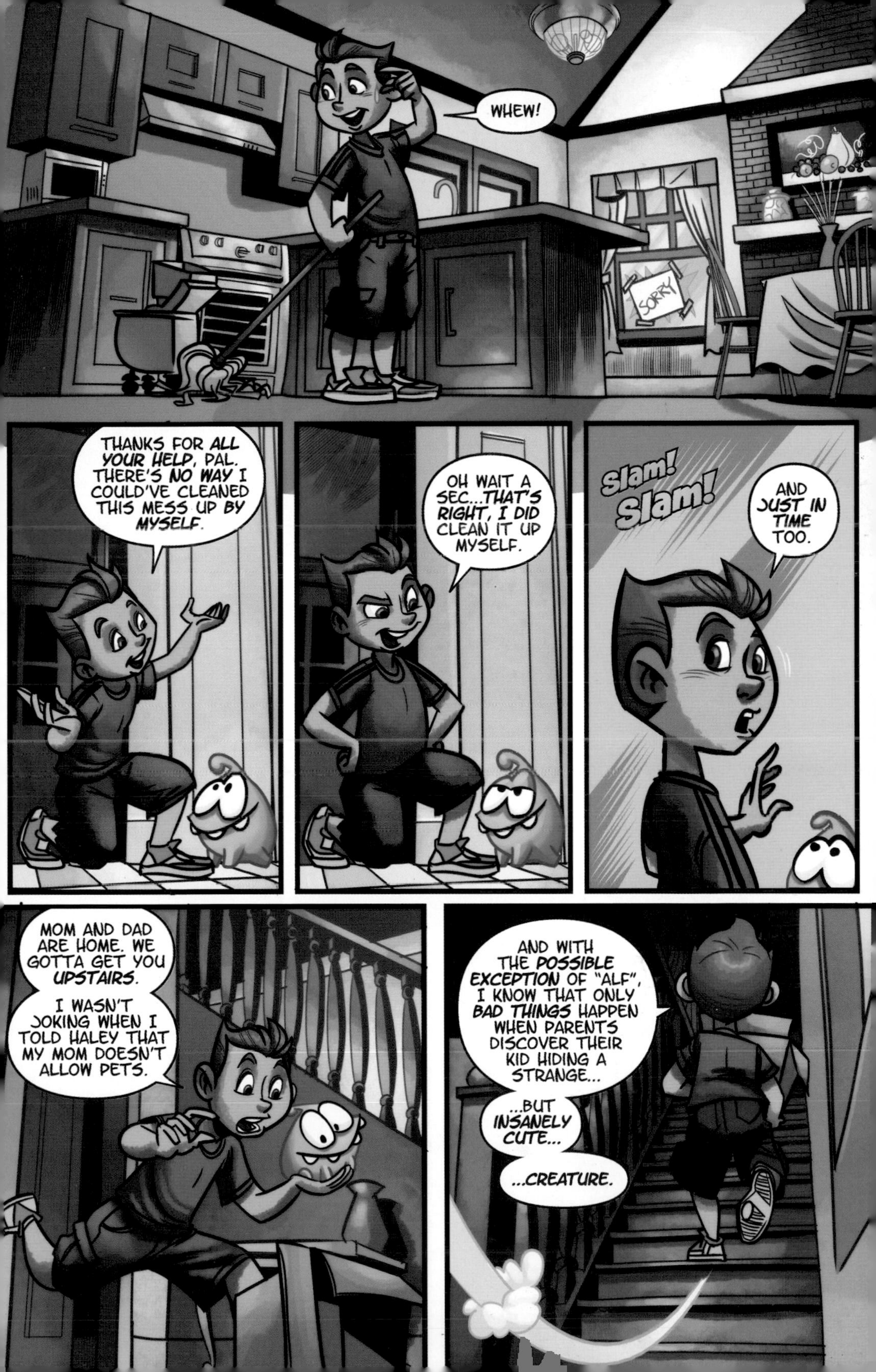
WHEW!
SORRY
THANKS FOR ALL YOUR HELP, PAL. THERE'S NO WAY I COULD'VE CLEANED THIS MESS UP BY MYSELF.
OH WAIT A SEC...THAT'S RIGHT, I DID CLEAN IT UP MYSELF.
Slam! Slam!
AND JUST IN TIME TOO.
MOM AND DAD ARE HOME. WE GOTTA GET YOU UPSTAIRS.
I WASN'T JOKING WHEN I TOLD HALEY THAT MY MOM DOESN'T ALLOW PETS.
AND WITH THE POSSIBLE EXCEPTION OF "ALF", I KNOW THAT ONLY BAD THINGS HAPPEN WHEN PARENTS DISCOVER THEIR KID HIDING A STRANGE...
...BUT INSANELY CUTE...
...CREATURE.

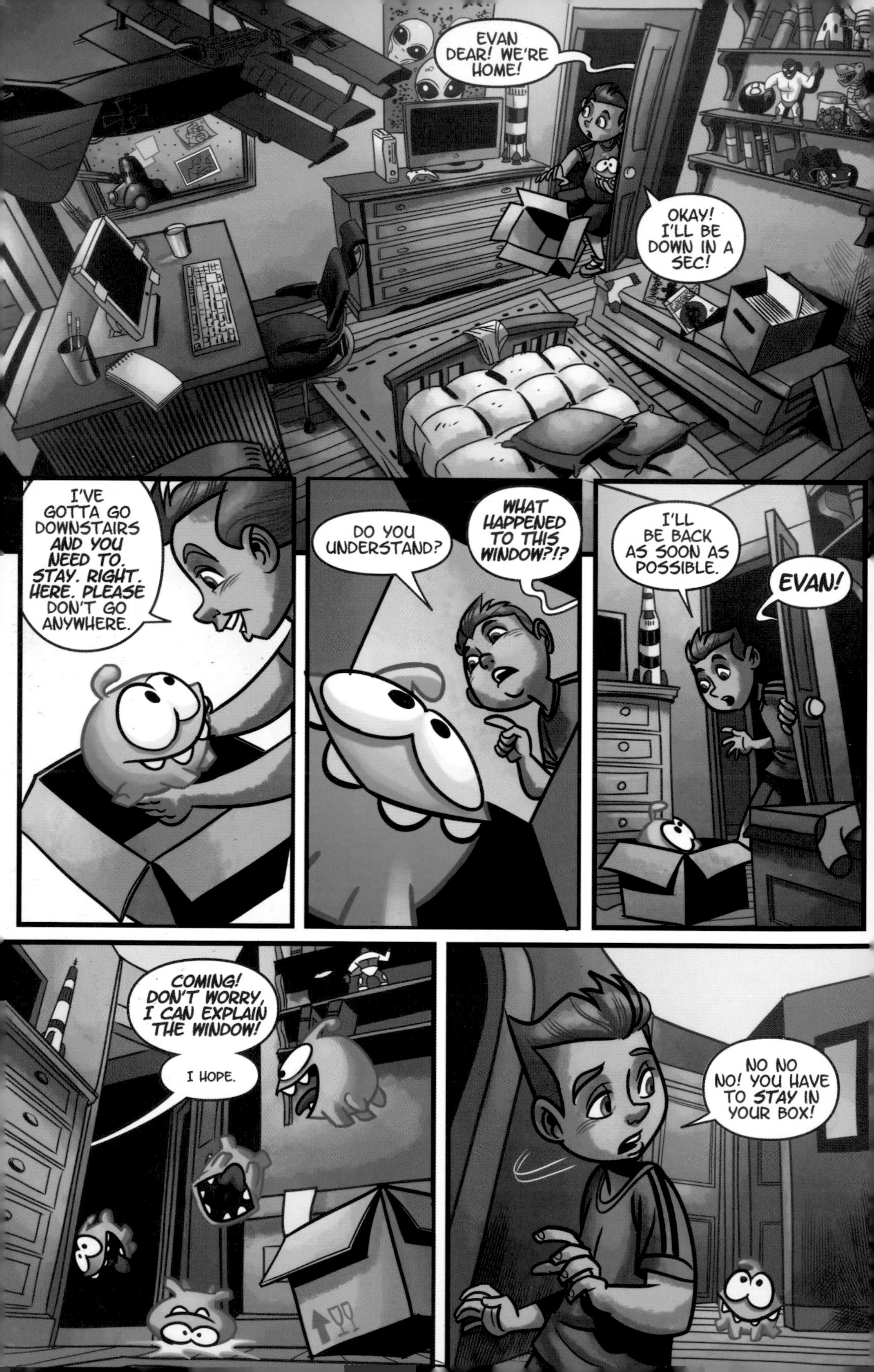
EVAN DEAR! WE'RE HOME!
OKAY! I'LL BE DOWN IN A SEC!
I'VE GOTTA GO DOWNSTAIRS AND YOU NEED TO. STAY. RIGHT. HERE. PLEASE DON'T GO ANYWHERE.
DO YOU UNDERSTAND?
WHAT HAPPENED TO THIS WINDOW?!?
I'LL BE BACK AS SOON AS POSSIBLE.
EVAN!
COMING! DON'T WORRY, I CAN EXPLAIN THE WINDOW!
I HOPE.
NO NO NO! YOU HAVE TO STAY IN YOUR BOX!

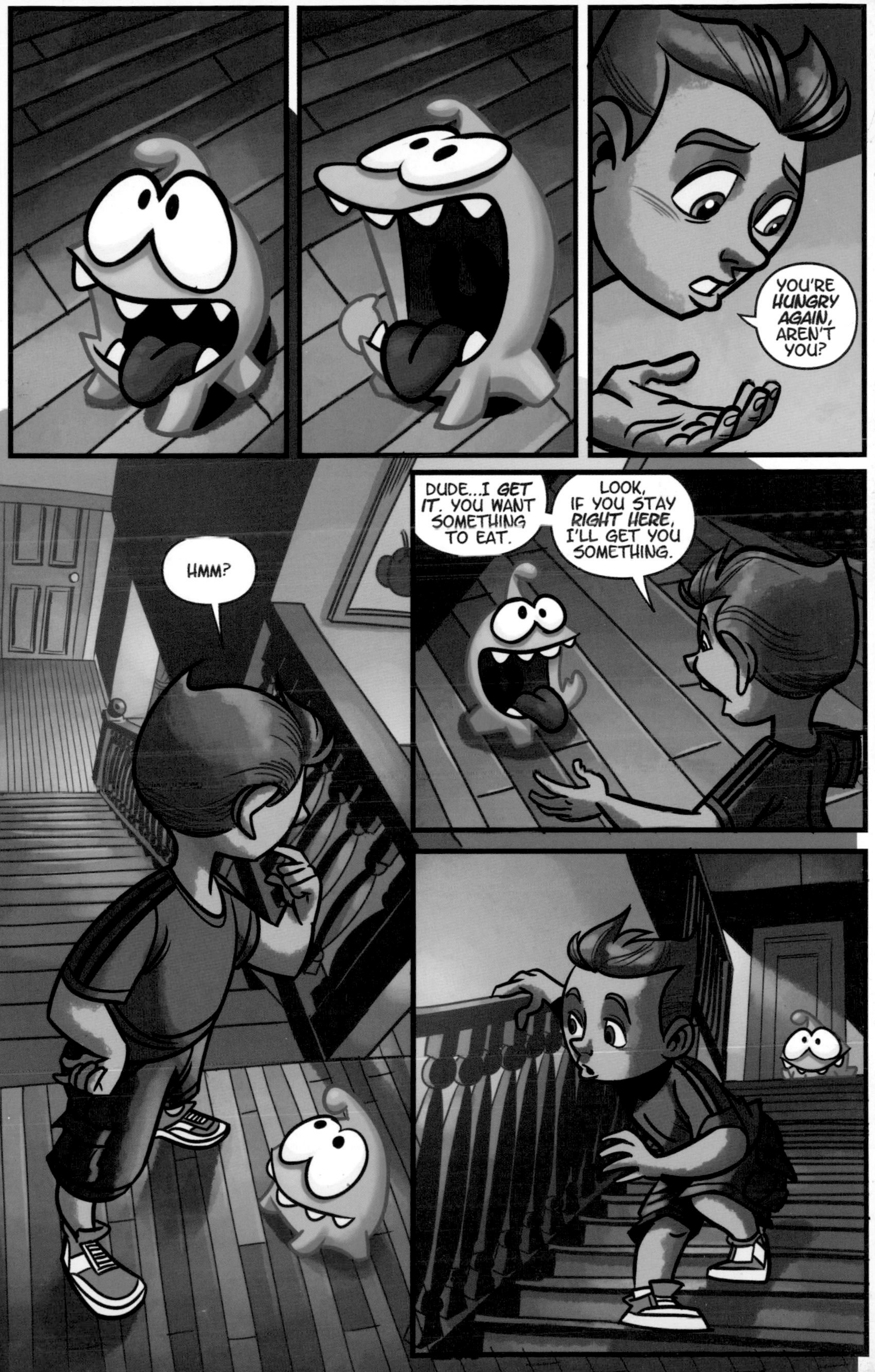
YOU'RE HUNGRY AGAIN, AREN'T YOU?
HMM?
DUDE...I GET IT. YOU WANT SOMETHING TO EAT.
LOOK, IF YOU STAY RIGHT HERE, I'LL GET YOU SOMETHING.

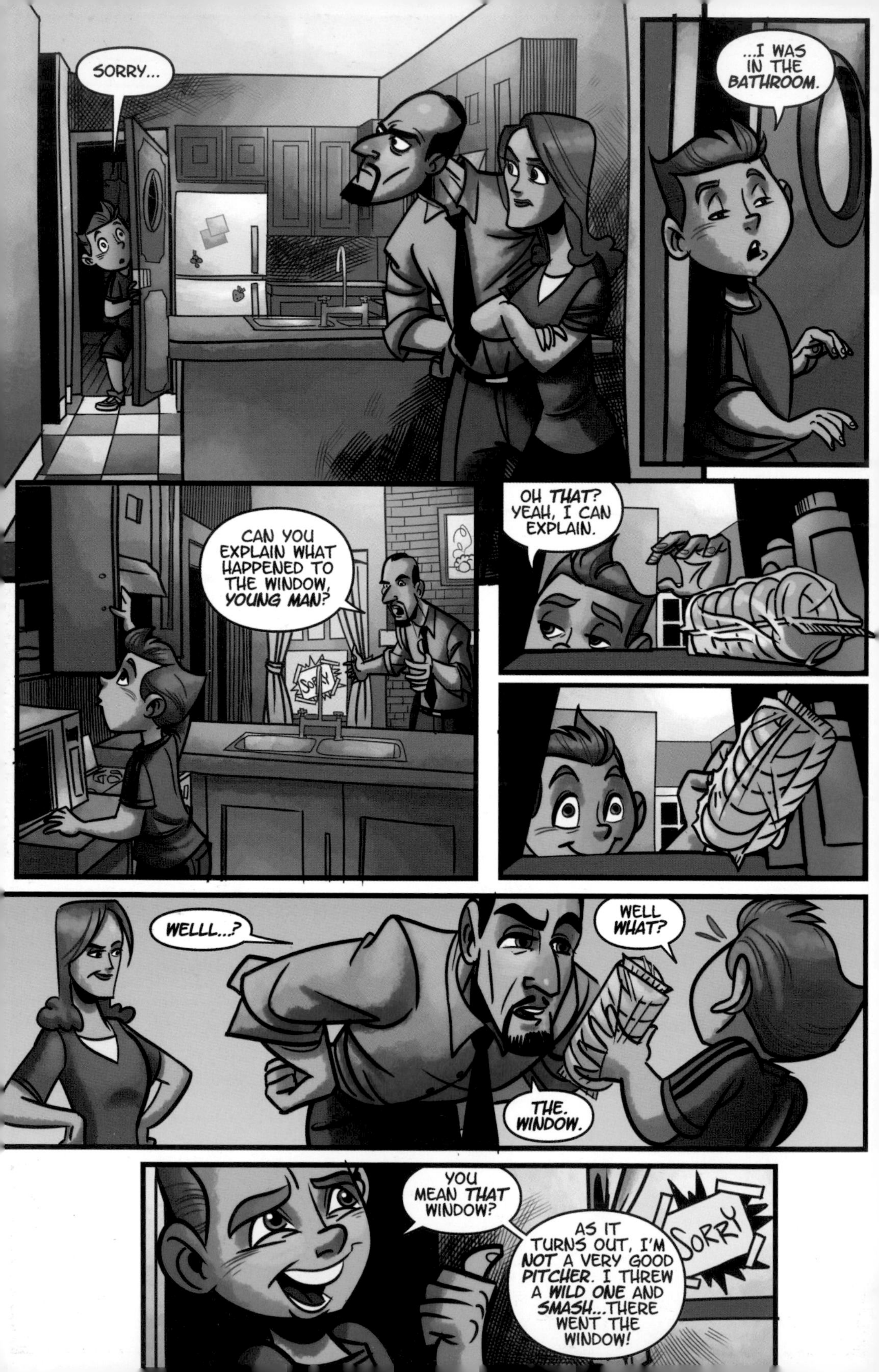
SORRY...
...I WAS IN THE BATHROOM.
CAN YOU EXPLAIN WHAT HAPPENED TO THE WINDOW, YOUNG MAN?
SORRY
OH THAT? YEAH, I CAN EXPLAIN.
WELLL...?
WELL WHAT?
THE. WINDOW.
YOU MEAN THAT WINDOW?
AS IT TURNS OUT, I'M NOT A VERY GOOD PITCHER. I THREW A WILD ONE AND SMASH...THERE WENT THE WINDOW!
SORRY

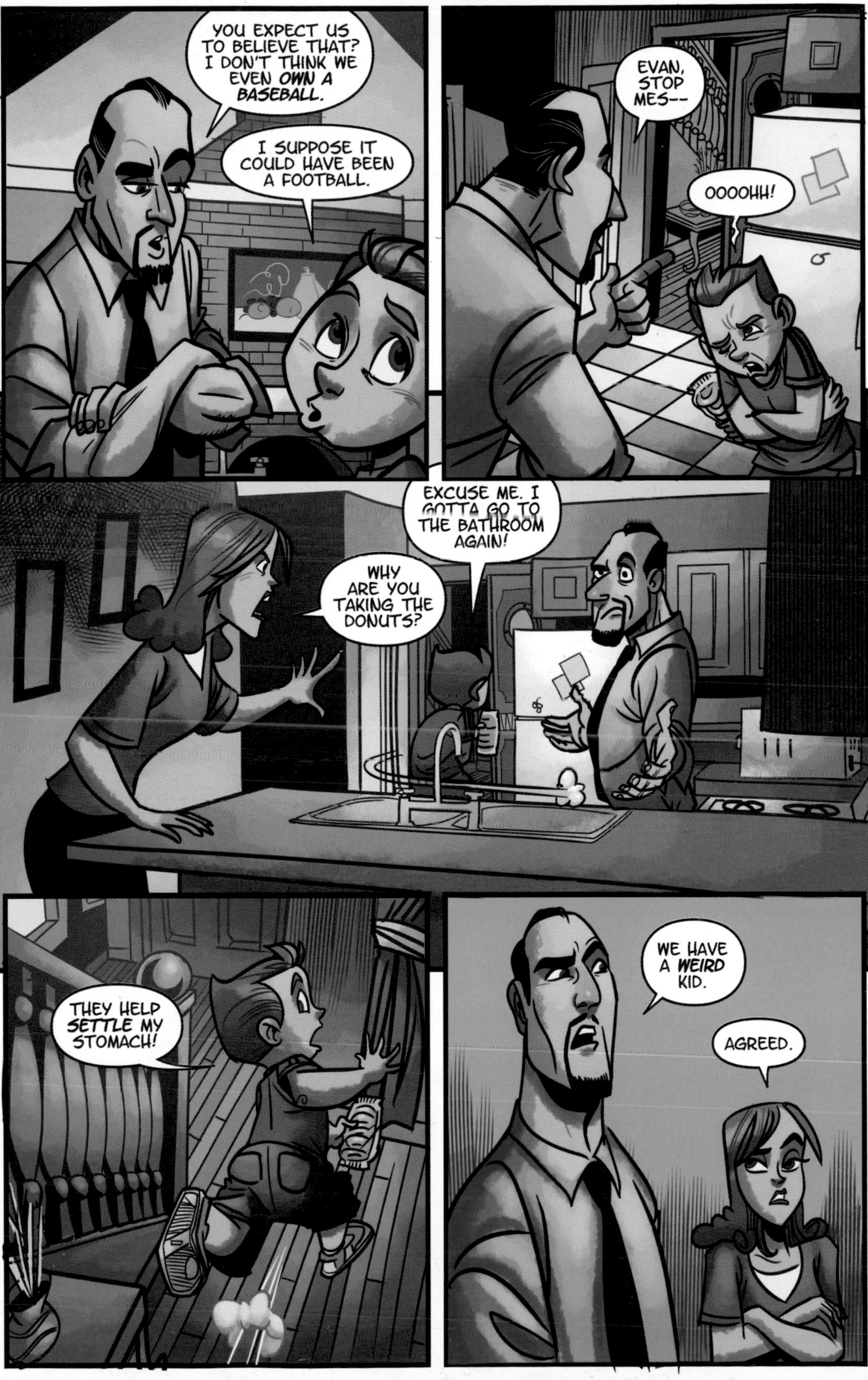
YOU EXPECT US TO BELIEVE THAT? I DON'T THINK WE EVEN OWN A BASEBALL.
I SUPPOSE IT COULD HAVE BEEN A FOOTBALL.
EVAN, STOP MES--
OOOOHH!
WHY ARE YOU TAKING THE DONUTS?
EXCUSE ME. I GOTTA GO TO THE BATHROOM AGAIN!
THEY HELP SETTLE MY STOMACH!
WE HAVE A WEIRD KID.
AGREED.

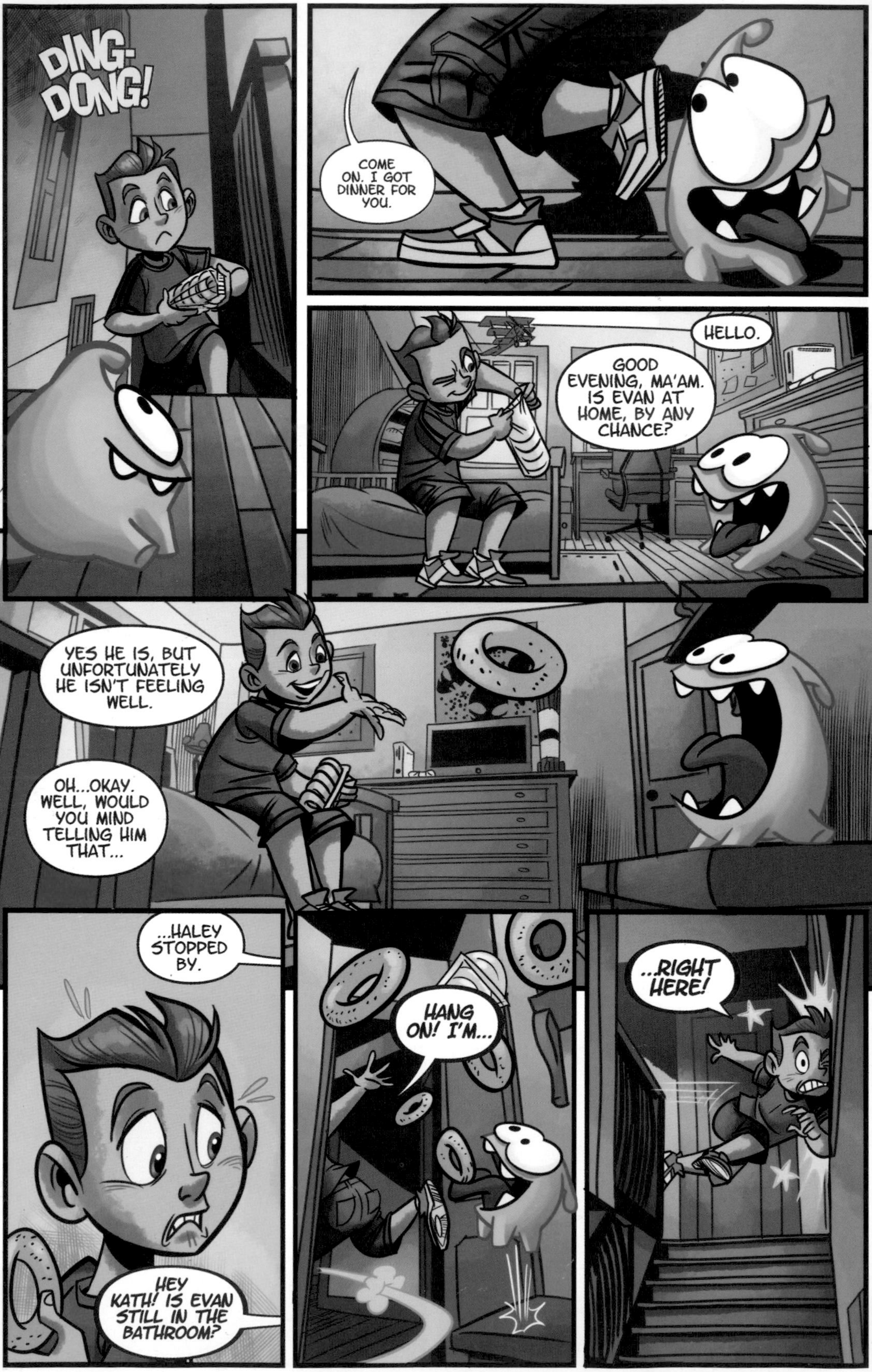
DING-DONG!
COME ON. I GOT DINNER FOR YOU.
HELLO.
GOOD EVENING, MA'AM. IS EVAN AT HOME, BY ANY CHANCE?
YES HE IS, BUT UNFORTUNATELY HE ISN'T FEELING WELL.
OH...OKAY. WELL, WOULD YOU MIND TELLING HIM THAT...
...HALEY STOPPED BY.
HEY KATH! IS EVAN STILL IN THE BATHROOM?
HANG ON! I'M...
...RIGHT HERE!

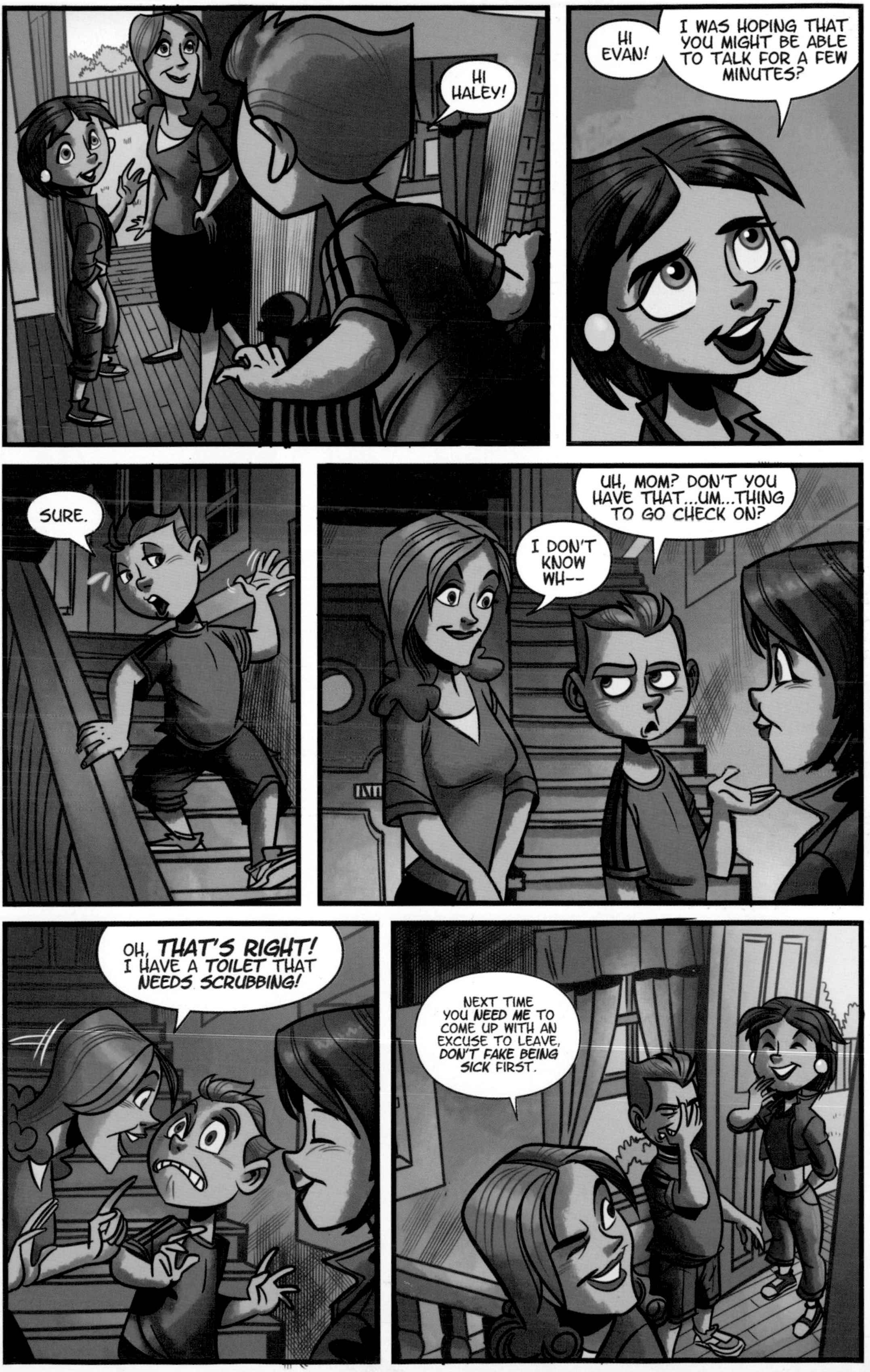
HI HALEY!
HI EVAN!
I WAS HOPING THAT YOU MIGHT BE ABLE TO TALK FOR A FEW MINUTES?
SURE.
UH, MOM? DON'T YOU HAVE THAT...UM...THING TO GO CHECK ON?
I DON'T KNOW WH--
OH, THAT'S RIGHT! I HAVE A TOILET THAT NEEDS SCRUBBING!
NEXT TIME YOU NEED ME TO COME UP WITH AN EXCUSE TO LEAVE, DON'T FAKE BEING SICK FIRST.

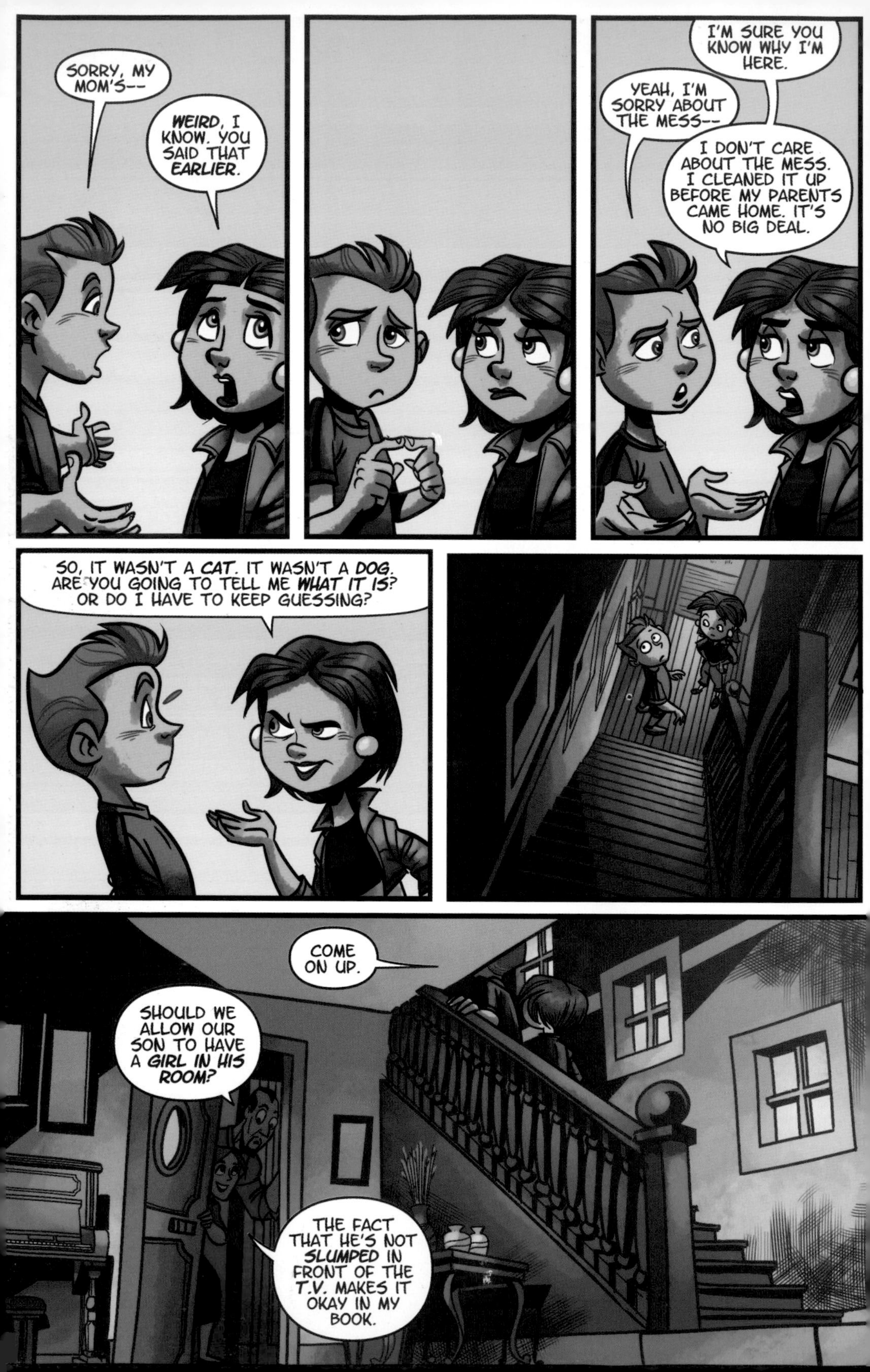
SORRY, MY MOM'S--
WEIRD, I KNOW. YOU SAID THAT EARLIER.
YEAH, I'M SORRY ABOUT THE MESS--
I'M SURE YOU KNOW WHY I'M HERE.
I DON'T CARE ABOUT THE MESS. I CLEANED IT UP BEFORE MY PARENTS CAME HOME. IT'S NO BIG DEAL.
SO, IT WASN'T A CAT. IT WASN'T A DOG. ARE YOU GOING TO TELL ME WHAT IT IS? OR DO I HAVE TO KEEP GUESSING?
COME ON UP.
SHOULD WE ALLOW OUR SON TO HAVE A GIRL IN HIS ROOM?
THE FACT THAT HE'S NOT SLUMPED IN FRONT OF THE T.V. MAKES IT OKAY IN MY BOOK.

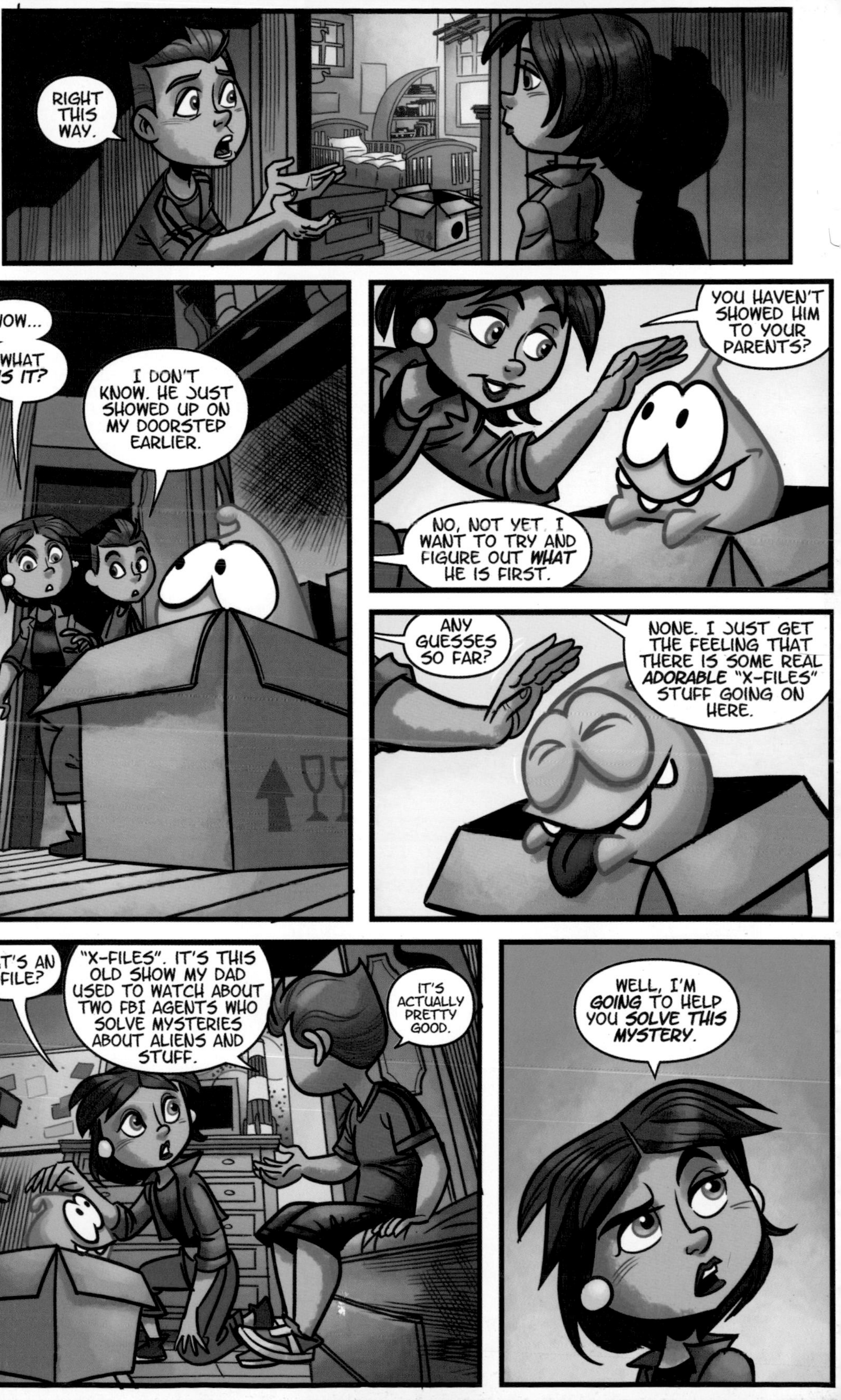
RIGHT THIS WAY.
WOW...
WHAT IS IT?
I DON'T KNOW. HE JUST SHOWED UP ON MY DOORSTEP EARLIER.
YOU HAVEN'T SHOWED HIM TO YOUR PARENTS?
NO, NOT YET. I WANT TO TRY AND FIGURE OUT WHAT HE IS FIRST.
ANY GUESSES SO FAR?
NONE. I JUST GET THE FEELING THAT THERE IS SOME REAL ADORABLE "X-FILES" STUFF GOING ON HERE.
WHAT'S AN X-FILE?
"X-FILES". IT'S THIS OLD SHOW MY DAD USED TO WATCH ABOUT TWO FBI AGENTS WHO SOLVE MYSTERIES ABOUT ALIENS AND STUFF.
IT'S ACTUALLY PRETTY GOOD.
WELL, I'M GOING TO HELP YOU SOLVE THIS MYSTERY.

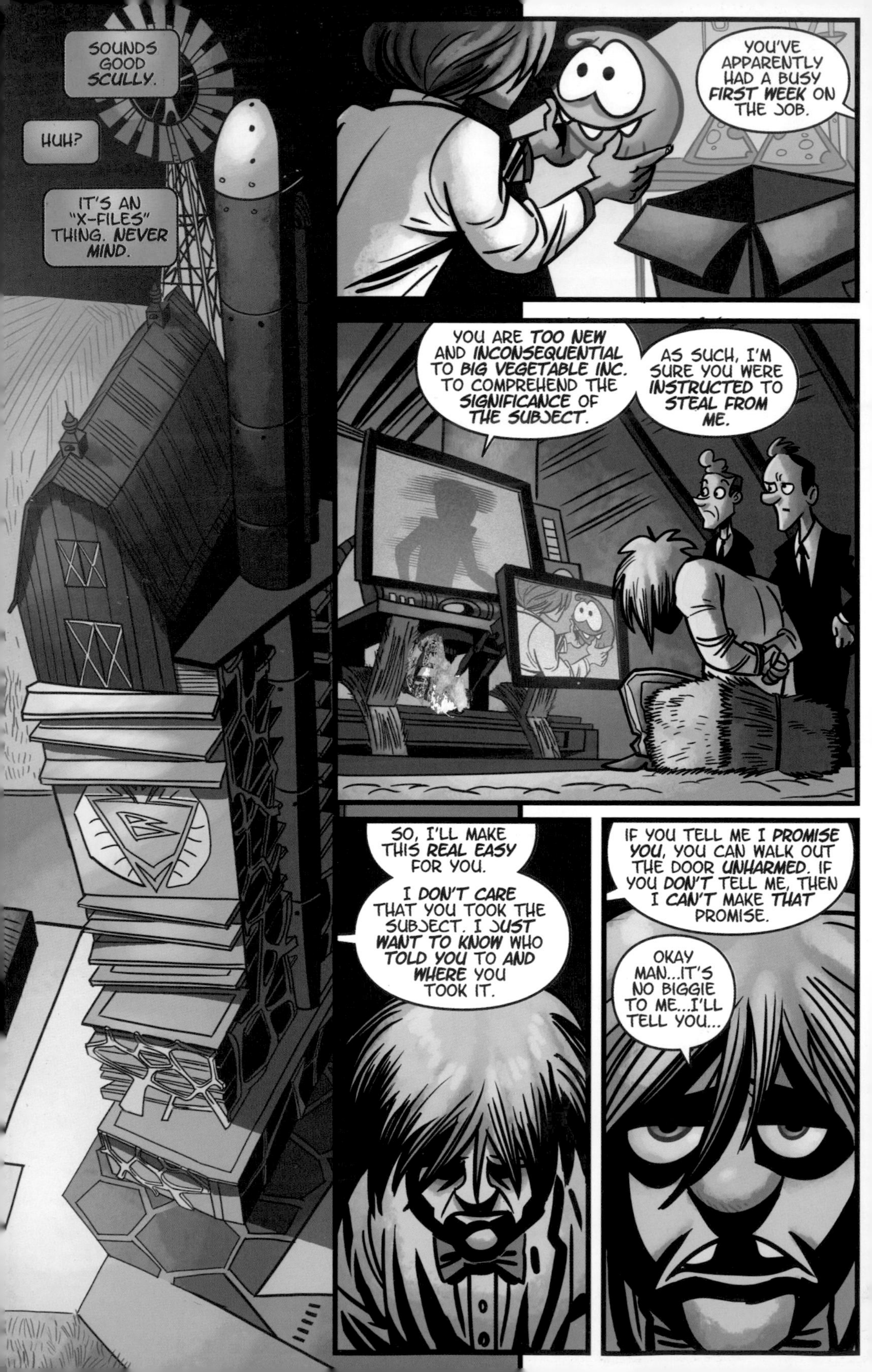
SOUNDS GOOD SCULLY.
HUH?
IT'S AN "X-FILES" THING. NEVER MIND.
YOU'VE APPARENTLY HAD A BUSY FIRST WEEK ON THE JOB.
YOU ARE TOO NEW AND INCONSEQUENTIAL TO BIG VEGETABLE INC. TO COMPREHEND THE SIGNIFICANCE OF THE SUBJECT.
AS SUCH, I'M SURE YOU WERE INSTRUCTED TO STEAL FROM ME.
SO, I'LL MAKE THIS REAL EASY FOR YOU.
I DON'T CARE THAT YOU TOOK THE SUBJECT. I JUST WANT TO KNOW WHO TOLD YOU TO AND WHERE YOU TOOK IT.
IF YOU TELL ME I PROMISE YOU, YOU CAN WALK OUT THE DOOR UNHARMED. IF YOU DON'T TELL ME, THEN I CAN'T MAKE THAT PROMISE.
OKAY MAN...IT'S NO BIGGIE TO ME...I'LL TELL YOU...

NOW, LISTEN...

...YOU HAVE TO STAY HERE WHILE I GO SPEND THE DAY AT THE PLACE I'M *STILL NOT CONVINCED* ISN'T SOME *CRAZILY ELABORATE* AND *LONG* PUNISHMENT FOR ALL THE NIGHTS I KEPT MY PARENTS AWAKE AFTER I WAS BORN.

THEY SAY IT'S "SCHOOL". I SAY THAT'S WHAT THEY WANT ME TO BELIEVE.

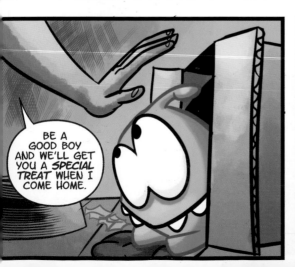

BE A GOOD BOY AND WE'LL GET YOU A *SPECIAL TREAT* WHEN I COME HOME.

SLAM

YAWN

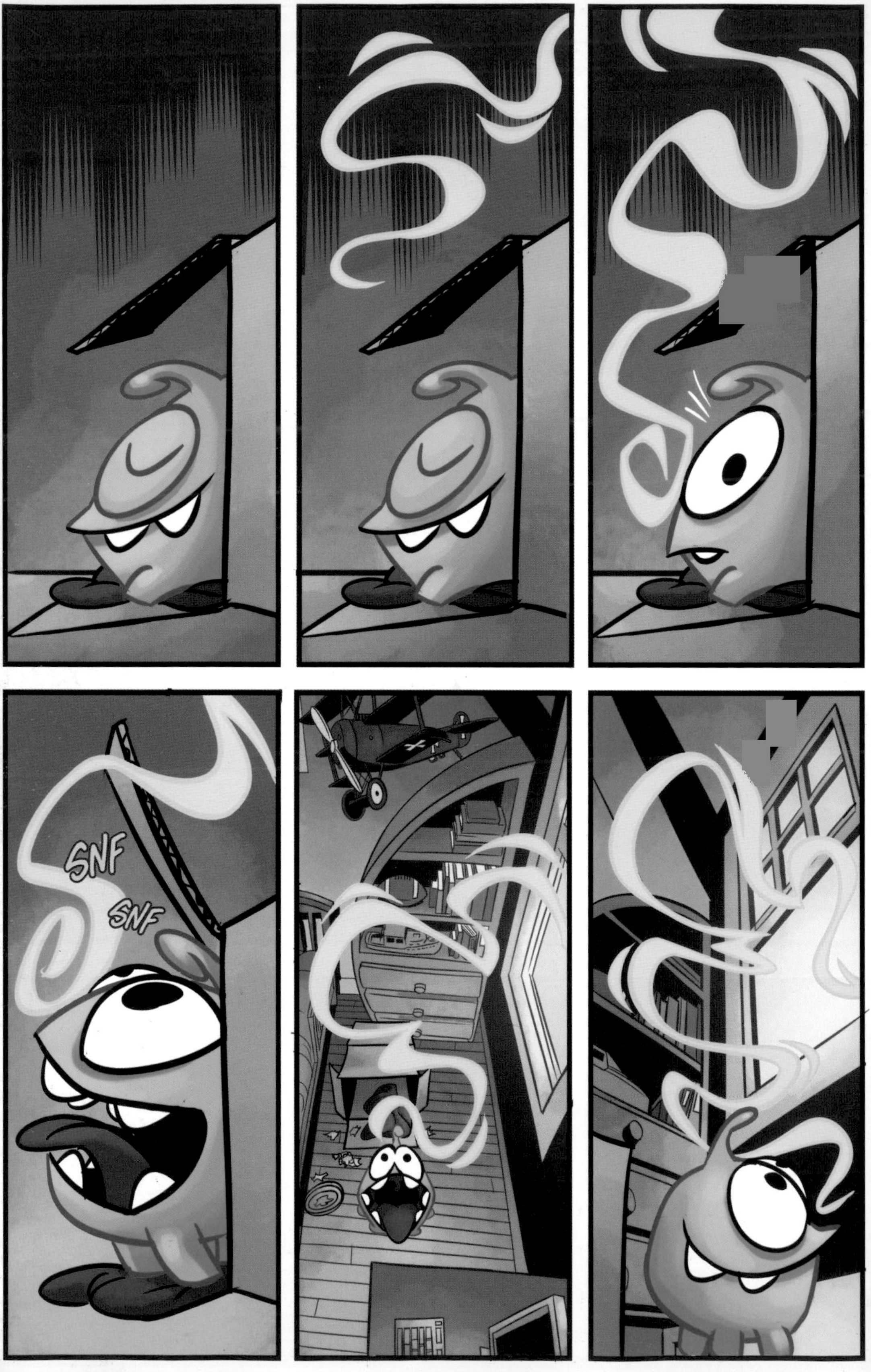
SNF
SNF

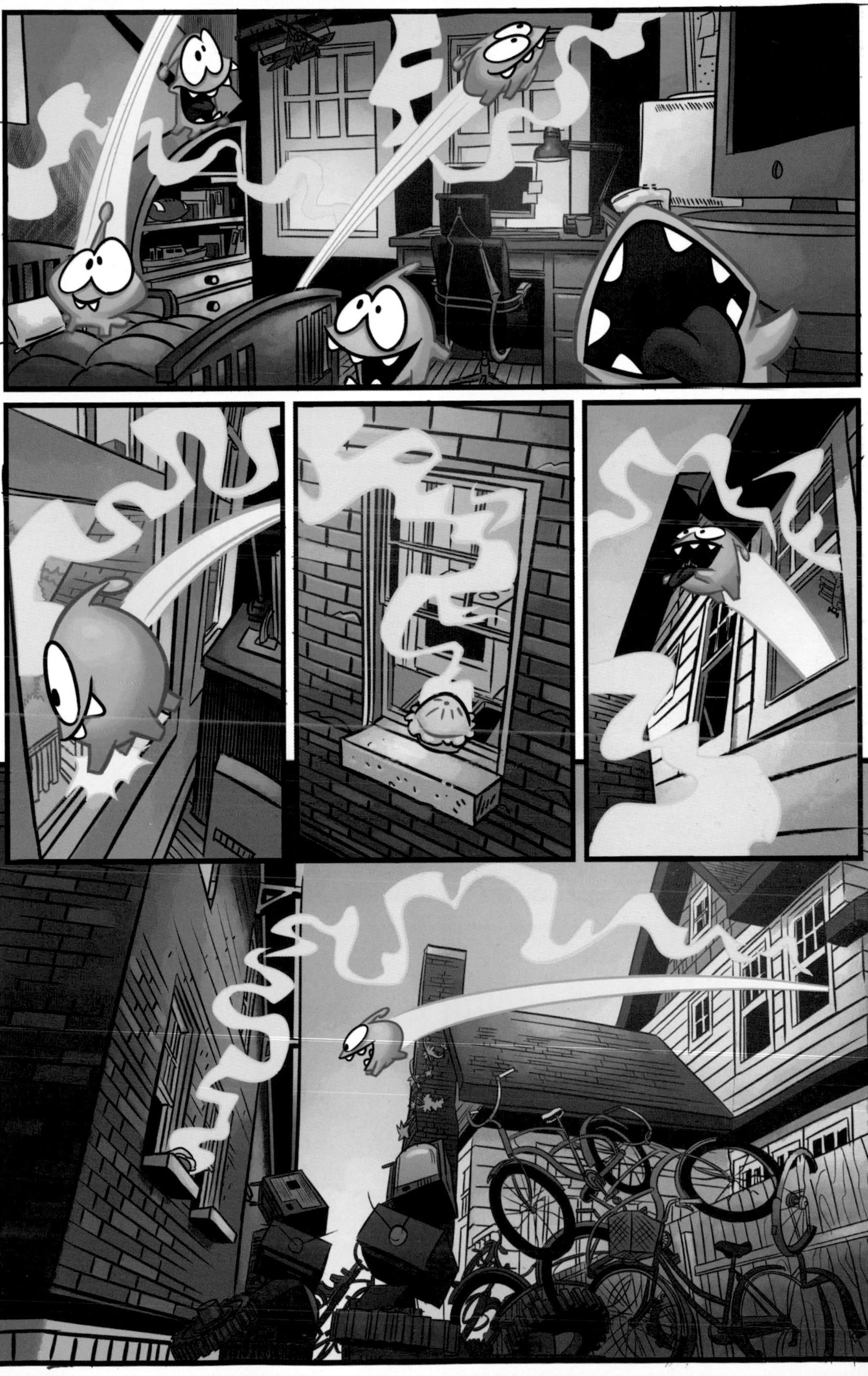

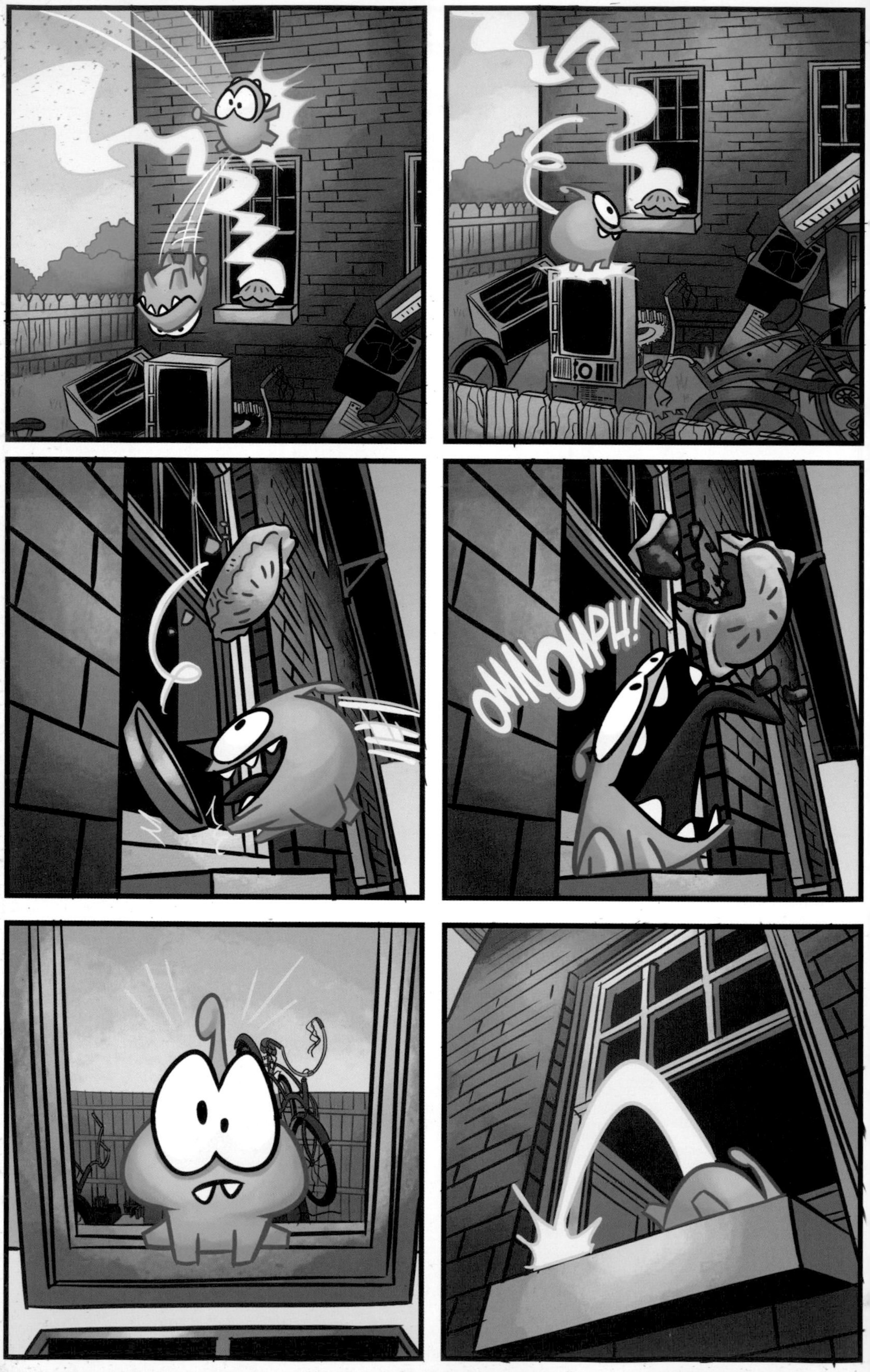
OMNOMPH!

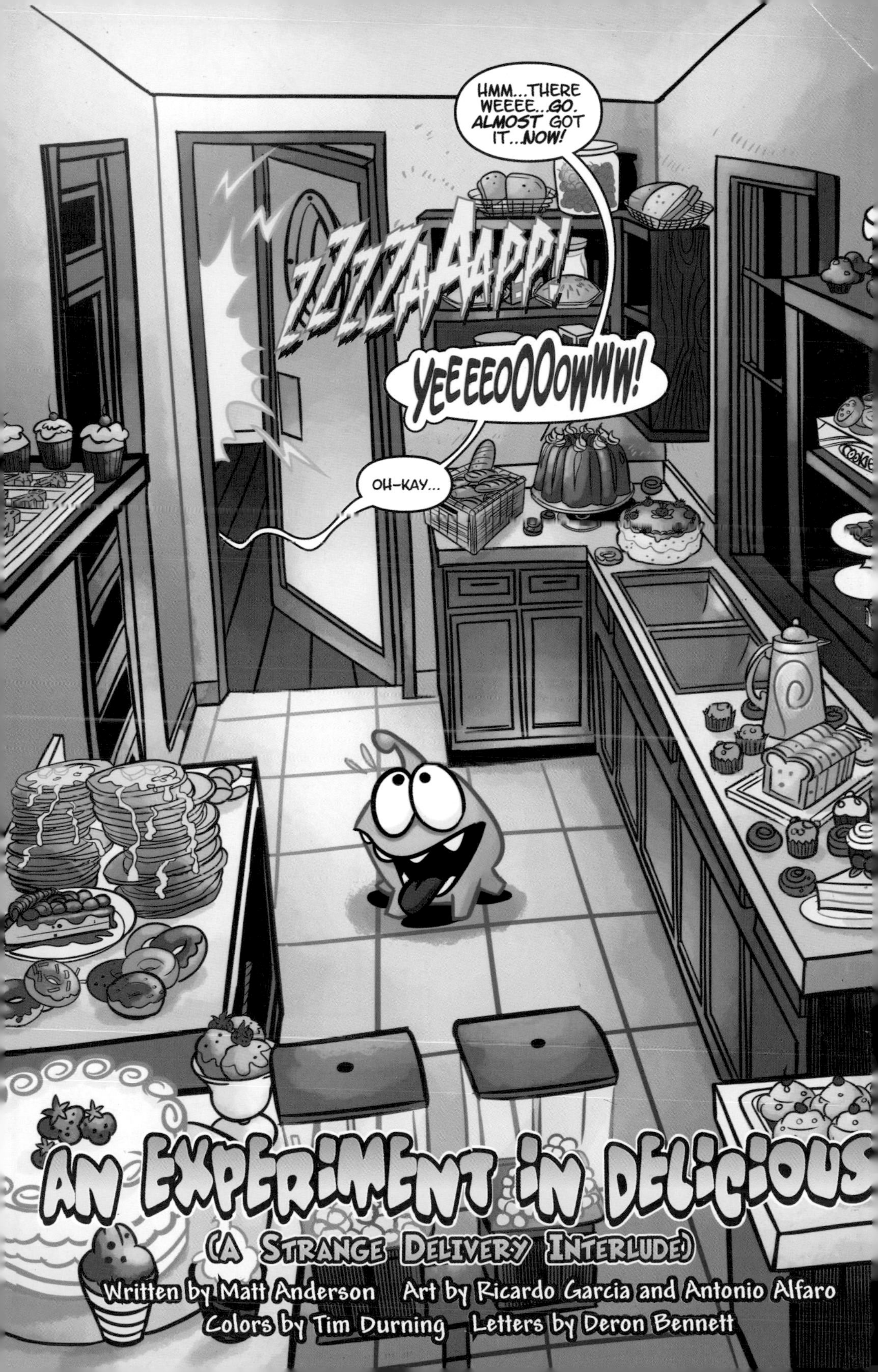

HMM...THERE WEEEE...GO. ALMOST GOT IT...NOW!
ZZZZAAAPP!
YEEEEOOOOWWW!
OH-KAY...
COOKIES
AN EXPERIMENT IN DELICIOUS
(A STRANGE DELIVERY INTERLUDE)
Written by Matt Anderson Art by Ricardo Garcia and Antonio Alfaro
Colors by Tim Durning Letters by Deron Bennett

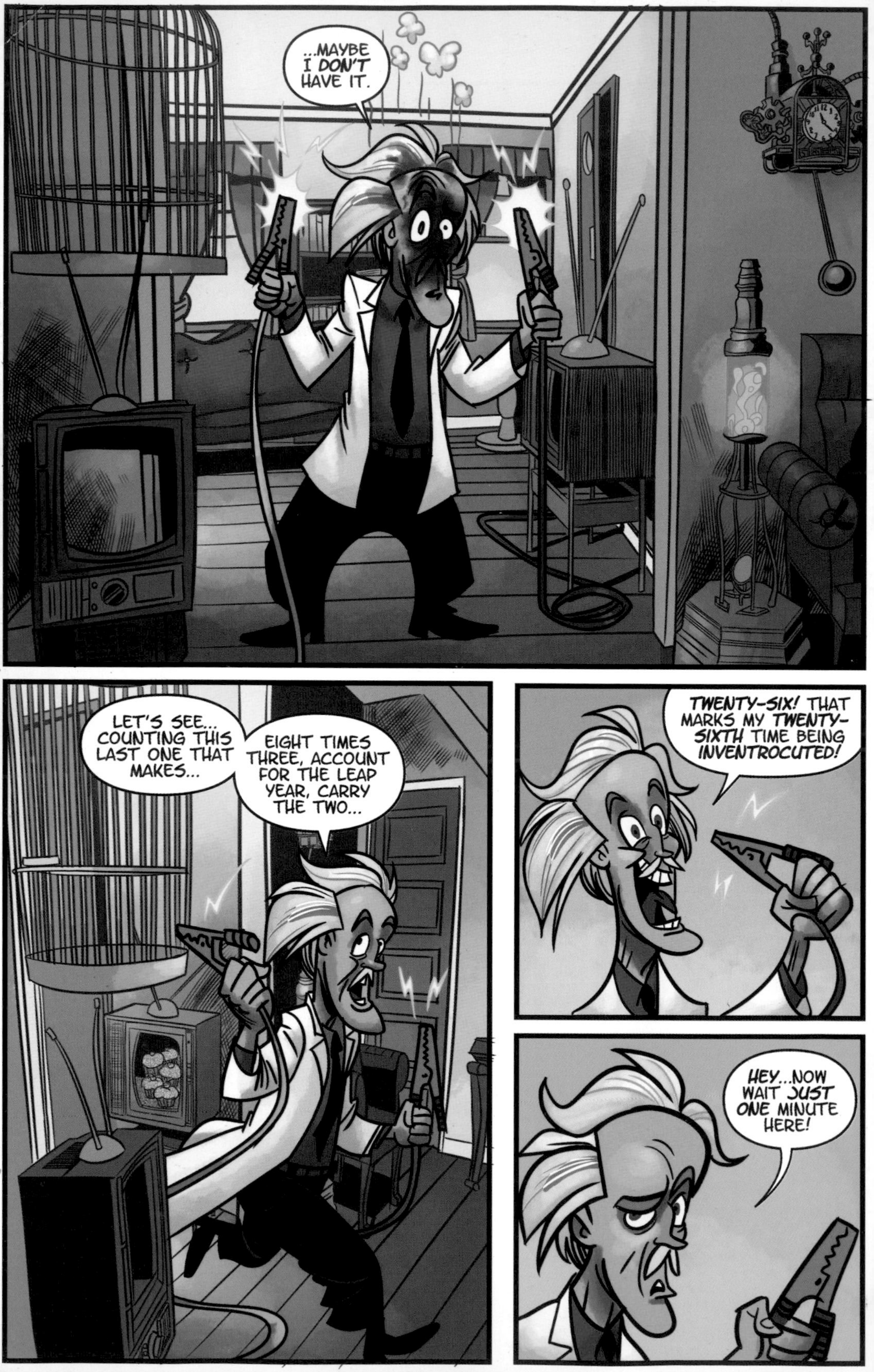

...MAYBE I DON'T HAVE IT.
LET'S SEE... COUNTING THIS LAST ONE THAT MAKES...
EIGHT TIMES THREE, ACCOUNT FOR THE LEAP YEAR, CARRY THE TWO...
TWENTY-SIX! THAT MARKS MY TWENTY-SIXTH TIME BEING INVENTROCUTED!
HEY...NOW WAIT JUST ONE MINUTE HERE!

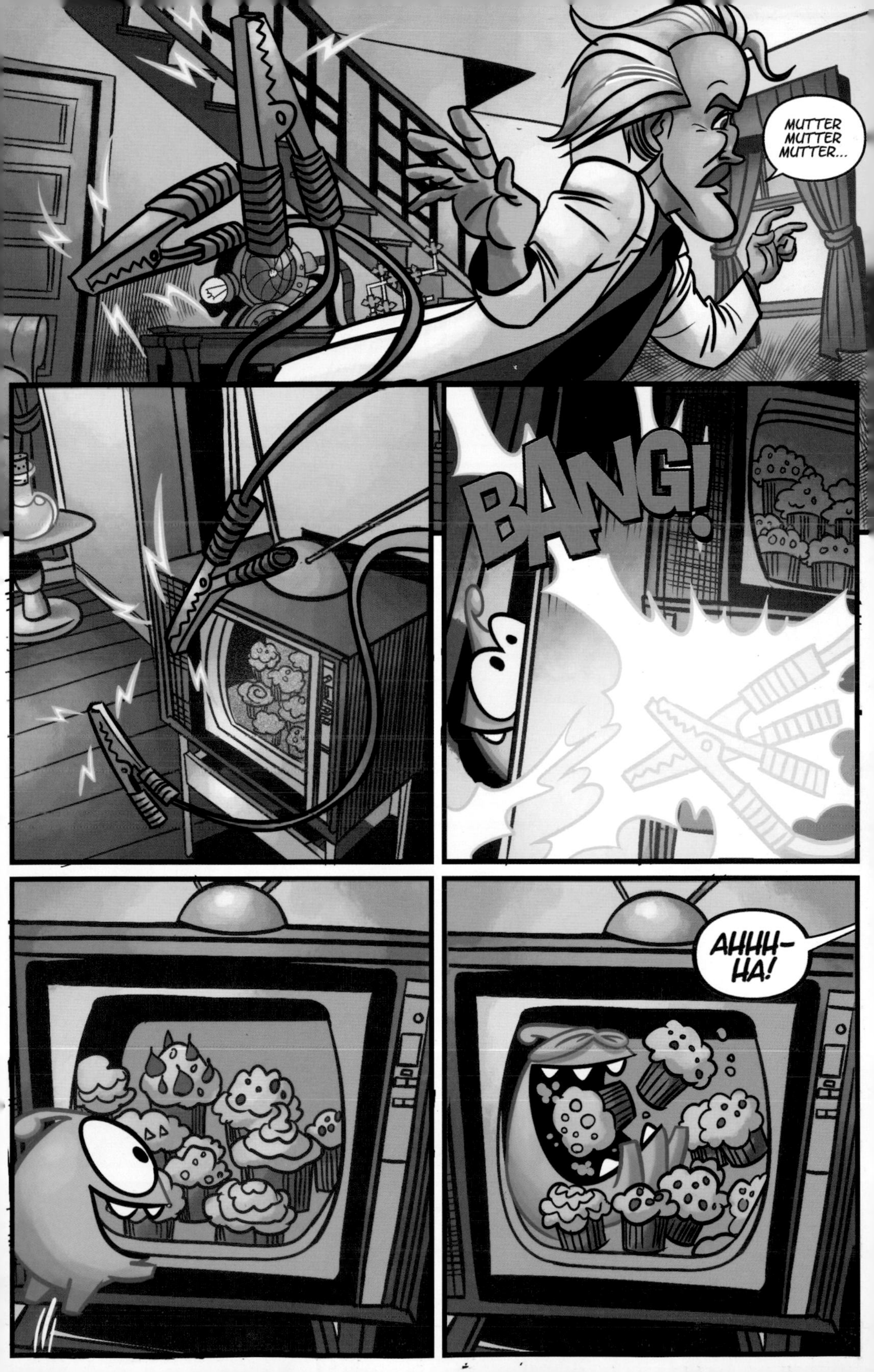
MUTTER MUTTER MUTTER...
BANG!
AHHH-HA!

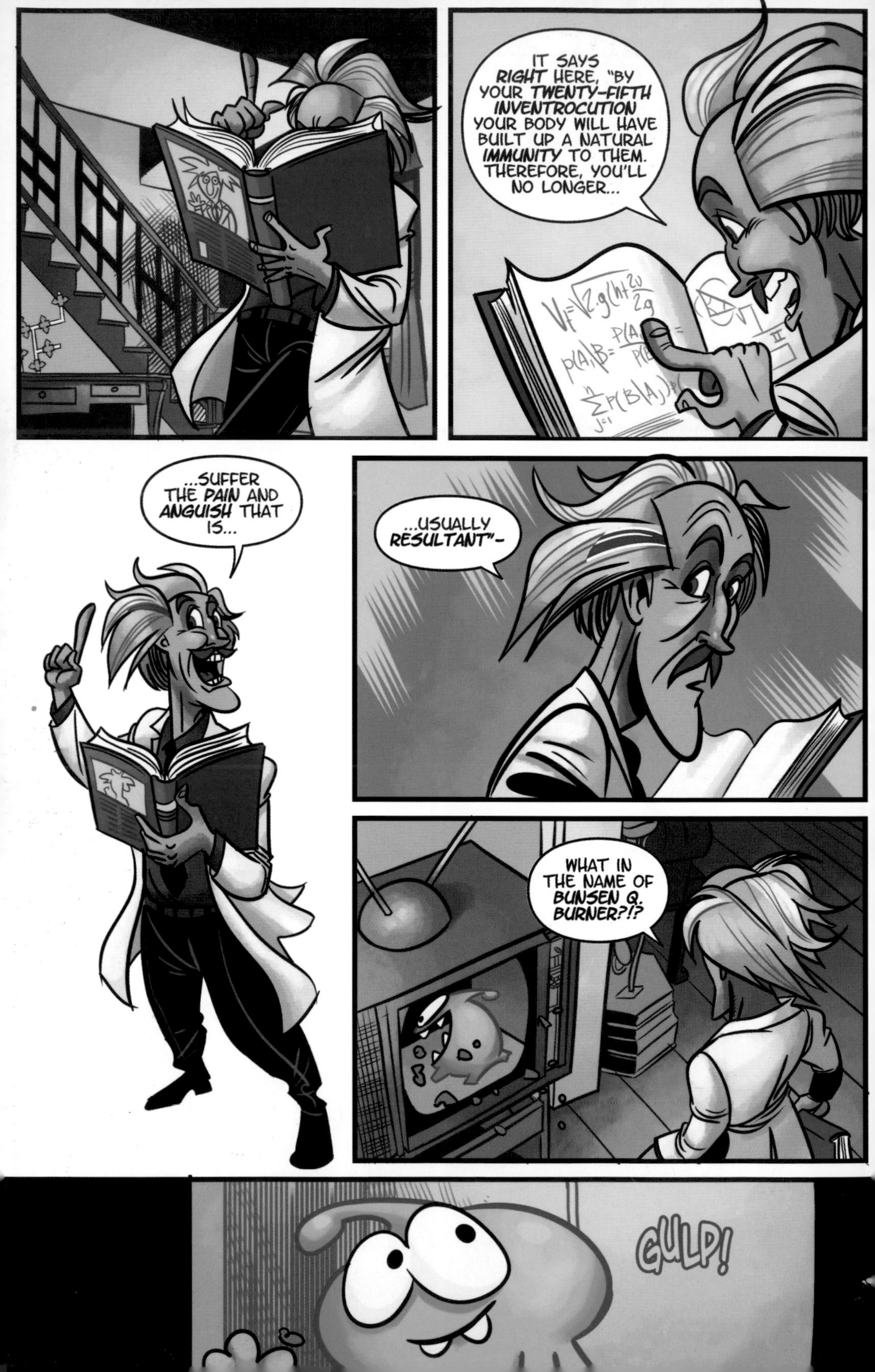
IT SAYS RIGHT HERE, "BY YOUR TWENTY-FIFTH INVENTROCUTION YOUR BODY WILL HAVE BUILT UP A NATURAL IMMUNITY TO THEM. THEREFORE, YOU'LL NO LONGER...
...SUFFER THE PAIN AND ANGUISH THAT IS...
...USUALLY RESULTANT"-
WHAT IN THE NAME OF BUNSEN Q. BURNER?!?
GULP!

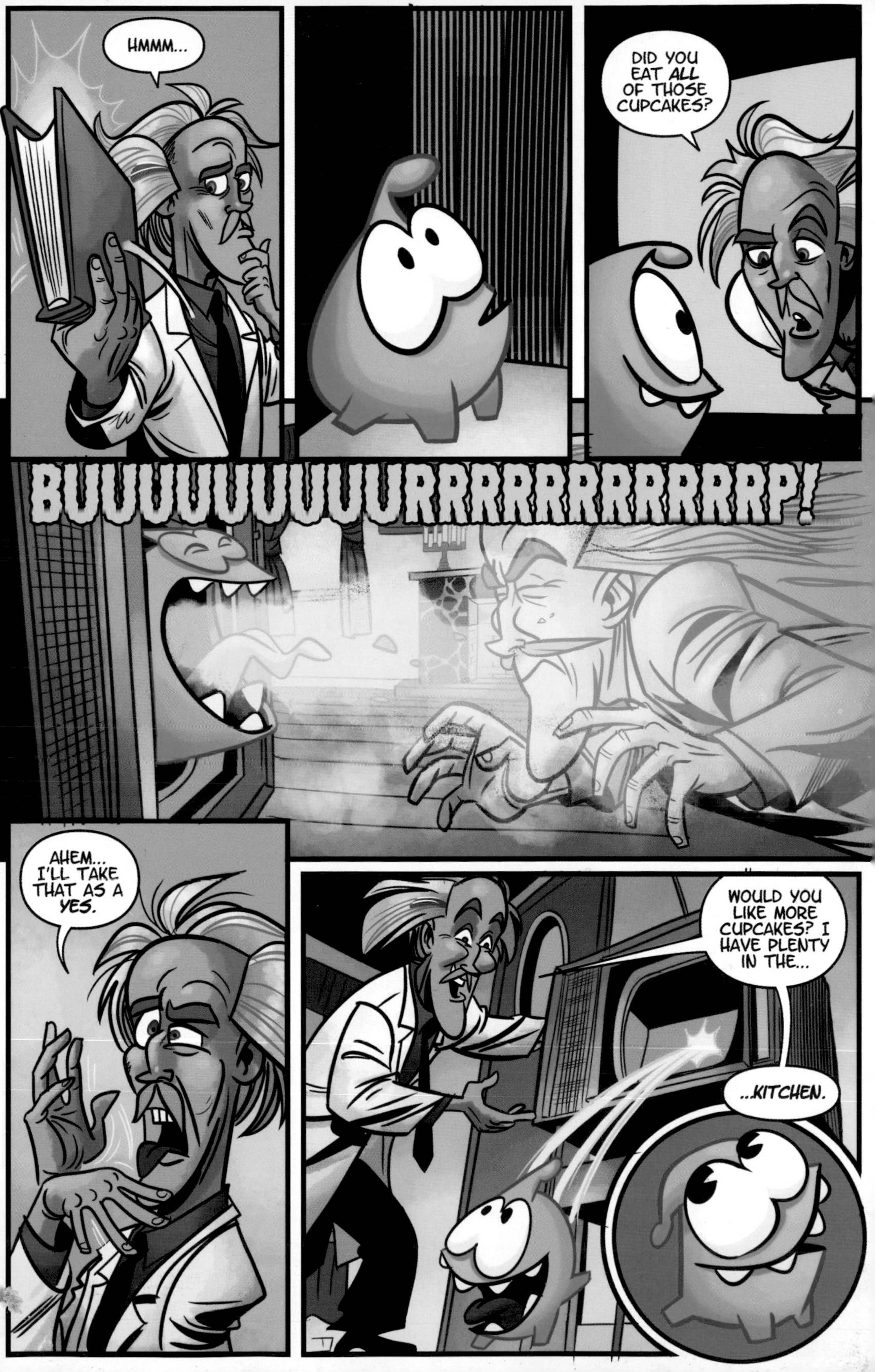
HMMM...
DID YOU EAT ALL OF THOSE CUPCAKES?
BUUUUUUUUUURRRRRRRRRRRRRP!
AHEM... I'LL TAKE THAT AS A YES.
WOULD YOU LIKE MORE CUPCAKES? I HAVE PLENTY IN THE...
...KITCHEN.

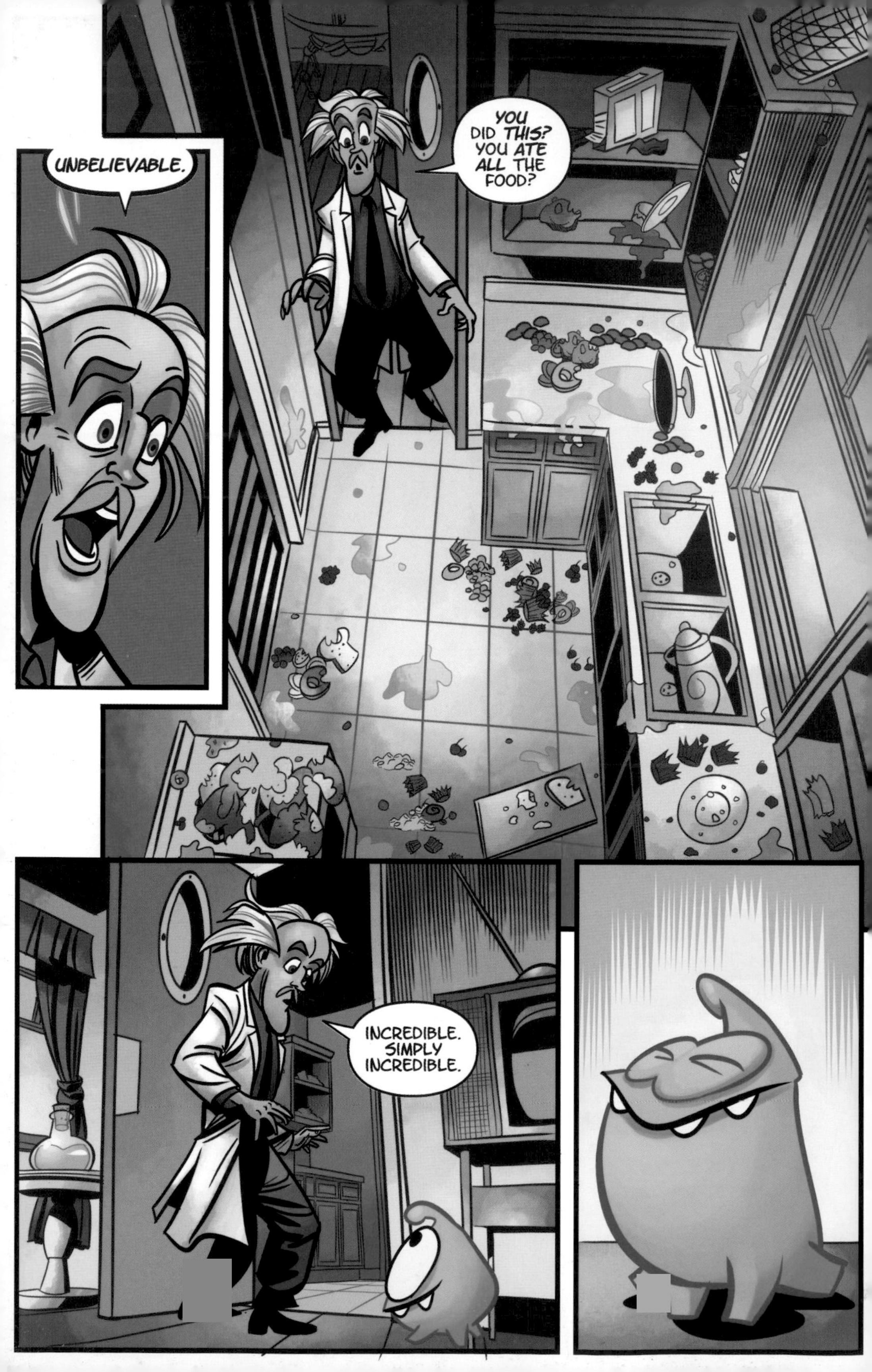
UNBELIEVABLE.
YOU DID THIS? YOU ATE ALL THE FOOD?
INCREDIBLE. SIMPLY INCREDIBLE.

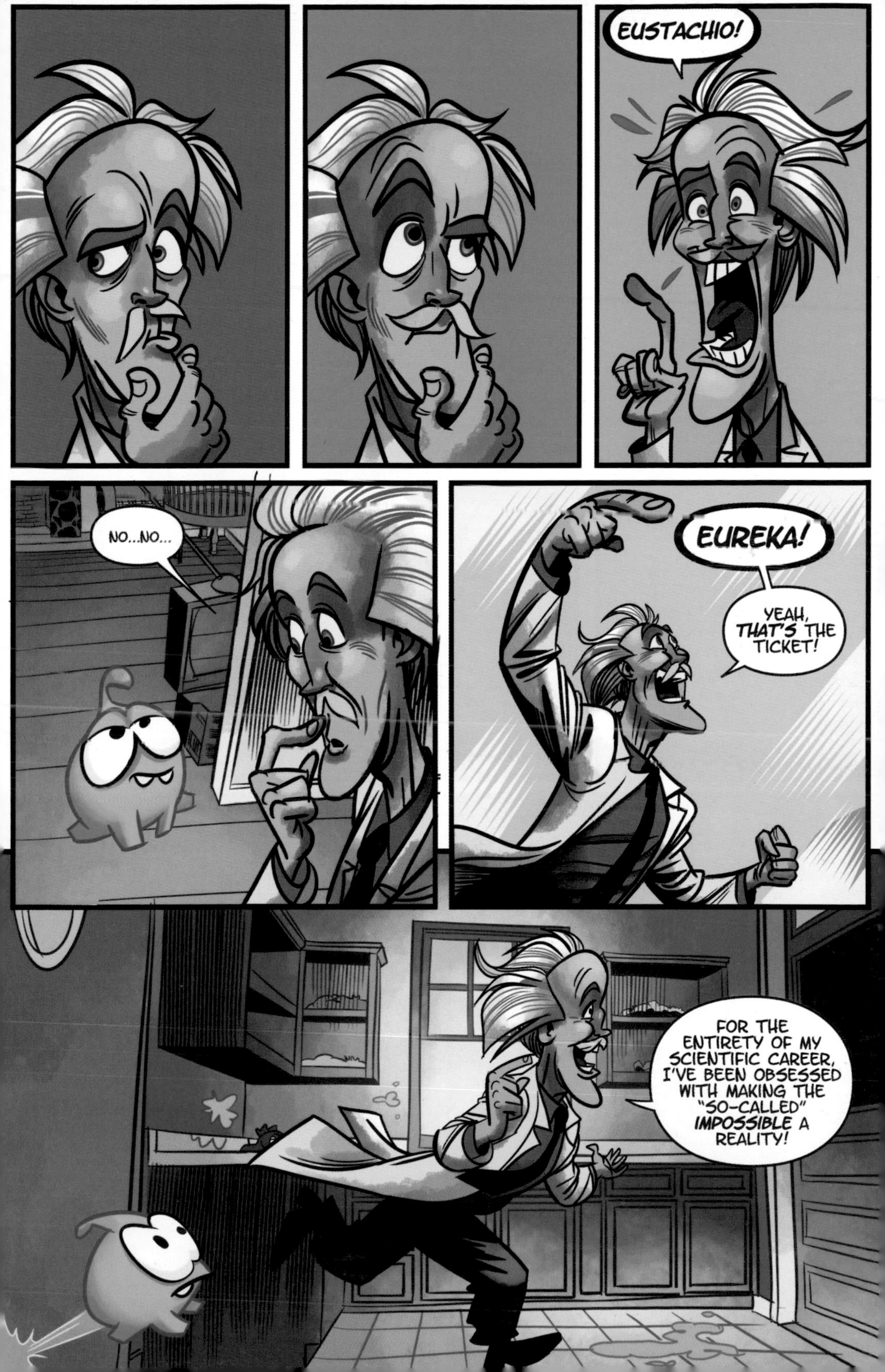
EUSTACHIO!
NO...NO...
EUREKA!
YEAH, THAT'S THE TICKET!
FOR THE ENTIRETY OF MY SCIENTIFIC CAREER, I'VE BEEN OBSESSED WITH MAKING THE "SO-CALLED" IMPOSSIBLE A REALITY!

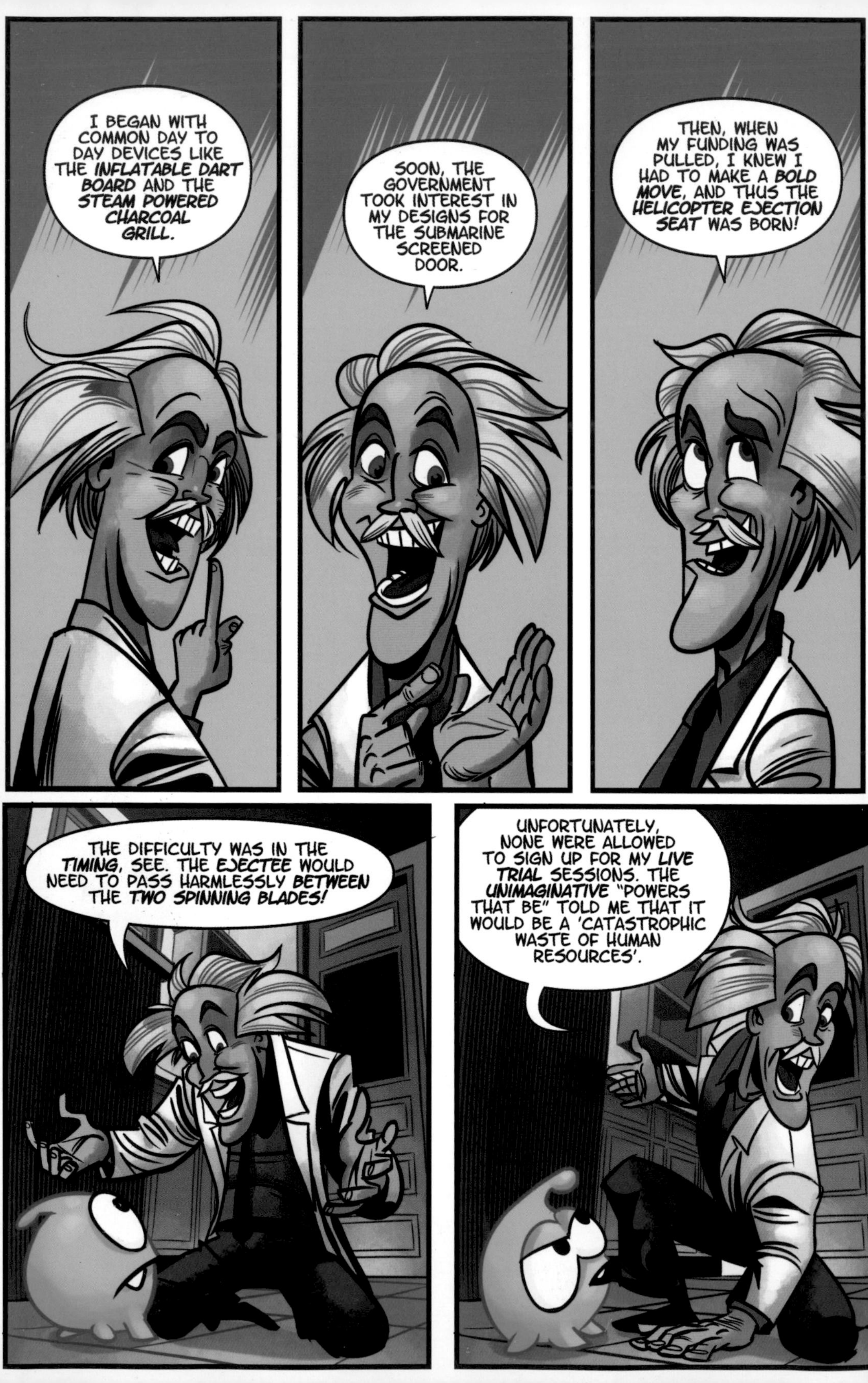
I BEGAN WITH COMMON DAY TO DAY DEVICES LIKE THE *INFLATABLE DART BOARD* AND THE *STEAM POWERED CHARCOAL GRILL.*
SOON, THE GOVERNMENT TOOK INTEREST IN MY DESIGNS FOR THE SUBMARINE SCREENED DOOR.
THEN, WHEN MY FUNDING WAS PULLED, I KNEW I HAD TO MAKE A *BOLD MOVE*, AND THUS THE *HELICOPTER EJECTION SEAT* WAS BORN!
THE DIFFICULTY WAS IN THE *TIMING*, SEE. THE *EJECTEE* WOULD NEED TO PASS HARMLESSLY *BETWEEN* THE *TWO SPINNING BLADES!*
UNFORTUNATELY, NONE WERE ALLOWED TO SIGN UP FOR MY *LIVE TRIAL* SESSIONS. THE *UNIMAGINATIVE* "POWERS THAT BE" TOLD ME THAT IT WOULD BE A 'CATASTROPHIC WASTE OF HUMAN RESOURCES'.

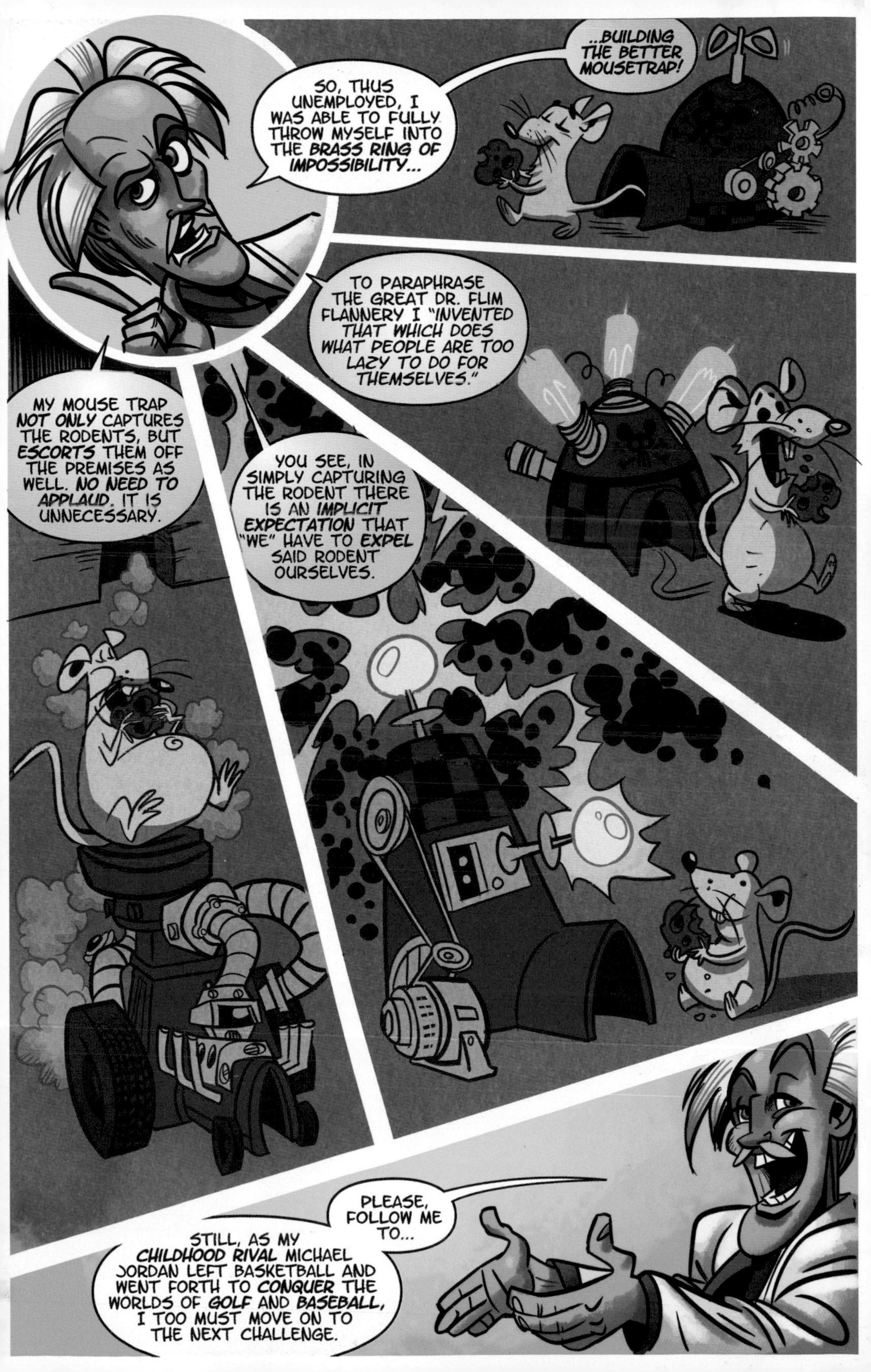
SO, THUS UNEMPLOYED, I WAS ABLE TO FULLY THROW MYSELF INTO THE BRASS RING OF IMPOSSIBILITY...
...BUILDING THE BETTER MOUSETRAP!
TO PARAPHRASE THE GREAT DR. FLIM FLANNERY I "INVENTED THAT WHICH DOES WHAT PEOPLE ARE TOO LAZY TO DO FOR THEMSELVES."
YOU SEE, IN SIMPLY CAPTURING THE RODENT THERE IS AN IMPLICIT EXPECTATION THAT "WE" HAVE TO EXPEL SAID RODENT OURSELVES.
MY MOUSE TRAP NOT ONLY CAPTURES THE RODENTS, BUT ESCORTS THEM OFF THE PREMISES AS WELL. NO NEED TO APPLAUD. IT IS UNNECESSARY.
STILL, AS MY CHILDHOOD RIVAL MICHAEL JORDAN LEFT BASKETBALL AND WENT FORTH TO CONQUER THE WORLDS OF GOLF AND BASEBALL, I TOO MUST MOVE ON TO THE NEXT CHALLENGE.
PLEASE, FOLLOW ME TO...

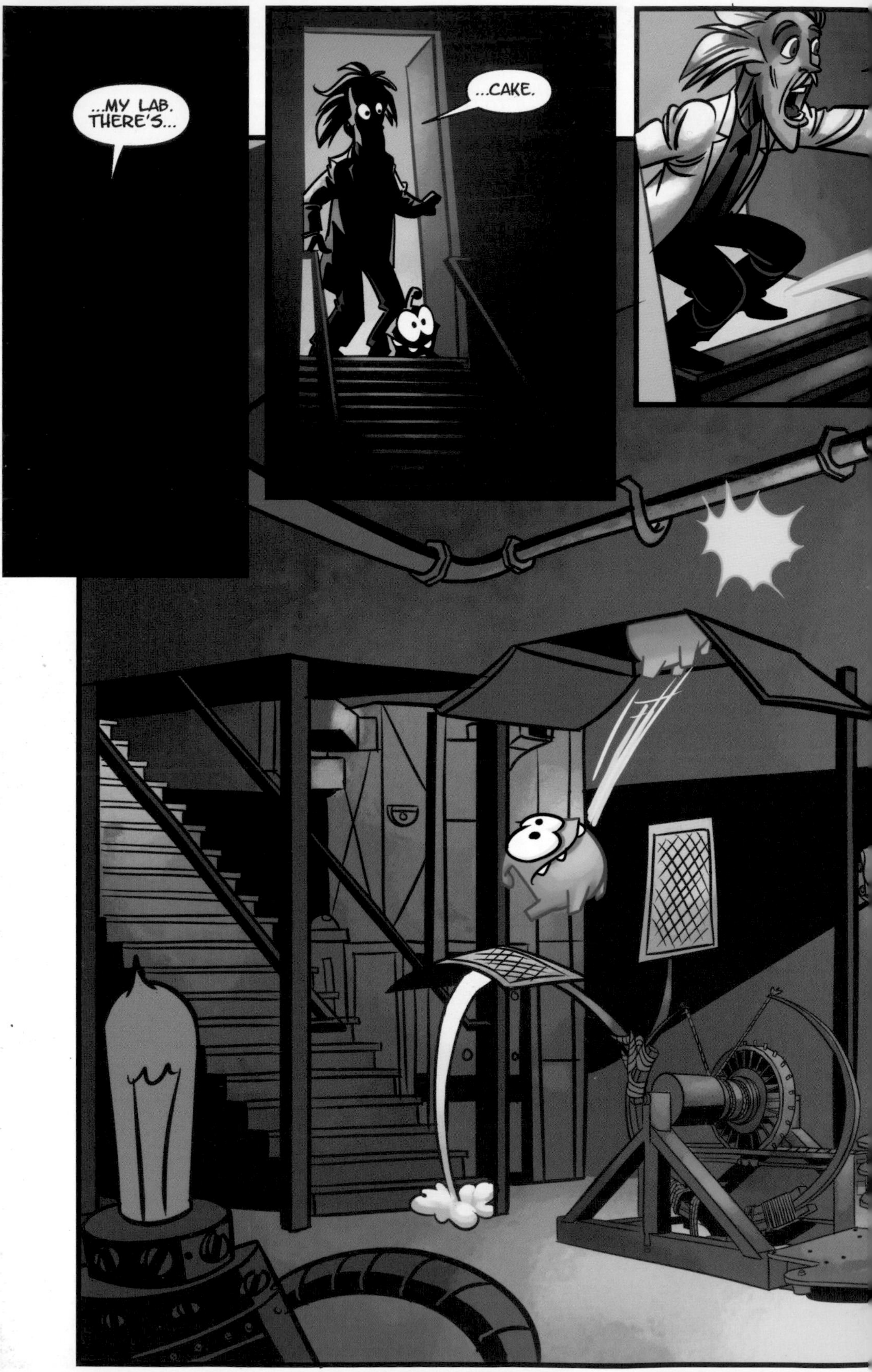
...MY LAB. THERE'S...
...CAKE.

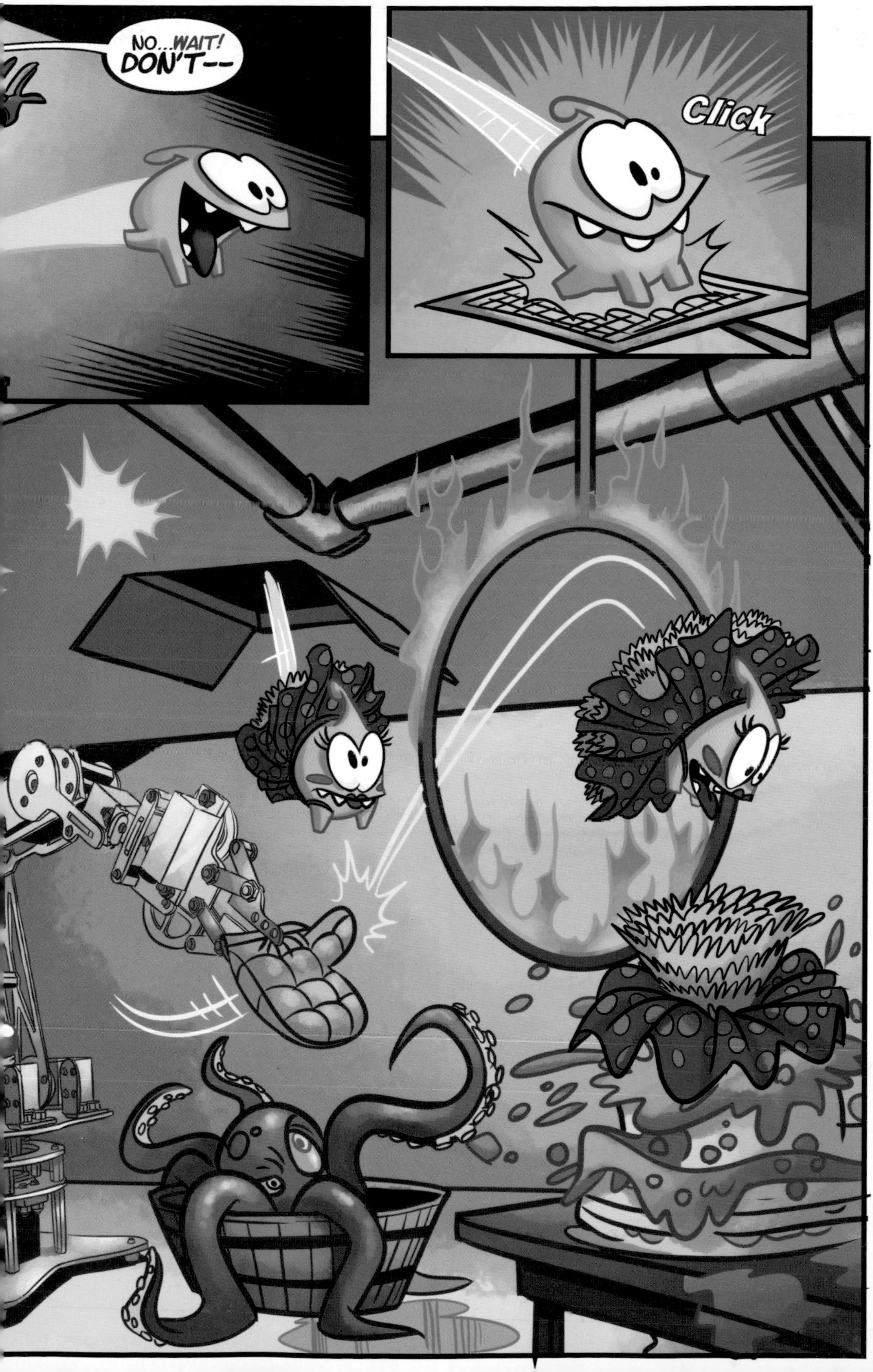
NO...WAIT! DON'T--
Click

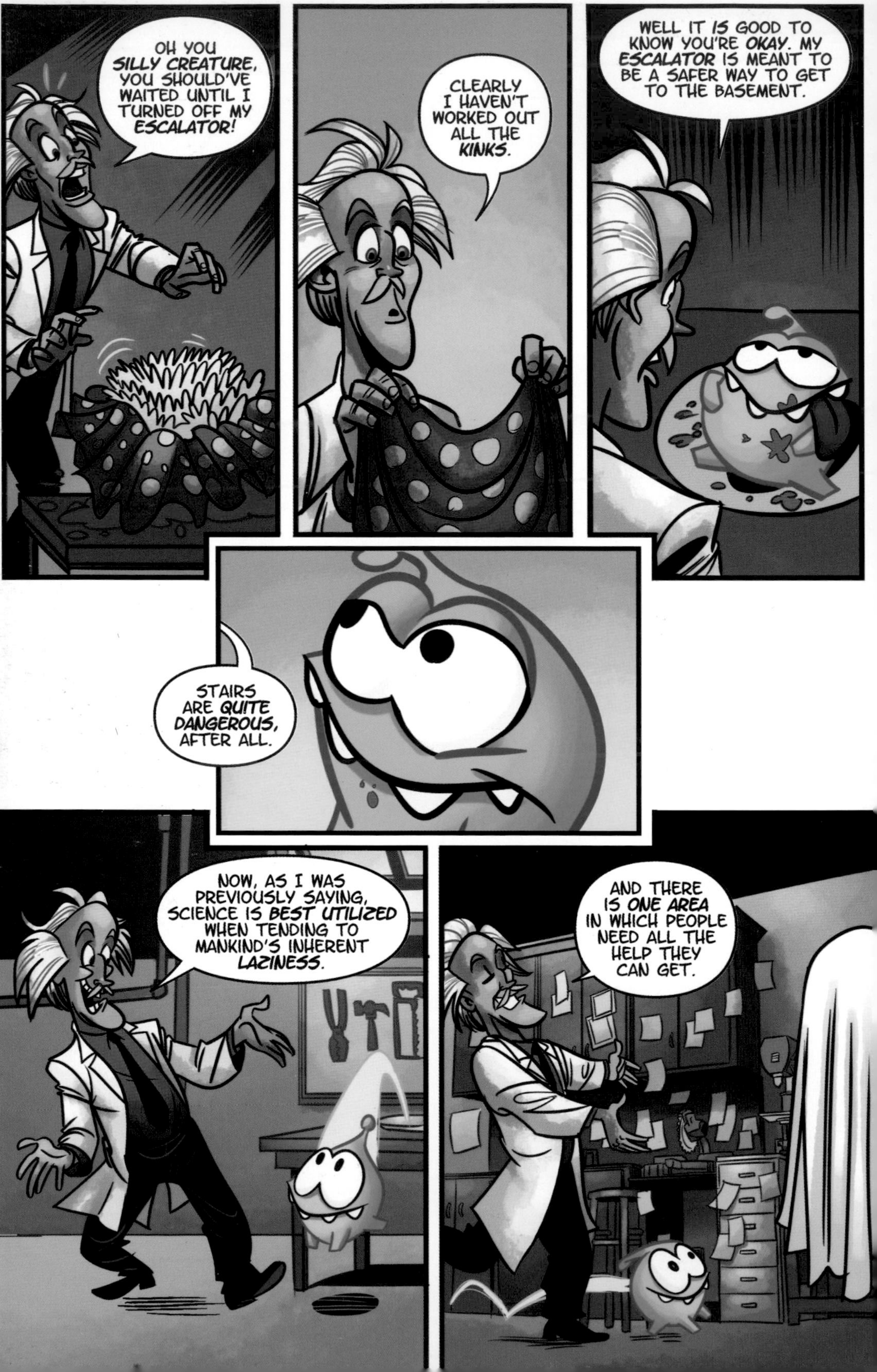
OH YOU SILLY CREATURE, YOU SHOULD'VE WAITED UNTIL I TURNED OFF MY ESCALATOR!
CLEARLY I HAVEN'T WORKED OUT ALL THE KINKS.
WELL IT IS GOOD TO KNOW YOU'RE OKAY. MY ESCALATOR IS MEANT TO BE A SAFER WAY TO GET TO THE BASEMENT.
STAIRS ARE QUITE DANGEROUS, AFTER ALL.
NOW, AS I WAS PREVIOUSLY SAYING, SCIENCE IS BEST UTILIZED WHEN TENDING TO MANKIND'S INHERENT LAZINESS.
AND THERE IS ONE AREA IN WHICH PEOPLE NEED ALL THE HELP THEY CAN GET.

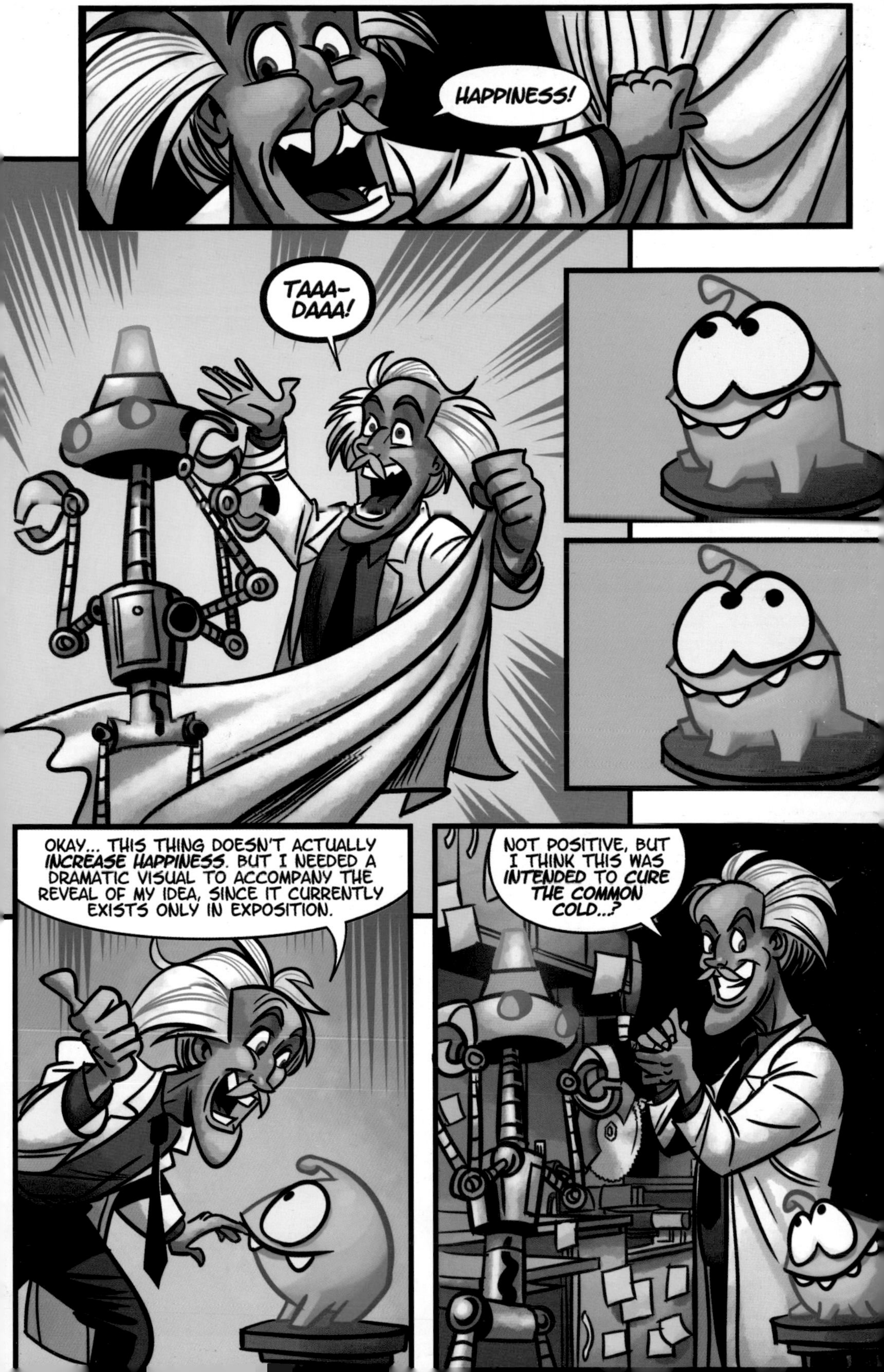
HAPPINESS!
TAAA-DAAA!
OKAY... THIS THING DOESN'T ACTUALLY *INCREASE HAPPINESS*. BUT I NEEDED A DRAMATIC VISUAL TO ACCOMPANY THE REVEAL OF MY IDEA, SINCE IT CURRENTLY EXISTS ONLY IN EXPOSITION.
NOT POSITIVE, BUT I THINK THIS WAS *INTENDED TO CURE THE COMMON COLD...?*

NOW! LET'S GET TO IT, SHALL WE?

CLAP!

I ESTIMATE THE NUMBER OF BAKED GOODS IN MY KITCHEN TO HAVE EASILY EXCEEDED 1000!

ASTONISHINGLY, YOU SEEM TO BE SUFFERING ZERO ILL EFFECTS. NOT EVEN THE USUAL FEELINGS OF REGRET AND SELF-LOATHING.

IRONICALLY...

I NEVER KNOW IF I'M USING THAT WORD CORRECTLY.

...INCREASED HAPPINESS IS WHAT USUALLY MOTIVATES ONE TO SEEK OUT SWEETS, EVEN THOUGH SWEETS RARELY IMPART THE HAPPINESS ONE DESIRES.

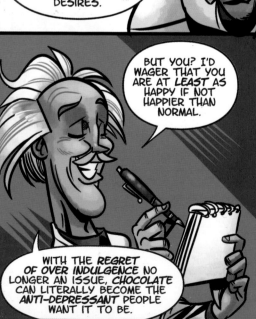

BUT YOU? I'D WAGER THAT YOU ARE AT LEAST AS HAPPY IF NOT HAPPIER THAN NORMAL.

WITH THE REGRET OF OVER INDULGENCE NO LONGER AN ISSUE, CHOCOLATE CAN LITERALLY BECOME THE ANTI-DEPRESSANT PEOPLE WANT IT TO BE.

IF I CAN UNRAVEL THE MYSTERY OF YOUR METABOLIC RATE IN RELATION TO YOUR SEROTONIN PRODUCTION, WHY...

YOU AND I COULD MAKE EVERY SINGLE PERSON ON THIS PLANET HAPPIER, MY SMALL-GREEN-SQUISHY FRIEND!

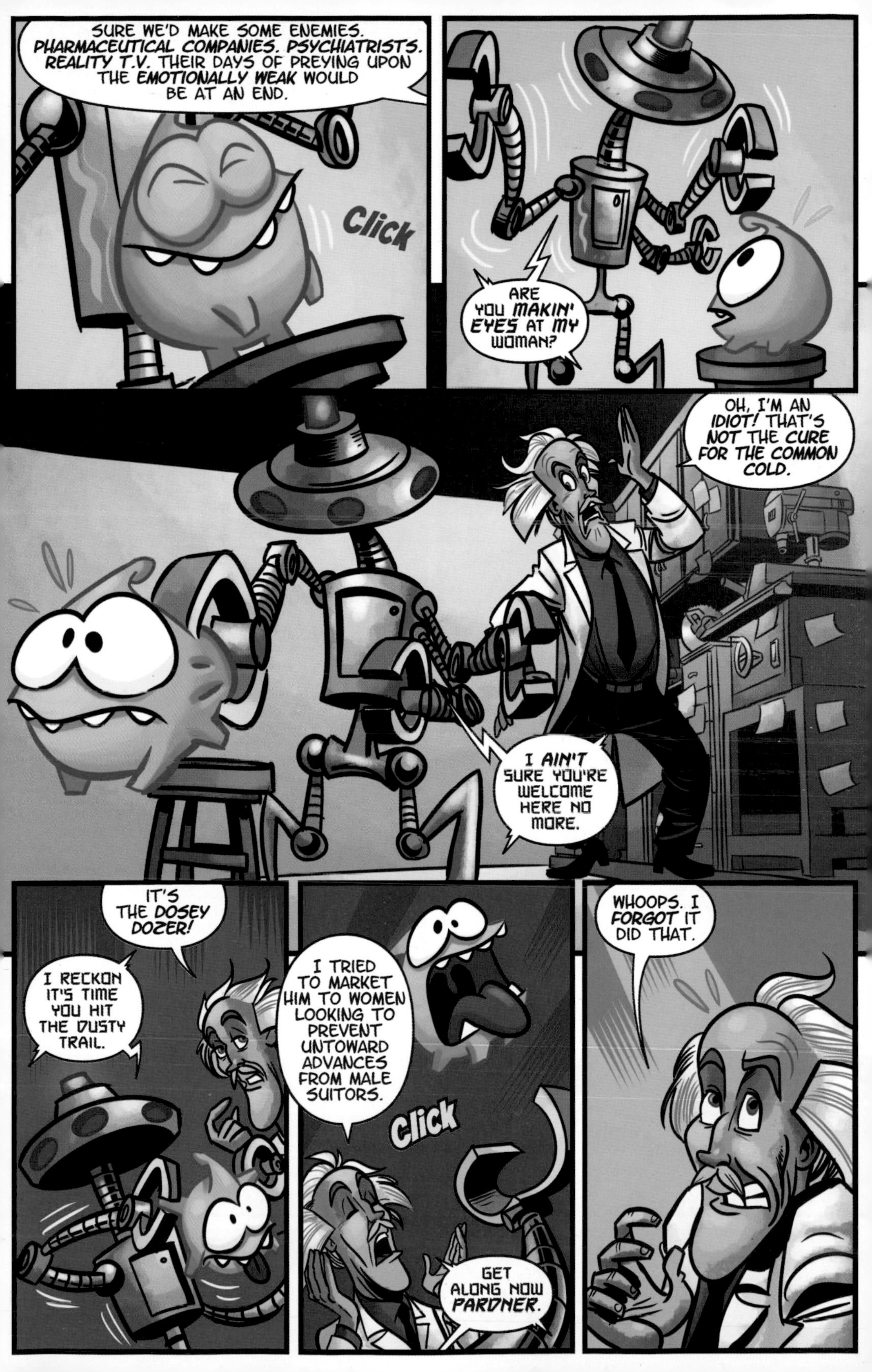
SURE WE'D MAKE SOME ENEMIES. PHARMACEUTICAL COMPANIES. PSYCHIATRISTS. REALITY T.V. THEIR DAYS OF PREYING UPON THE EMOTIONALLY WEAK WOULD BE AT AN END.
Click
ARE YOU MAKIN' EYES AT MY WOMAN?
OH, I'M AN IDIOT! THAT'S NOT THE CURE FOR THE COMMON COLD.
I AIN'T SURE YOU'RE WELCOME HERE NO MORE.
IT'S THE DOSEY DOZER!
I RECKON IT'S TIME YOU HIT THE DUSTY TRAIL.
I TRIED TO MARKET HIM TO WOMEN LOOKING TO PREVENT UNTOWARD ADVANCES FROM MALE SUITORS.
Click
GET ALONG NOW PARDNER.
WHOOPS. I FORGOT IT DID THAT.

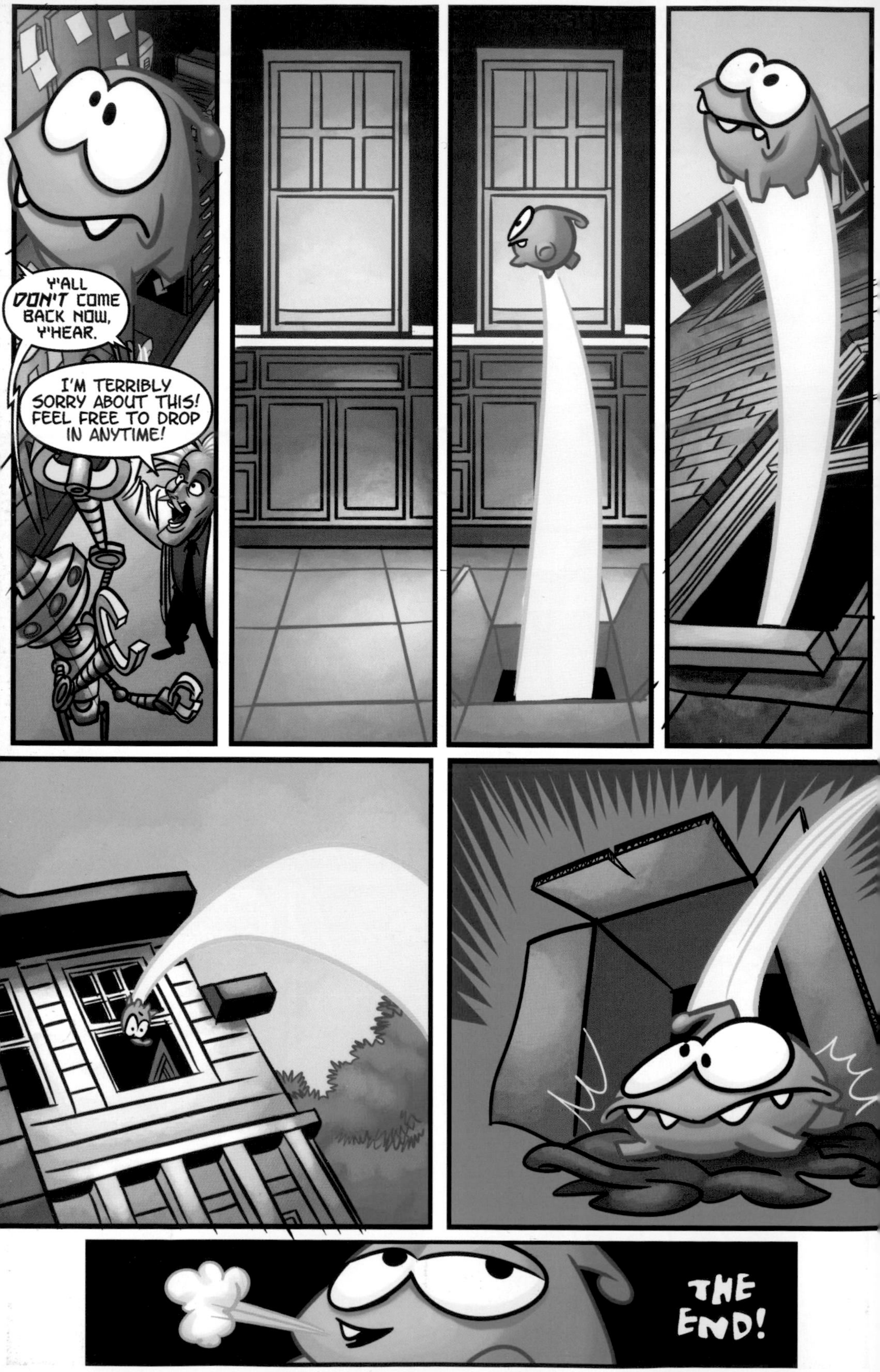
Y'ALL DON'T COME BACK NOW, Y'HEAR.
I'M TERRIBLY SORRY ABOUT THIS! FEEL FREE TO DROP IN ANYTIME!
THE END!

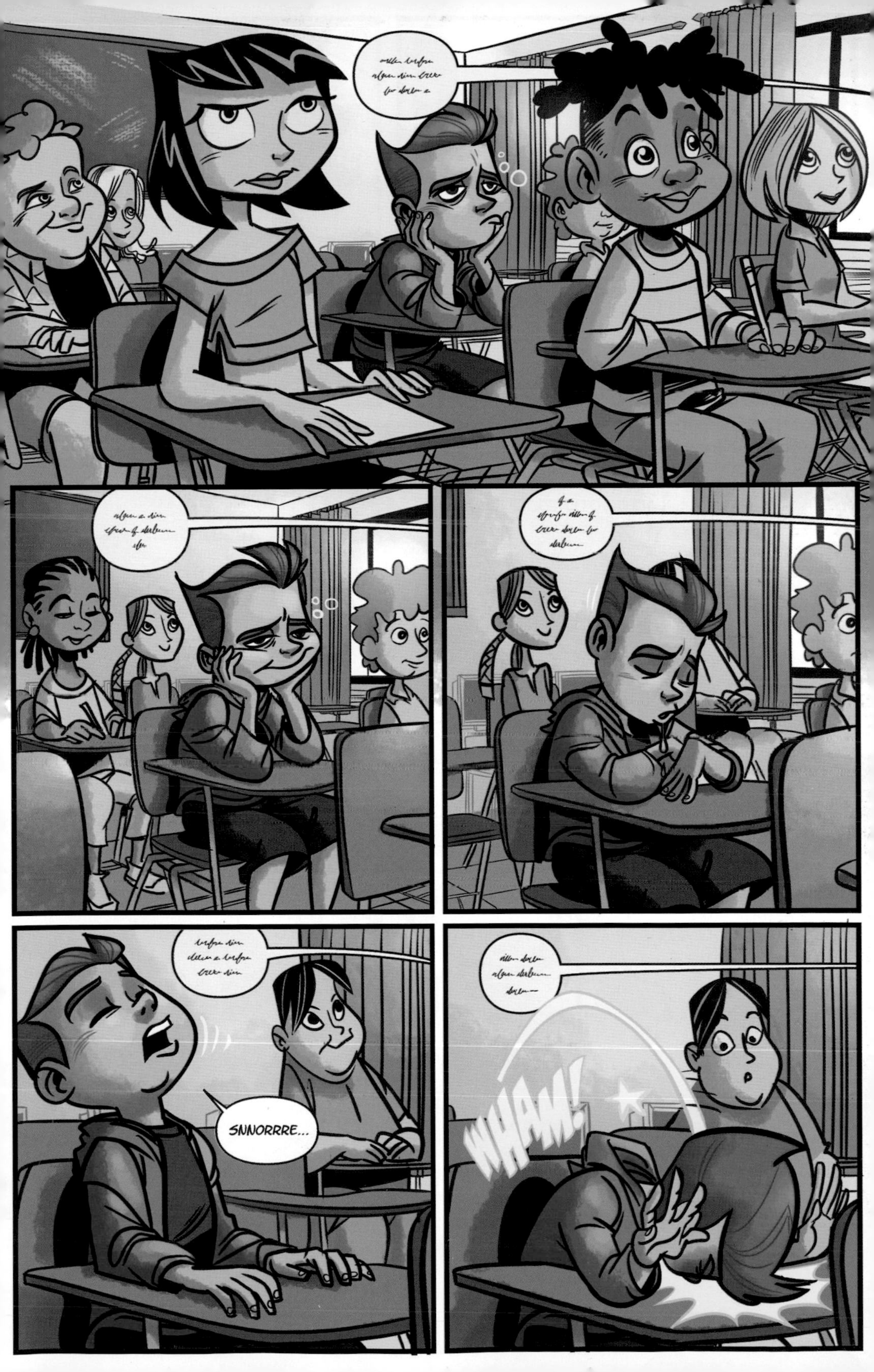
SNNORRRE...
WHAM!

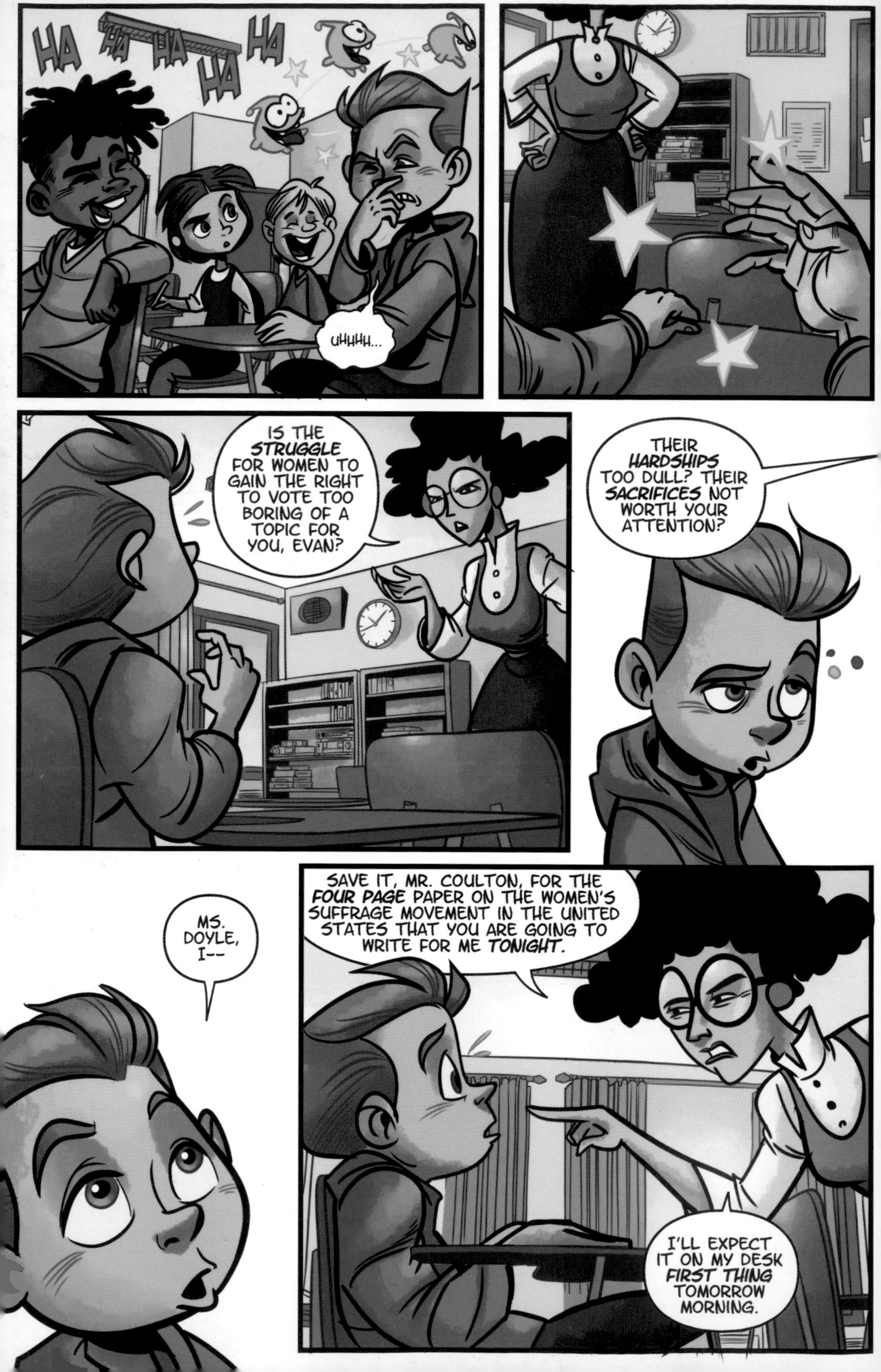
HA HA HA HA HA HA
UHHHH...
IS THE STRUGGLE FOR WOMEN TO GAIN THE RIGHT TO VOTE TOO BORING OF A TOPIC FOR YOU, EVAN?
THEIR HARDSHIPS TOO DULL? THEIR SACRIFICES NOT WORTH YOUR ATTENTION?
MS. DOYLE, I--
SAVE IT, MR. COULTON, FOR THE FOUR PAGE PAPER ON THE WOMEN'S SUFFRAGE MOVEMENT IN THE UNITED STATES THAT YOU ARE GOING TO WRITE FOR ME TONIGHT.
I'LL EXPECT IT ON MY DESK FIRST THING TOMORROW MORNING.

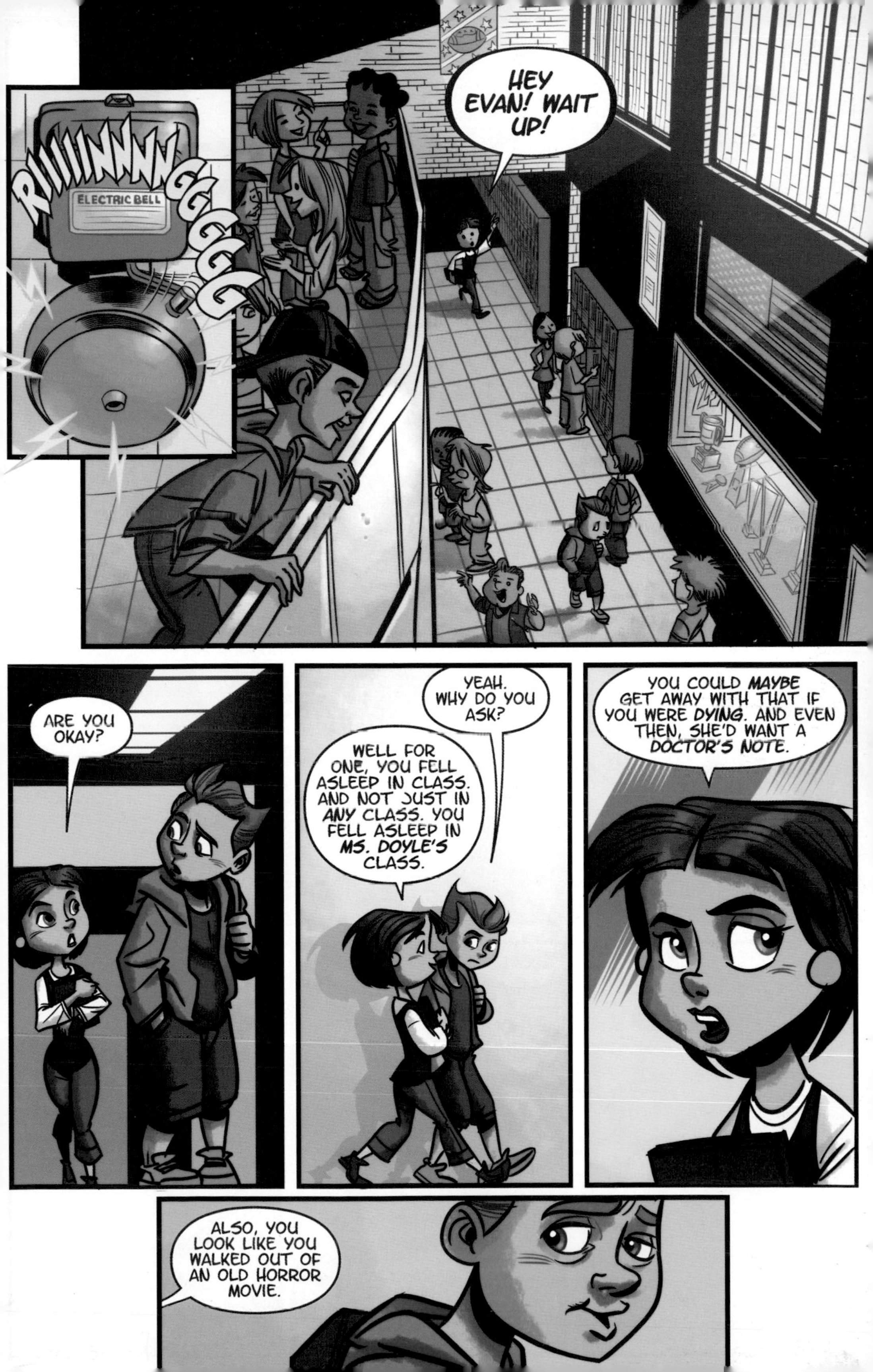
RIIIIINNNNGGGGG
ELECTRIC BELL
HEY EVAN! WAIT UP!
ARE YOU OKAY?
YEAH. WHY DO YOU ASK?
WELL FOR ONE, YOU FELL ASLEEP IN CLASS. AND NOT JUST IN ANY CLASS. YOU FELL ASLEEP IN MS. DOYLE'S CLASS.
YOU COULD MAYBE GET AWAY WITH THAT IF YOU WERE DYING. AND EVEN THEN, SHE'D WANT A DOCTOR'S NOTE.
ALSO, YOU LOOK LIKE YOU WALKED OUT OF AN OLD HORROR MOVIE.

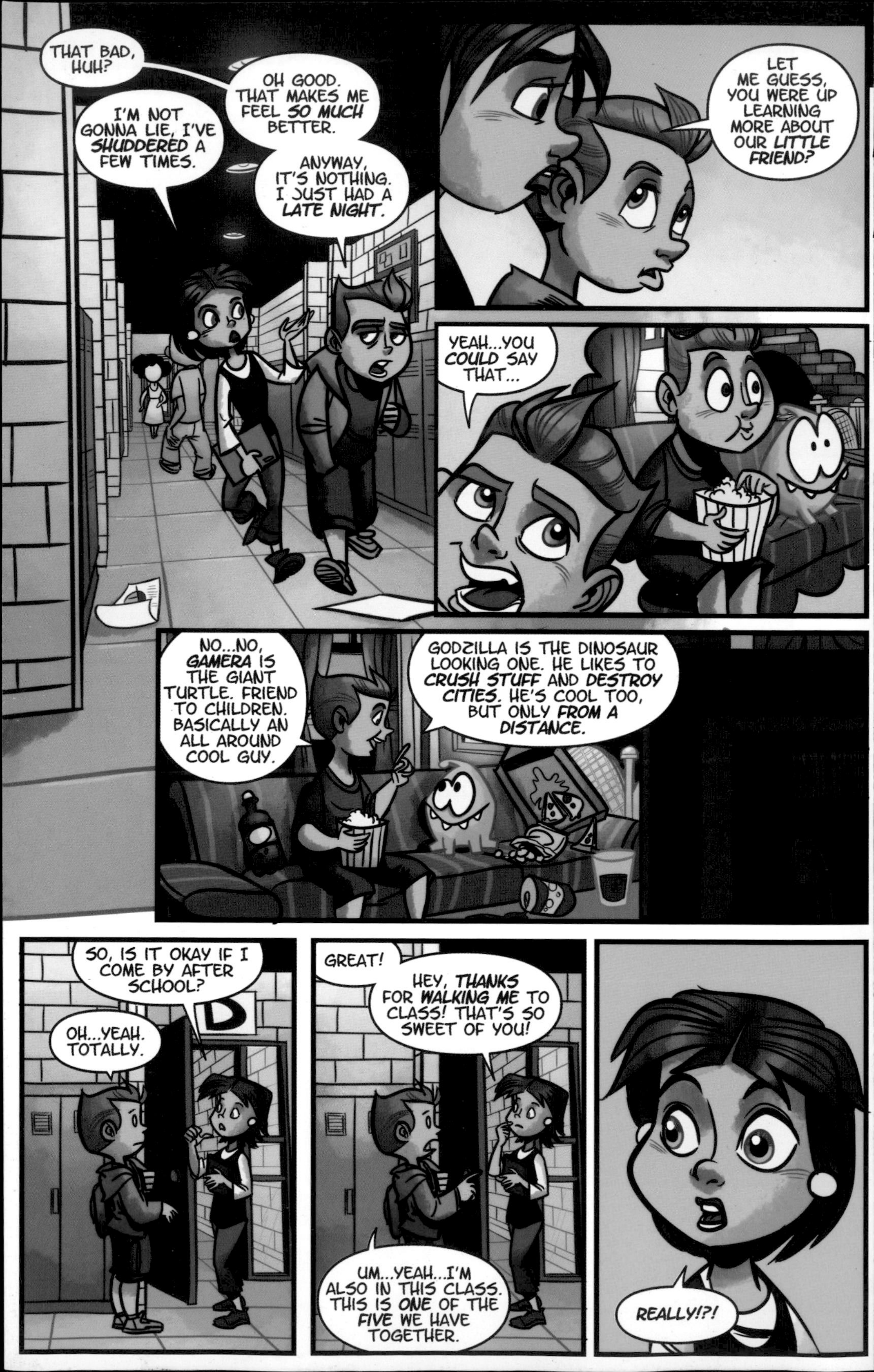
THAT BAD, HUH?
I'M NOT GONNA LIE, I'VE SHUDDERED A FEW TIMES.
OH GOOD. THAT MAKES ME FEEL SO MUCH BETTER.
ANYWAY, IT'S NOTHING. I JUST HAD A LATE NIGHT.
LET ME GUESS, YOU WERE UP LEARNING MORE ABOUT OUR LITTLE FRIEND?
YEAH...YOU COULD SAY THAT...
NO...NO, GAMERA IS THE GIANT TURTLE. FRIEND TO CHILDREN. BASICALLY AN ALL AROUND COOL GUY.
GODZILLA IS THE DINOSAUR LOOKING ONE. HE LIKES TO CRUSH STUFF AND DESTROY CITIES. HE'S COOL TOO, BUT ONLY FROM A DISTANCE.
SO, IS IT OKAY IF I COME BY AFTER SCHOOL?
OH...YEAH. TOTALLY.
GREAT!
HEY, THANKS FOR WALKING ME TO CLASS! THAT'S SO SWEET OF YOU!
UM...YEAH...I'M ALSO IN THIS CLASS. THIS IS ONE OF THE FIVE WE HAVE TOGETHER.
REALLY!?!

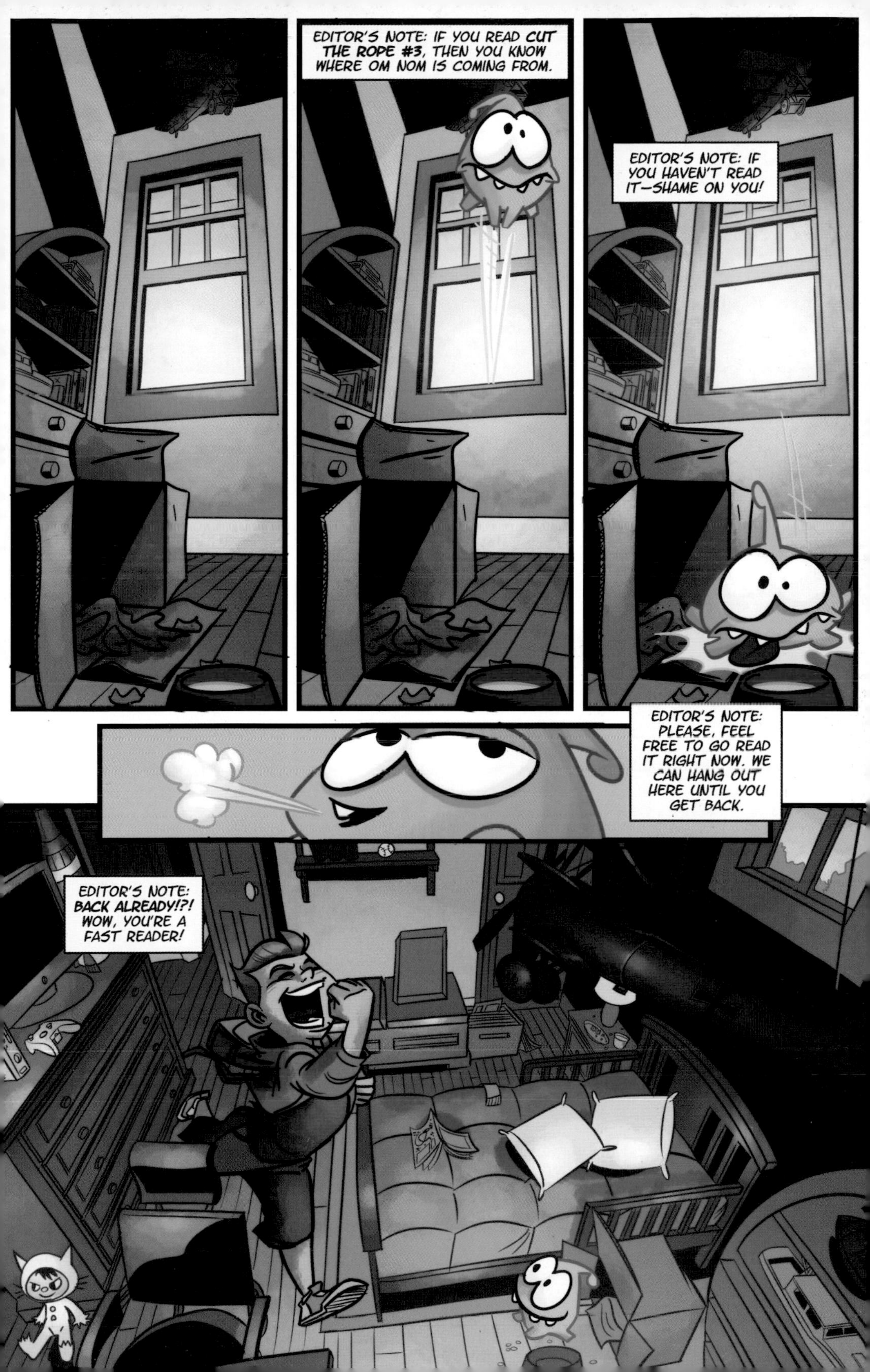
EDITOR'S NOTE: IF YOU READ CUT THE ROPE #3, THEN YOU KNOW WHERE OM NOM IS COMING FROM.
EDITOR'S NOTE: IF YOU HAVEN'T READ IT—SHAME ON YOU!
EDITOR'S NOTE: PLEASE, FEEL FREE TO GO READ IT RIGHT NOW. WE CAN HANG OUT HERE UNTIL YOU GET BACK.
EDITOR'S NOTE: BACK ALREADY!?! WOW, YOU'RE A FAST READER!

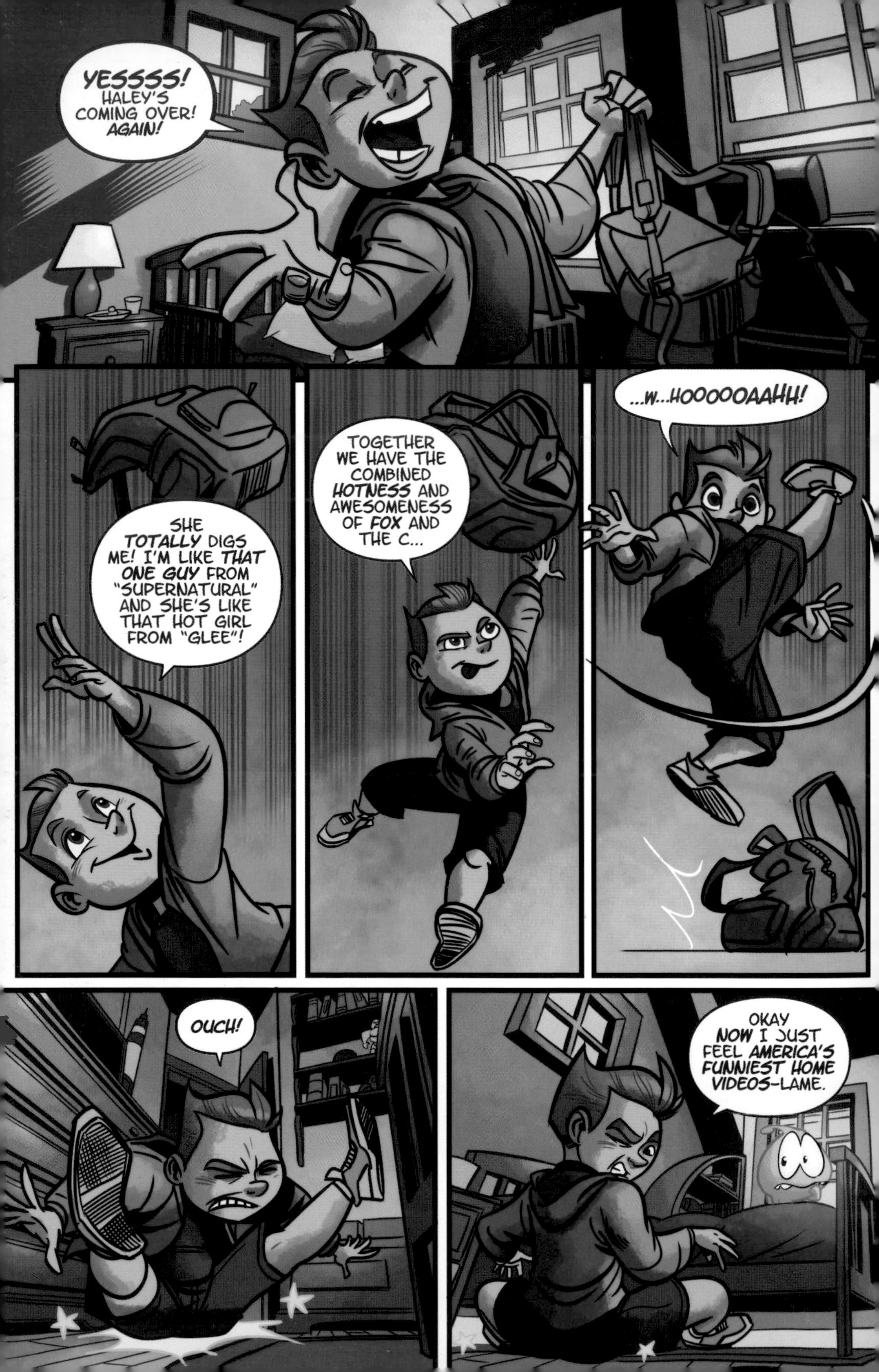
YESSSS! HALEY'S COMING OVER! AGAIN!
SHE TOTALLY DIGS ME! I'M LIKE THAT ONE GUY FROM "SUPERNATURAL" AND SHE'S LIKE THAT HOT GIRL FROM "GLEE"!
TOGETHER WE HAVE THE COMBINED HOTNESS AND AWESOMENESS OF FOX AND THE C...
...W...HOOOOOAAHH!
OUCH!
OKAY NOW I JUST FEEL AMERICA'S FUNNIEST HOME VIDEOS-LAME.

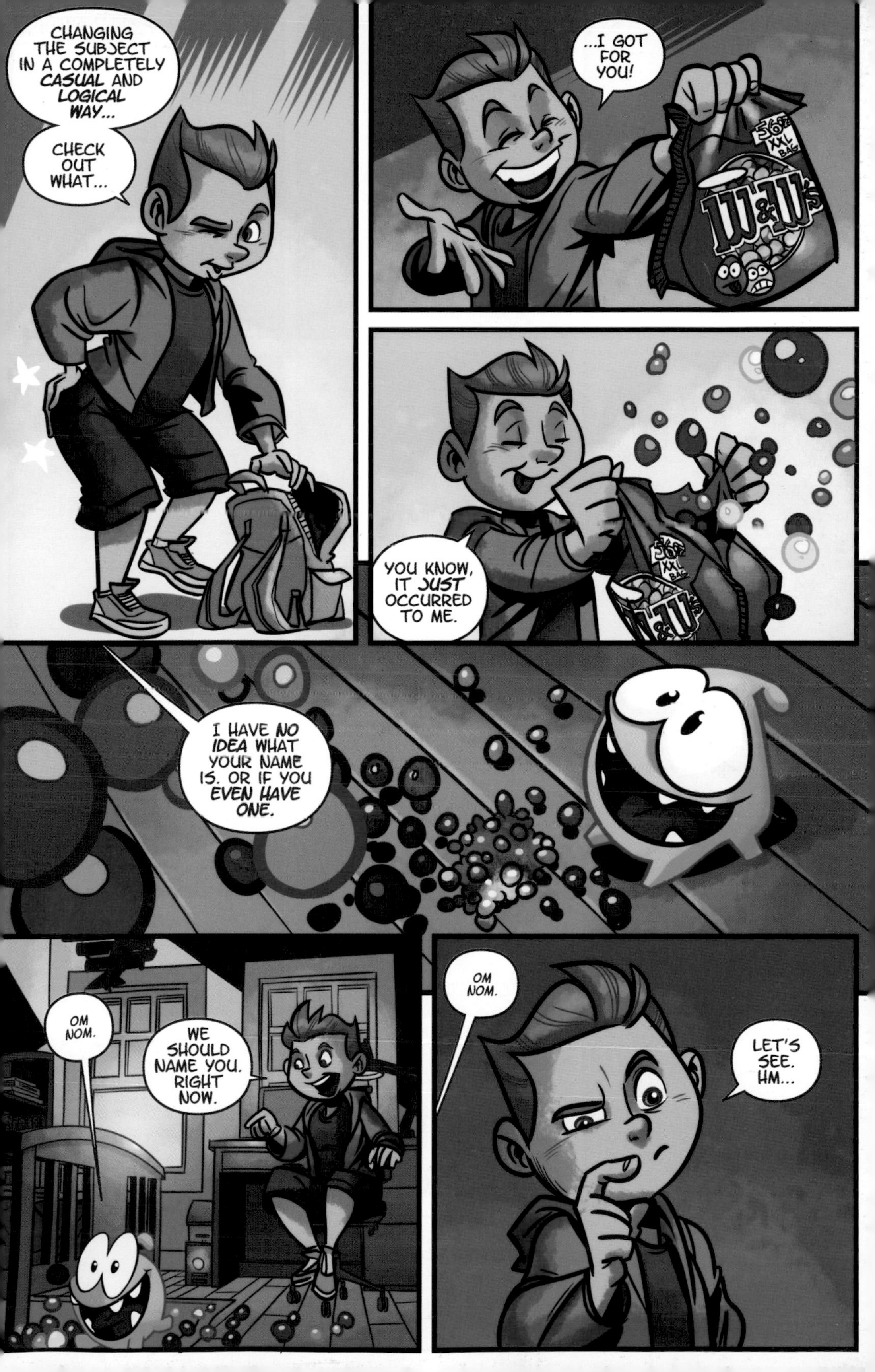
CHANGING THE SUBJECT IN A COMPLETELY CASUAL AND LOGICAL WAY...
CHECK OUT WHAT...
...I GOT FOR YOU!
56oz XXL BAG
M&M's
YOU KNOW, IT JUST OCCURRED TO ME.
I HAVE NO IDEA WHAT YOUR NAME IS. OR IF YOU EVEN HAVE ONE.
OM NOM.
WE SHOULD NAME YOU. RIGHT NOW.
OM NOM.
LET'S SEE. HM...

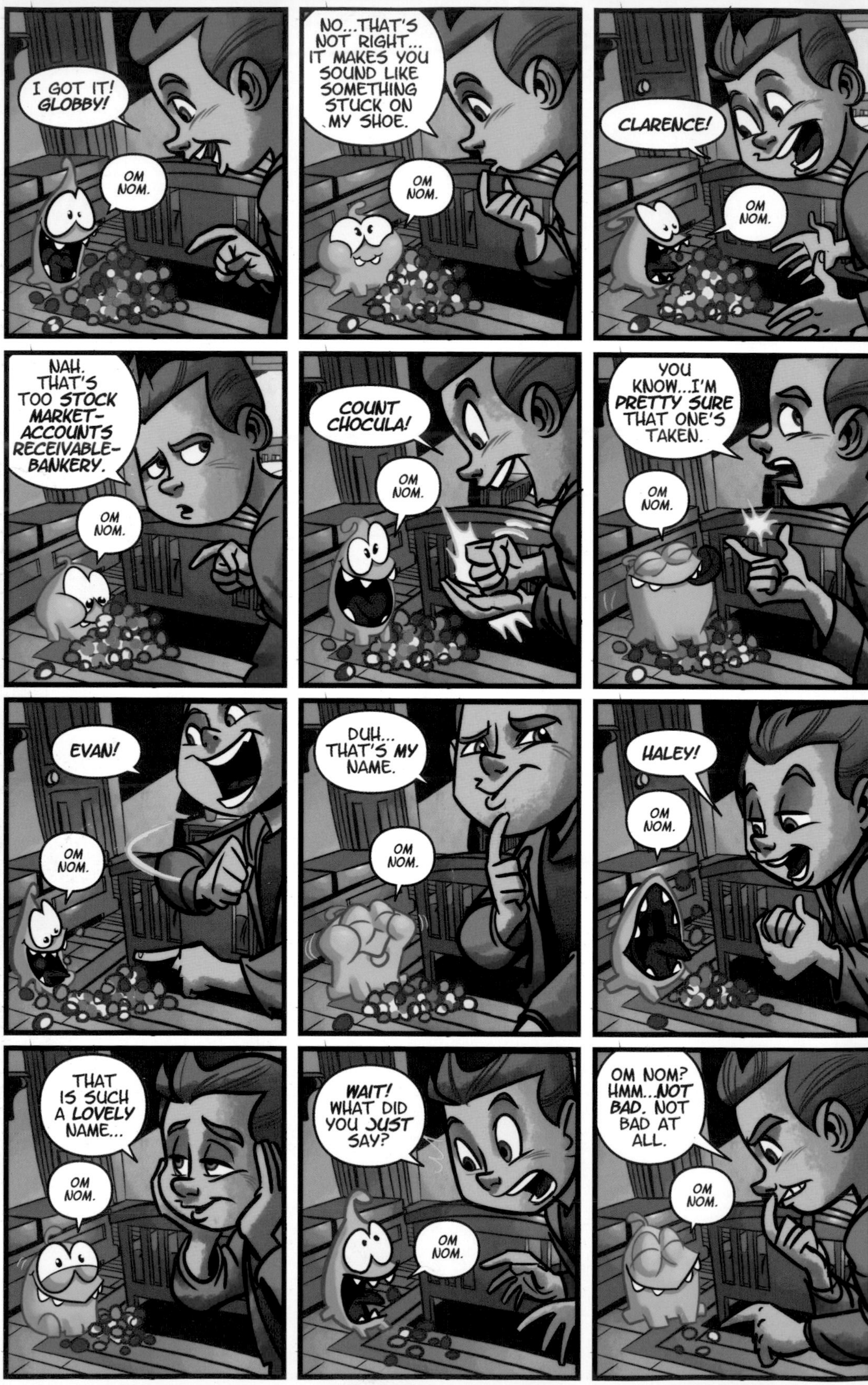
I GOT IT! GLOBBY!
OM NOM.
NO...THAT'S NOT RIGHT... IT MAKES YOU SOUND LIKE SOMETHING STUCK ON MY SHOE.
OM NOM.
CLARENCE!
OM NOM.
NAH. THAT'S TOO STOCK MARKET-ACCOUNTS RECEIVABLE-BANKERY.
OM NOM.
COUNT CHOCULA!
OM NOM.
YOU KNOW...I'M PRETTY SURE THAT ONE'S TAKEN.
OM NOM.
EVAN!
OM NOM.
DUH... THAT'S MY NAME.
OM NOM.
HALEY!
OM NOM.
THAT IS SUCH A LOVELY NAME...
OM NOM.
WAIT! WHAT DID YOU JUST SAY?
OM NOM.
OM NOM? HMM...NOT BAD. NOT BAD AT ALL.
OM NOM.

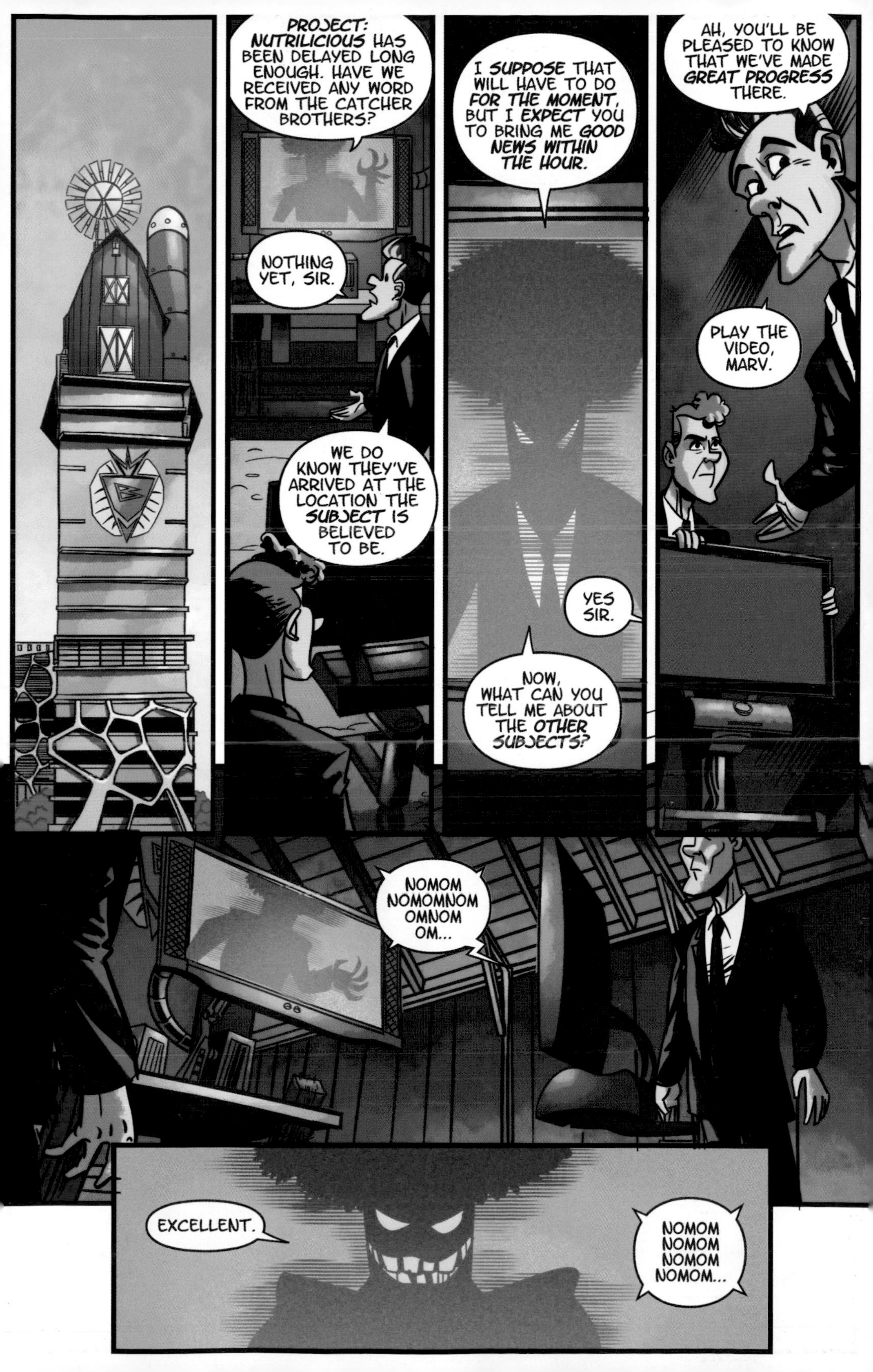
PROJECT: NUTRILICIOUS HAS BEEN DELAYED LONG ENOUGH. HAVE WE RECEIVED ANY WORD FROM THE CATCHER BROTHERS?
NOTHING YET, SIR.
WE DO KNOW THEY'VE ARRIVED AT THE LOCATION THE SUBJECT IS BELIEVED TO BE.
I SUPPOSE THAT WILL HAVE TO DO FOR THE MOMENT, BUT I EXPECT YOU TO BRING ME GOOD NEWS WITHIN THE HOUR.
YES SIR.
NOW, WHAT CAN YOU TELL ME ABOUT THE OTHER SUBJECTS?
AH, YOU'LL BE PLEASED TO KNOW THAT WE'VE MADE GREAT PROGRESS THERE.
PLAY THE VIDEO, MARV.
NOMOM NOMOMNOM OMNOM OM...
EXCELLENT.
NOMOM NOMOM NOMOM NOMOM...

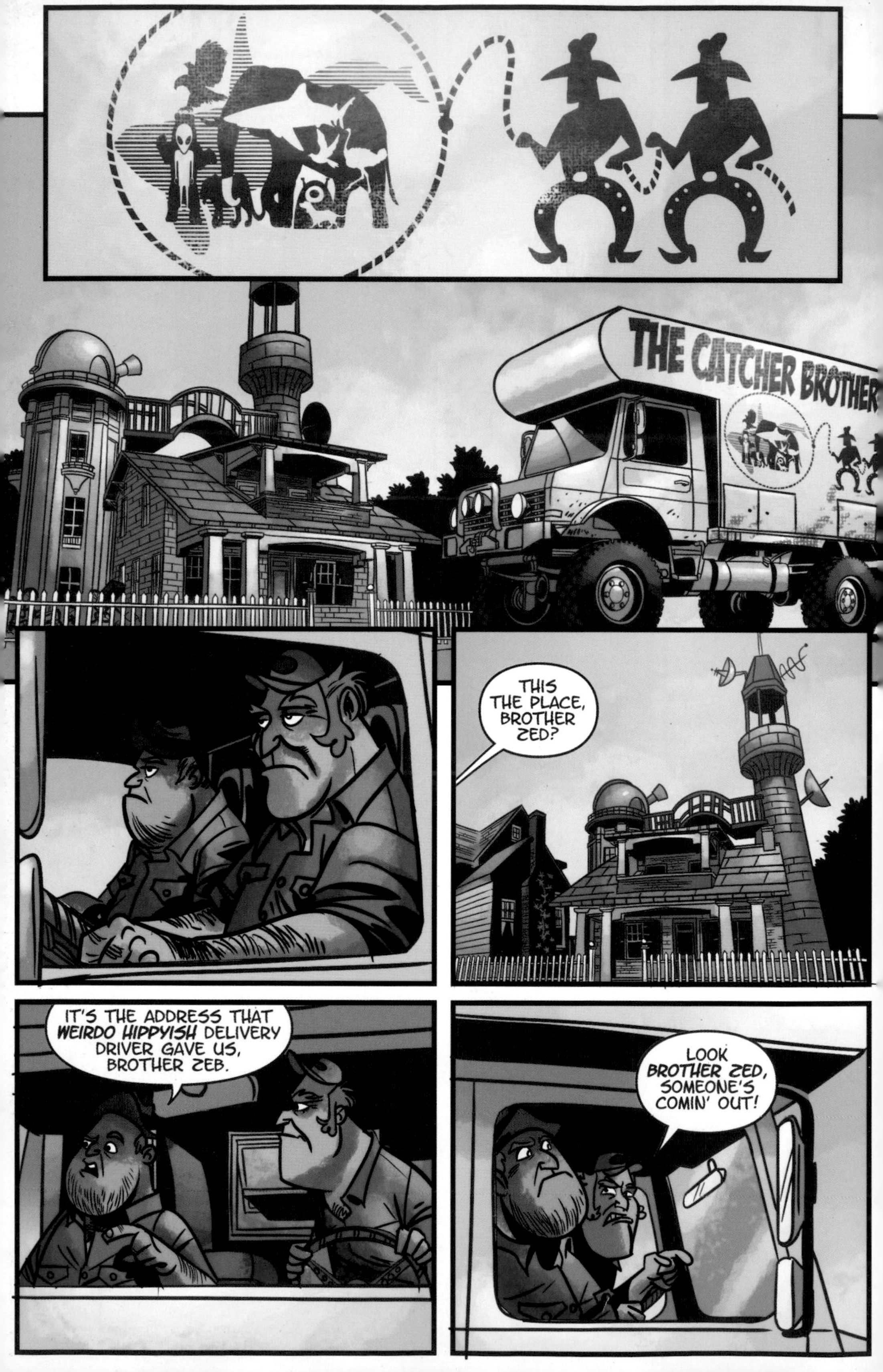
THE CATCHER BROTHER
THIS THE PLACE, BROTHER ZED?
IT'S THE ADDRESS THAT WEIRDO HIPPYISH DELIVERY DRIVER GAVE US, BROTHER ZEB.
LOOK BROTHER ZED, SOMEONE'S COMIN' OUT!

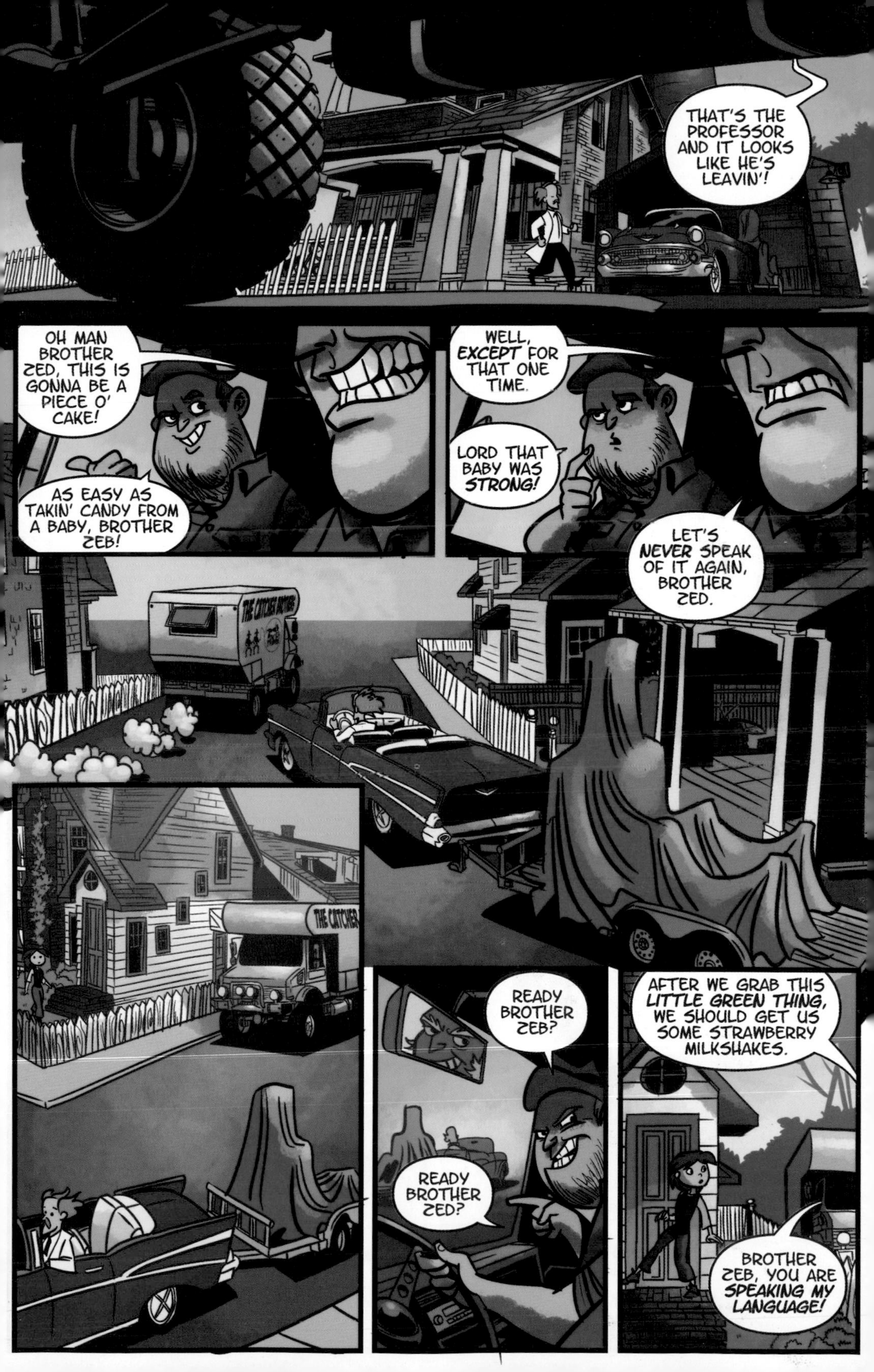
THAT'S THE PROFESSOR AND IT LOOKS LIKE HE'S LEAVIN'!
OH MAN BROTHER ZED, THIS IS GONNA BE A PIECE O' CAKE!
AS EASY AS TAKIN' CANDY FROM A BABY, BROTHER ZEB!
WELL, EXCEPT FOR THAT ONE TIME.
LORD THAT BABY WAS STRONG!
LET'S NEVER SPEAK OF IT AGAIN, BROTHER ZED.
THE CATCHER BROTHERS
THE CATCHER
READY BROTHER ZEB?
READY BROTHER ZED?
AFTER WE GRAB THIS LITTLE GREEN THING, WE SHOULD GET US SOME STRAWBERRY MILKSHAKES.
BROTHER ZEB, YOU ARE SPEAKING MY LANGUAGE!

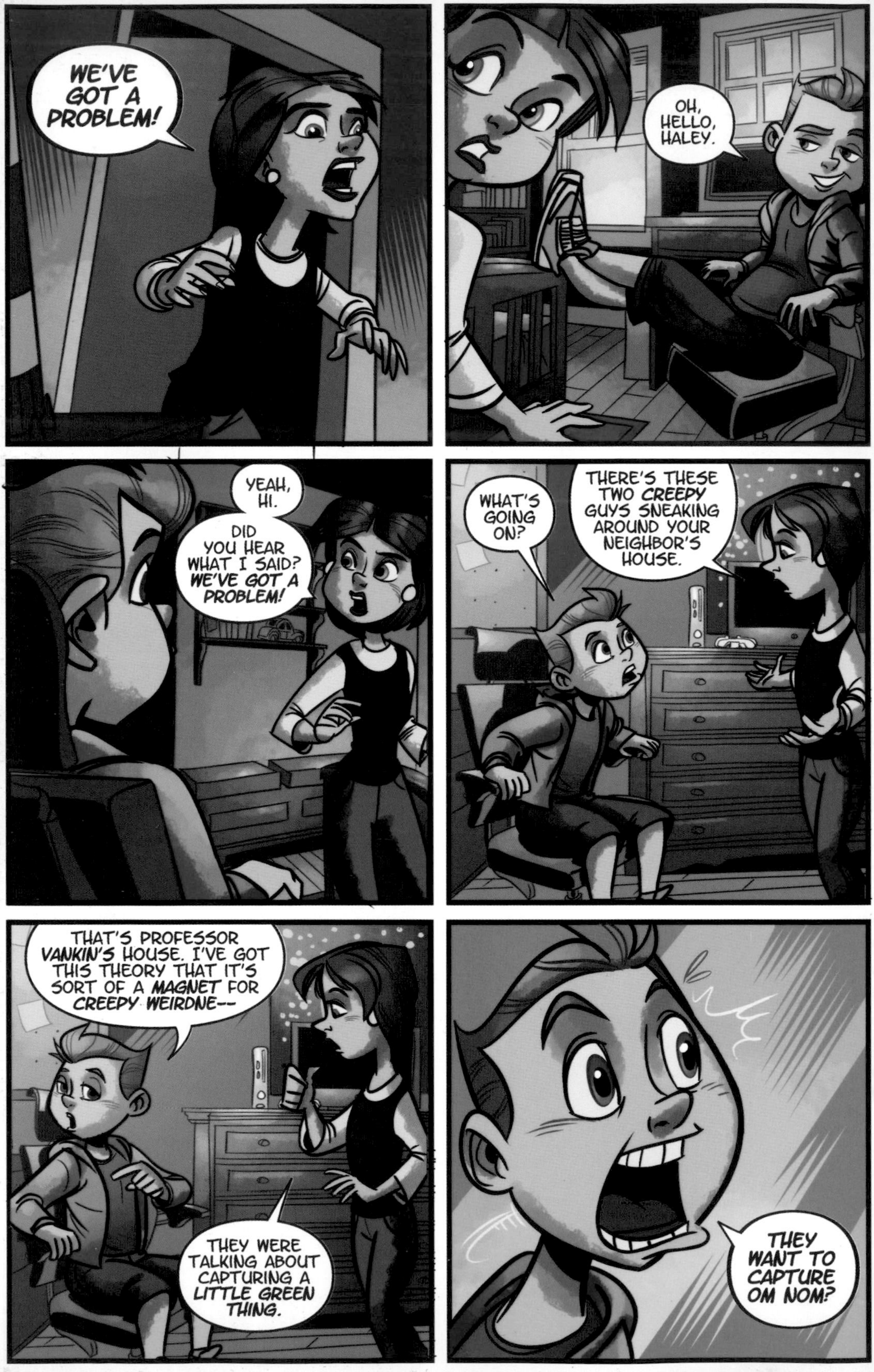
WE'VE GOT A PROBLEM!
OH, HELLO, HALEY.
YEAH, HI.
DID YOU HEAR WHAT I SAID? WE'VE GOT A PROBLEM!
WHAT'S GOING ON?
THERE'S THESE TWO CREEPY GUYS SNEAKING AROUND YOUR NEIGHBOR'S HOUSE.
THAT'S PROFESSOR VANKIN'S HOUSE. I'VE GOT THIS THEORY THAT IT'S SORT OF A MAGNET FOR CREEPY WEIRDNE--
THEY WERE TALKING ABOUT CAPTURING A LITTLE GREEN THING.
THEY WANT TO CAPTURE OM NOM?

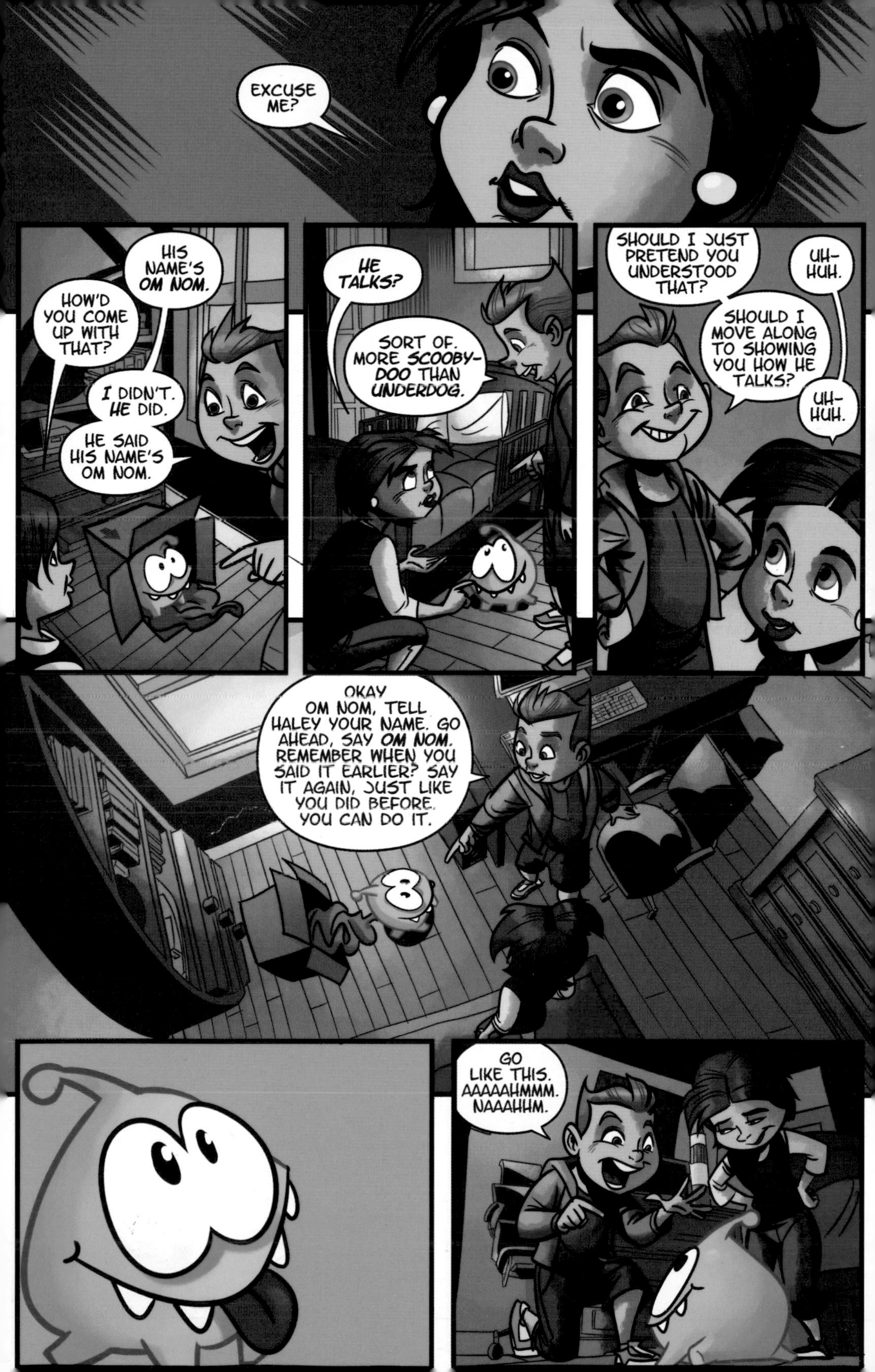

EXCUSE ME?
HOW'D YOU COME UP WITH THAT?
HIS NAME'S OM NOM.
I DIDN'T. HE DID.
HE SAID HIS NAME'S OM NOM.
HE TALKS?
SORT OF. MORE SCOOBY-DOO THAN UNDERDOG.
SHOULD I JUST PRETEND YOU UNDERSTOOD THAT?
UH-HUH.
SHOULD I MOVE ALONG TO SHOWING YOU HOW HE TALKS?
UH-HUH.
OKAY OM NOM, TELL HALEY YOUR NAME. GO AHEAD, SAY OM NOM. REMEMBER WHEN YOU SAID IT EARLIER? SAY IT AGAIN, JUST LIKE YOU DID BEFORE. YOU CAN DO IT.
GO LIKE THIS. AAAAAHMMM. NAAAHHM.

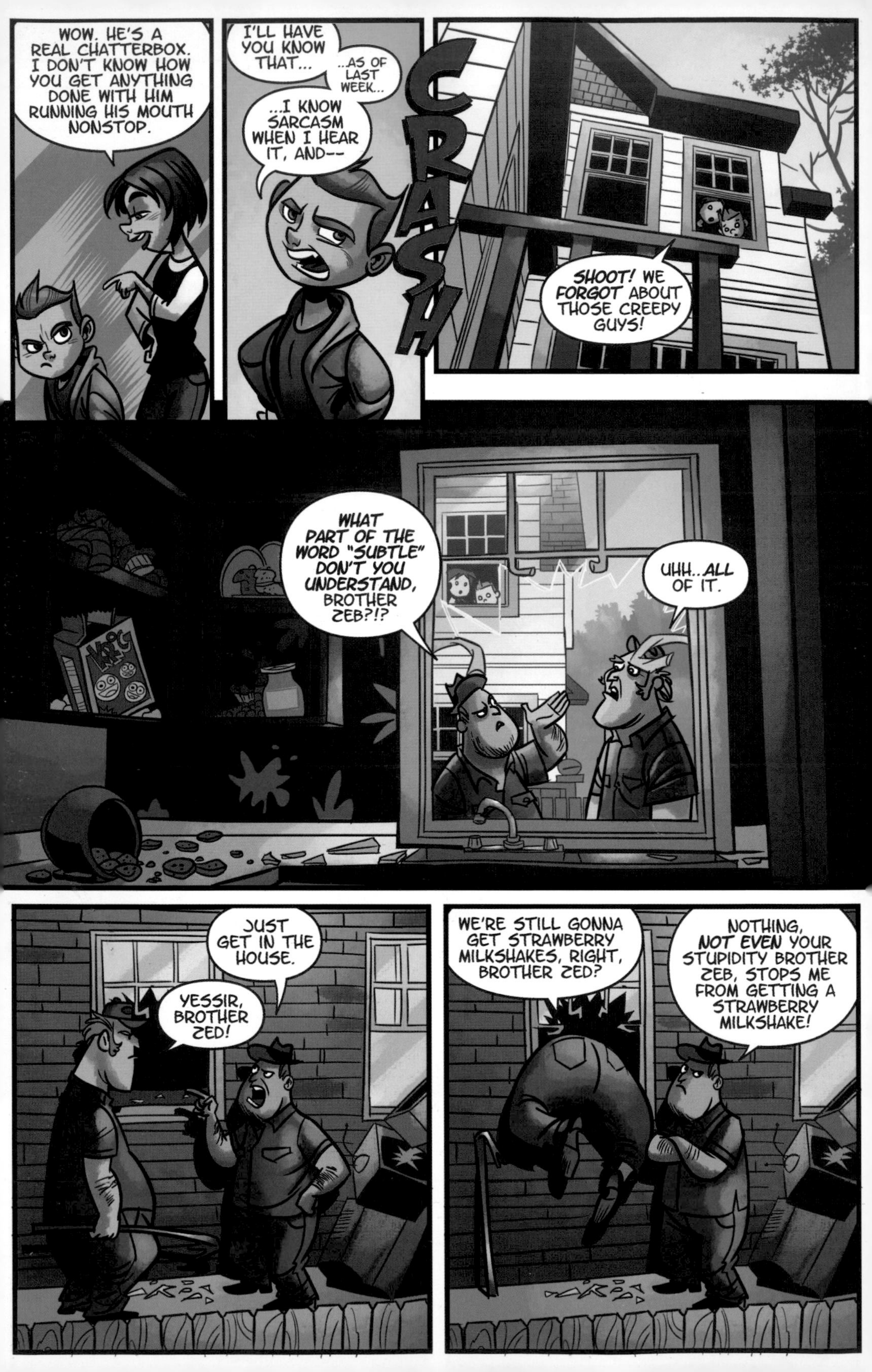
WOW. HE'S A REAL CHATTERBOX. I DON'T KNOW HOW YOU GET ANYTHING DONE WITH HIM RUNNING HIS MOUTH NONSTOP.
I'LL HAVE YOU KNOW THAT...
...AS OF LAST WEEK...
...I KNOW SARCASM WHEN I HEAR IT, AND--
CRASH
SHOOT! WE FORGOT ABOUT THOSE CREEPY GUYS!
WHAT PART OF THE WORD "SUBTLE" DON'T YOU UNDERSTAND, BROTHER ZEB?!?
UHH...ALL OF IT.
JUST GET IN THE HOUSE.
YESSIR, BROTHER ZED!
WE'RE STILL GONNA GET STRAWBERRY MILKSHAKES, RIGHT, BROTHER ZED?
NOTHING, NOT EVEN YOUR STUPIDITY BROTHER ZEB, STOPS ME FROM GETTING A STRAWBERRY MILKSHAKE!

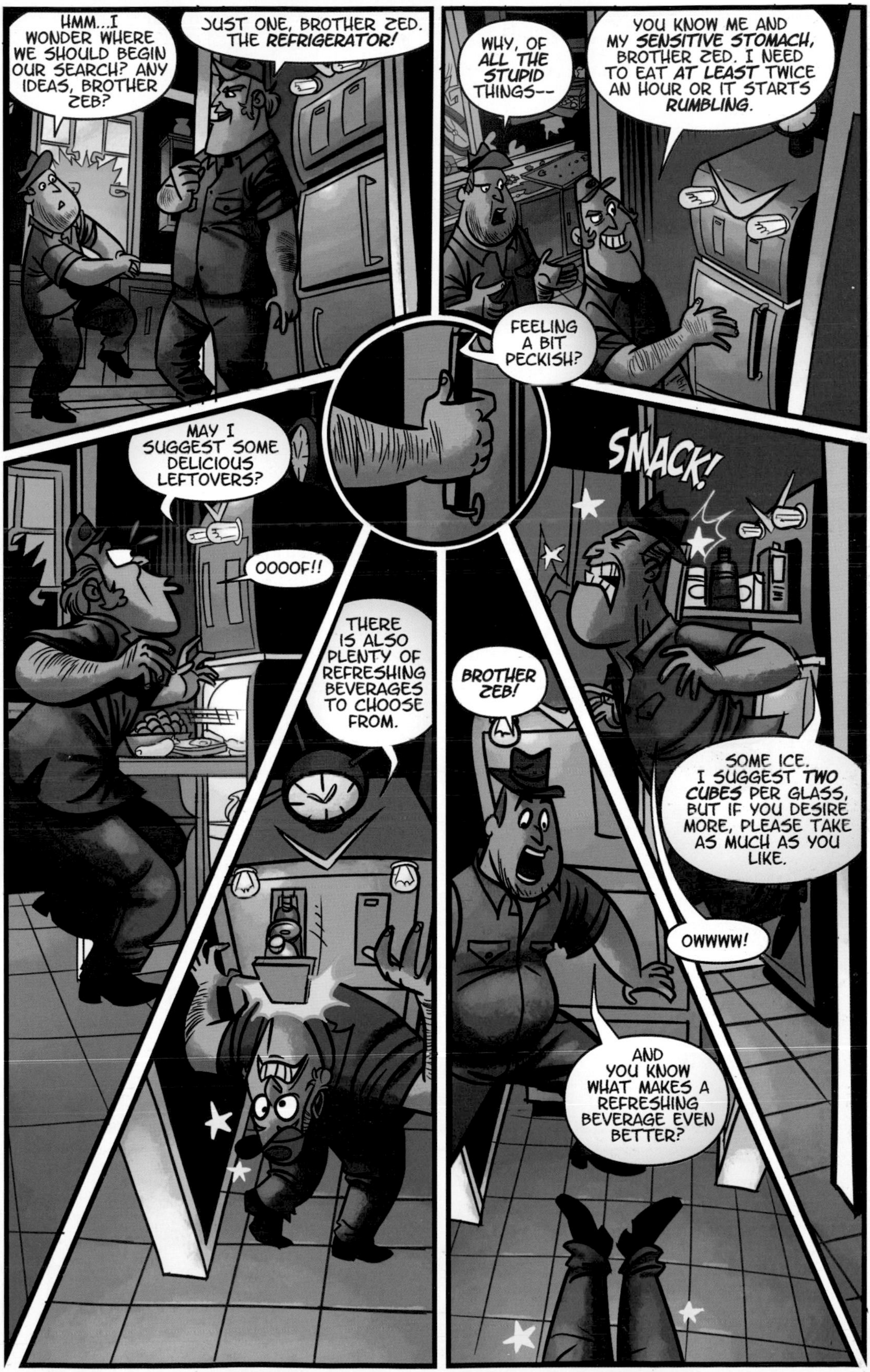
HMM...I WONDER WHERE WE SHOULD BEGIN OUR SEARCH? ANY IDEAS, BROTHER ZEB?
JUST ONE, BROTHER ZED. THE REFRIGERATOR!
WHY, OF ALL THE STUPID THINGS--
YOU KNOW ME AND MY SENSITIVE STOMACH, BROTHER ZED. I NEED TO EAT AT LEAST TWICE AN HOUR OR IT STARTS RUMBLING.
FEELING A BIT PECKISH?
MAY I SUGGEST SOME DELICIOUS LEFTOVERS?
OOOOF!!
SMACK!
THERE IS ALSO PLENTY OF REFRESHING BEVERAGES TO CHOOSE FROM.
BROTHER ZEB!
SOME ICE. I SUGGEST TWO CUBES PER GLASS, BUT IF YOU DESIRE MORE, PLEASE TAKE AS MUCH AS YOU LIKE.
OWWWW!
AND YOU KNOW WHAT MAKES A REFRESHING BEVERAGE EVEN BETTER?

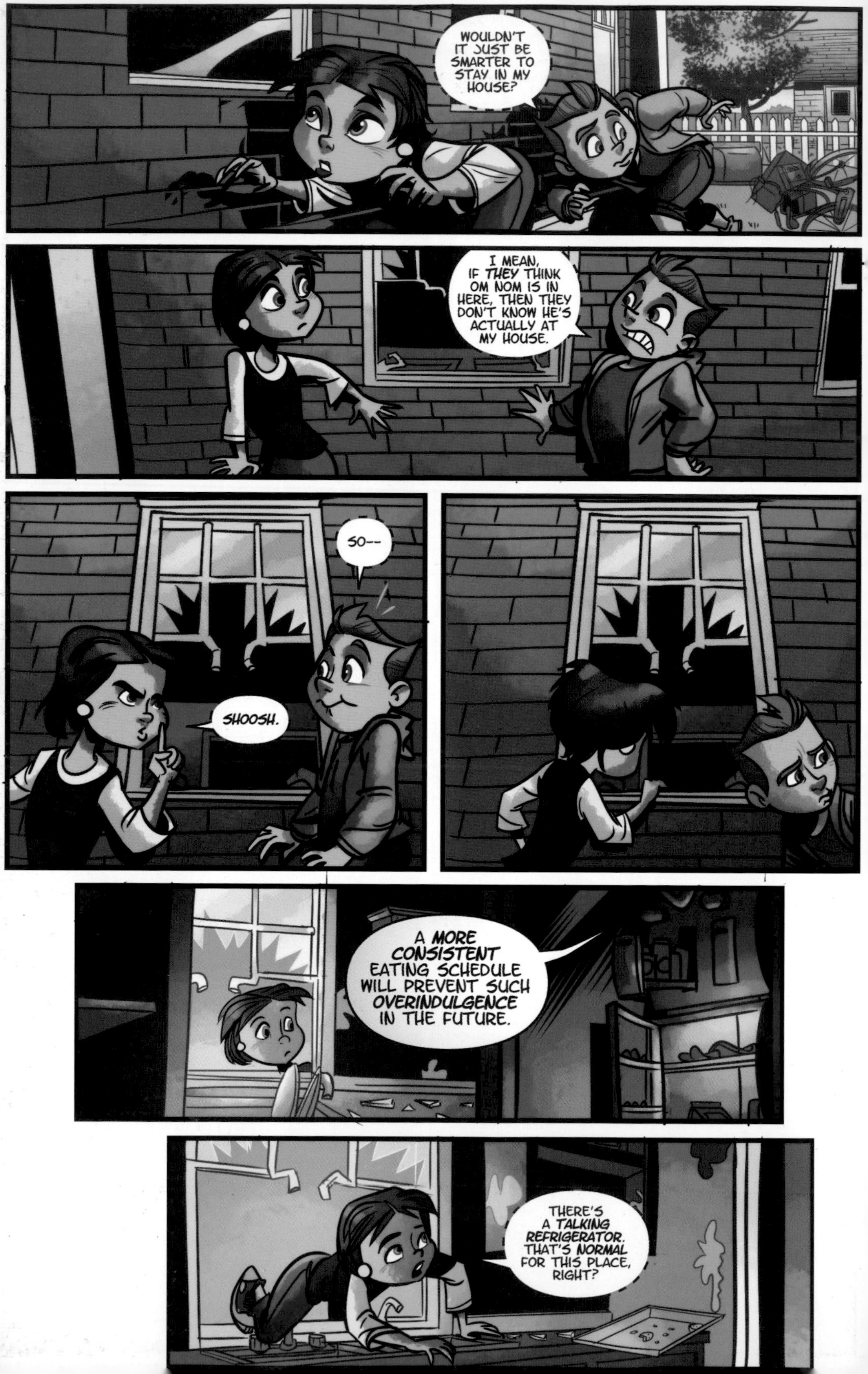

WOULDN'T IT JUST BE SMARTER TO STAY IN MY HOUSE?
I MEAN, IF THEY THINK OM NOM IS IN HERE, THEN THEY DON'T KNOW HE'S ACTUALLY AT MY HOUSE.
SO--
SHOOSH.
A MORE CONSISTENT EATING SCHEDULE WILL PREVENT SUCH OVERINDULGENCE IN THE FUTURE.
THERE'S A TALKING REFRIGERATOR. THAT'S NORMAL FOR THIS PLACE, RIGHT?

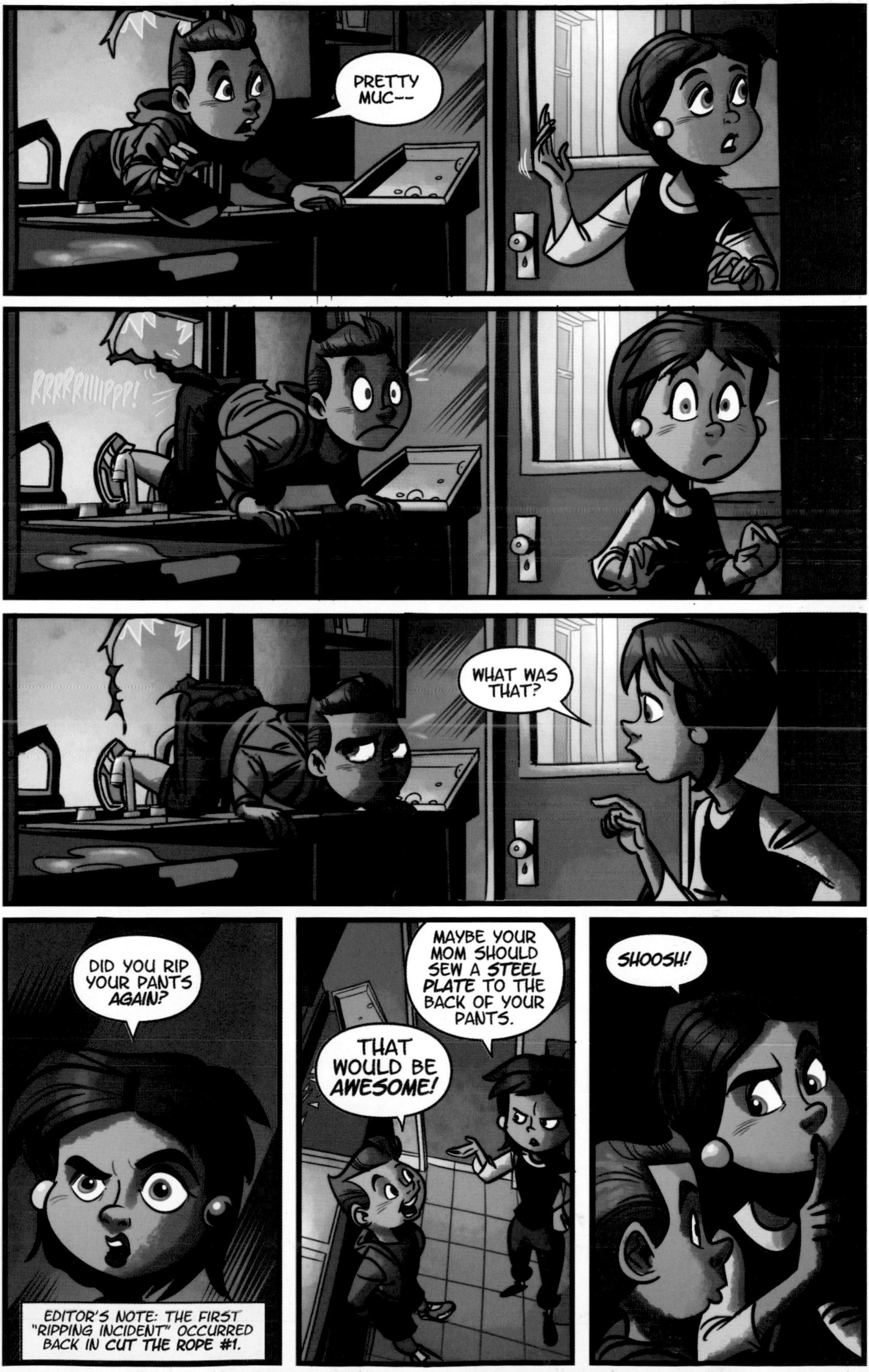
PRETTY MUC--
RRRRRIIIIPPP!
WHAT WAS THAT?
DID YOU RIP YOUR PANTS AGAIN?
EDITOR'S NOTE: THE FIRST "RIPPING INCIDENT" OCCURRED BACK IN CUT THE ROPE #1.
MAYBE YOUR MOM SHOULD SEW A STEEL PLATE TO THE BACK OF YOUR PANTS.
THAT WOULD BE AWESOME!
SHOOSH!

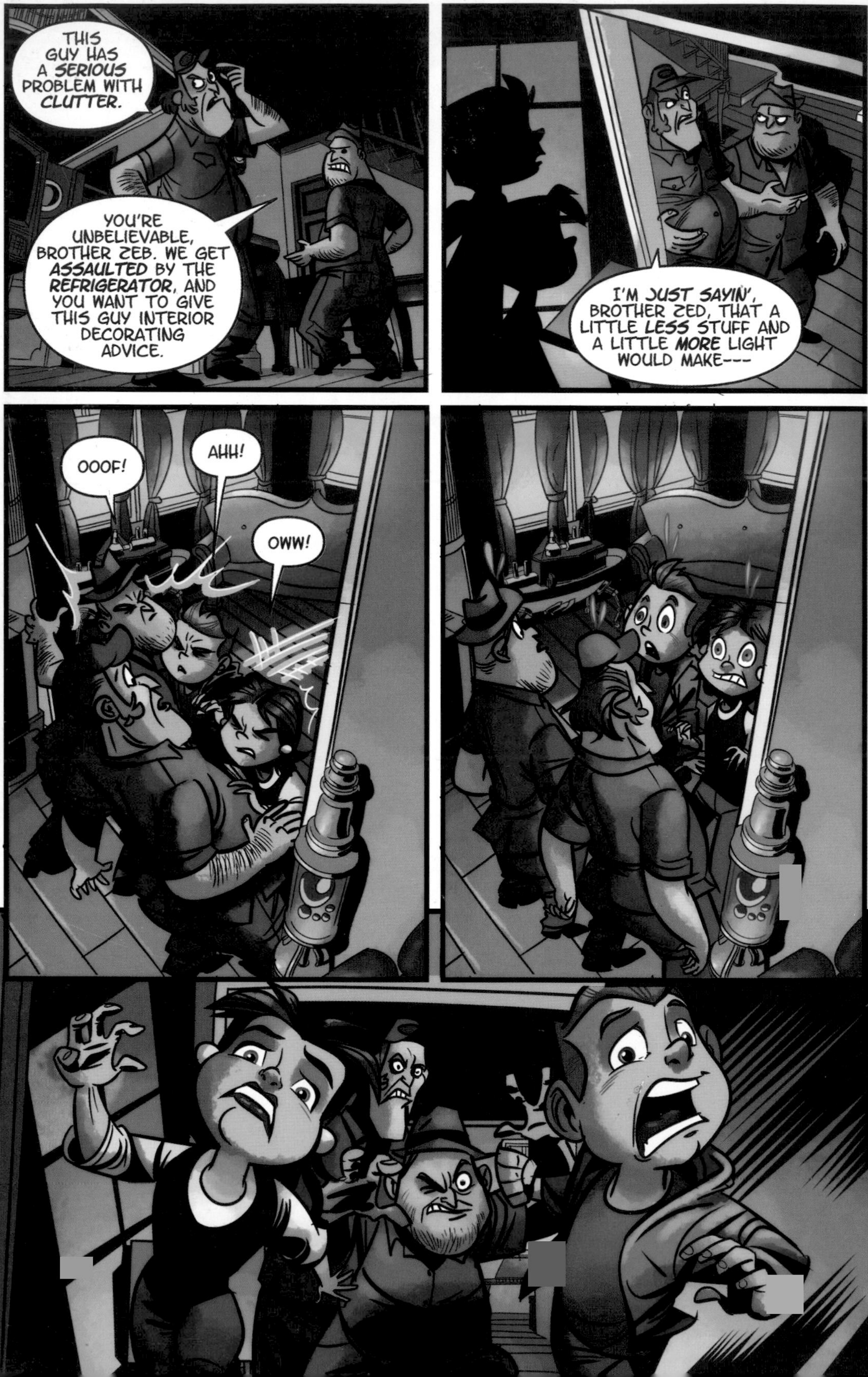
THIS GUY HAS A SERIOUS PROBLEM WITH CLUTTER.
YOU'RE UNBELIEVABLE, BROTHER ZEB. WE GET ASSAULTED BY THE REFRIGERATOR, AND YOU WANT TO GIVE THIS GUY INTERIOR DECORATING ADVICE.
I'M JUST SAYIN', BROTHER ZED, THAT A LITTLE LESS STUFF AND A LITTLE MORE LIGHT WOULD MAKE---
OOOF!
AHH!
OWW!

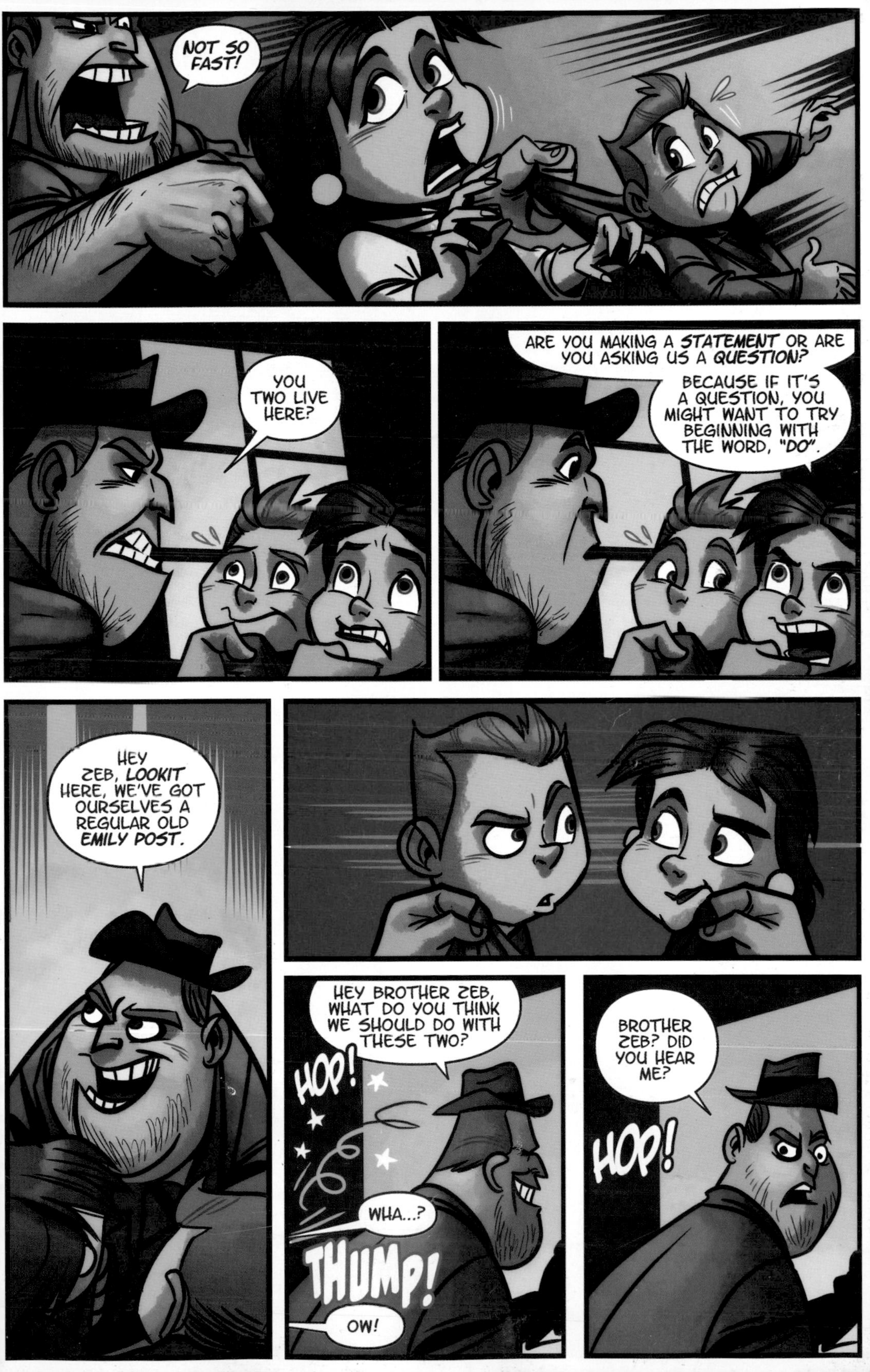

NOT SO FAST!
YOU TWO LIVE HERE?
ARE YOU MAKING A STATEMENT OR ARE YOU ASKING US A QUESTION?
BECAUSE IF IT'S A QUESTION, YOU MIGHT WANT TO TRY BEGINNING WITH THE WORD, "DO".
HEY ZEB, LOOKIT HERE, WE'VE GOT OURSELVES A REGULAR OLD EMILY POST.
HEY BROTHER ZEB, WHAT DO YOU THINK WE SHOULD DO WITH THESE TWO?
HOP!
WHA...?
THUMP!
OW!
BROTHER ZEB? DID YOU HEAR ME?
HOP!

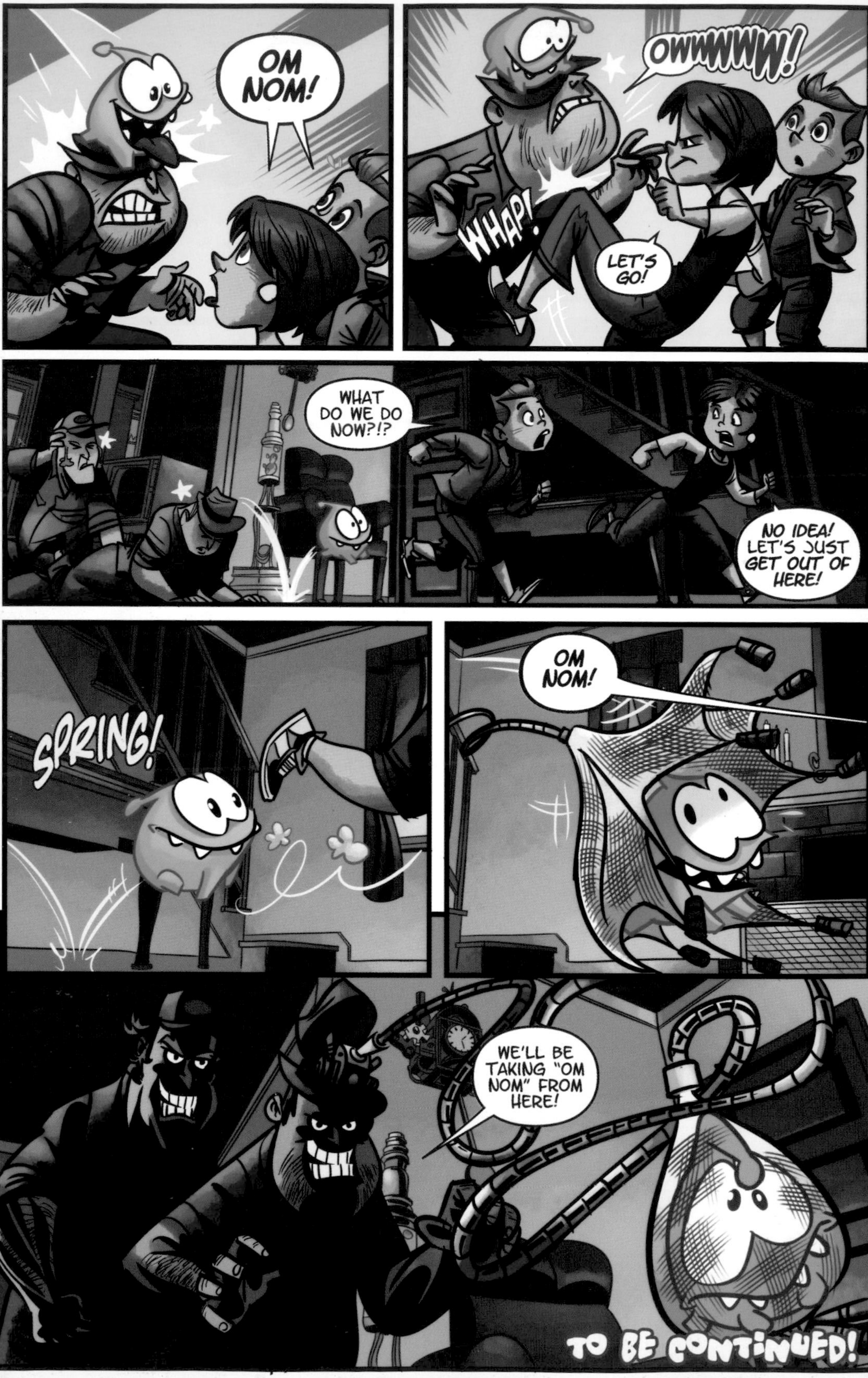
OM NOM!
OWWWWW!
WHAP!
LET'S GO!
WHAT DO WE DO NOW?!?
NO IDEA! LET'S JUST GET OUT OF HERE!
SPRING!
OM NOM!
WE'LL BE TAKING "OM NOM" FROM HERE!
TO BE CONTINUED!

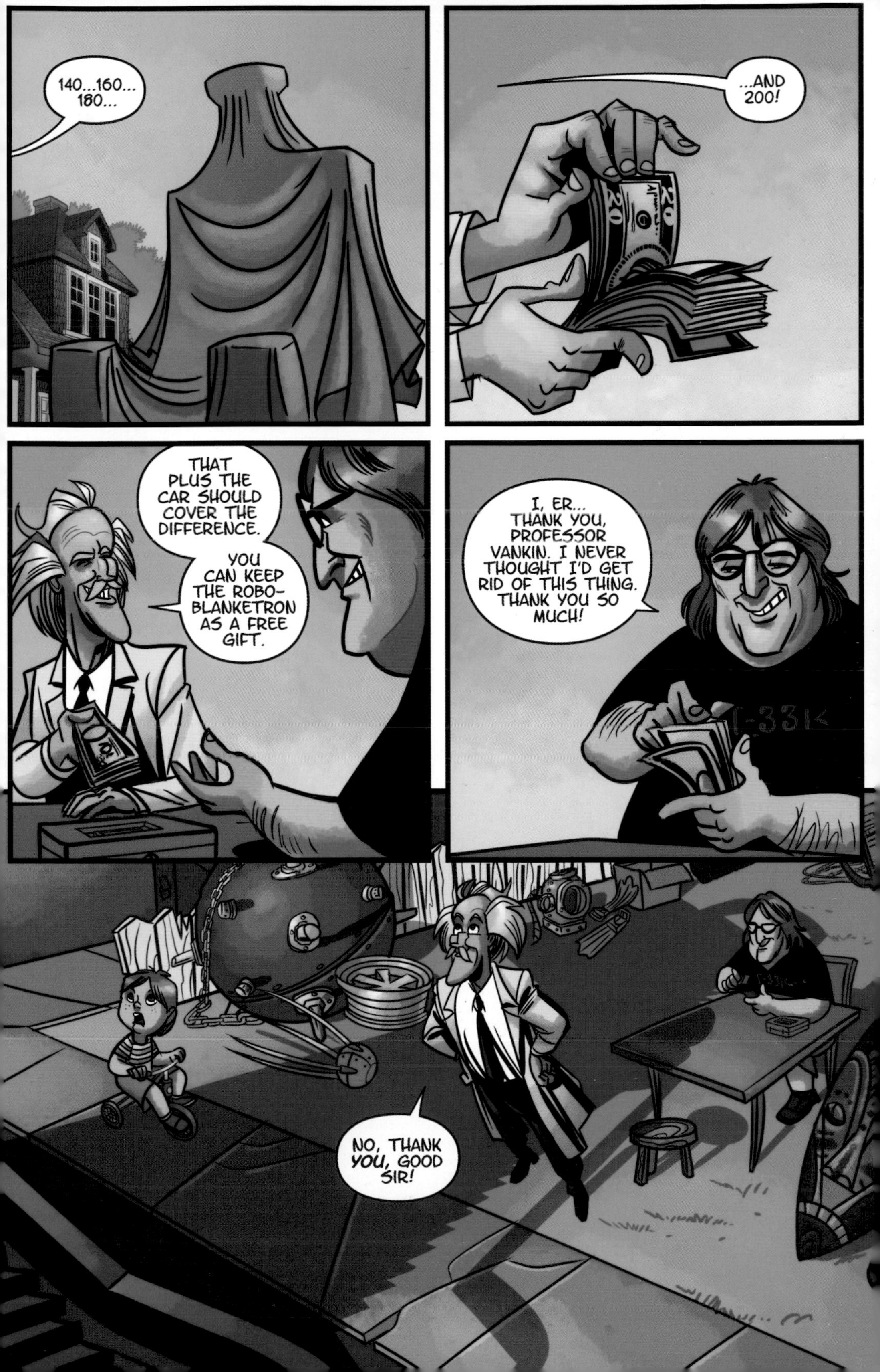
140...160... 180...
...AND 200!
THAT PLUS THE CAR SHOULD COVER THE DIFFERENCE.
YOU CAN KEEP THE ROBO-BLANKETRON AS A FREE GIFT.
I, ER... THANK YOU, PROFESSOR VANKIN. I NEVER THOUGHT I'D GET RID OF THIS THING. THANK YOU SO MUCH!
NO, THANK YOU, GOOD SIR!

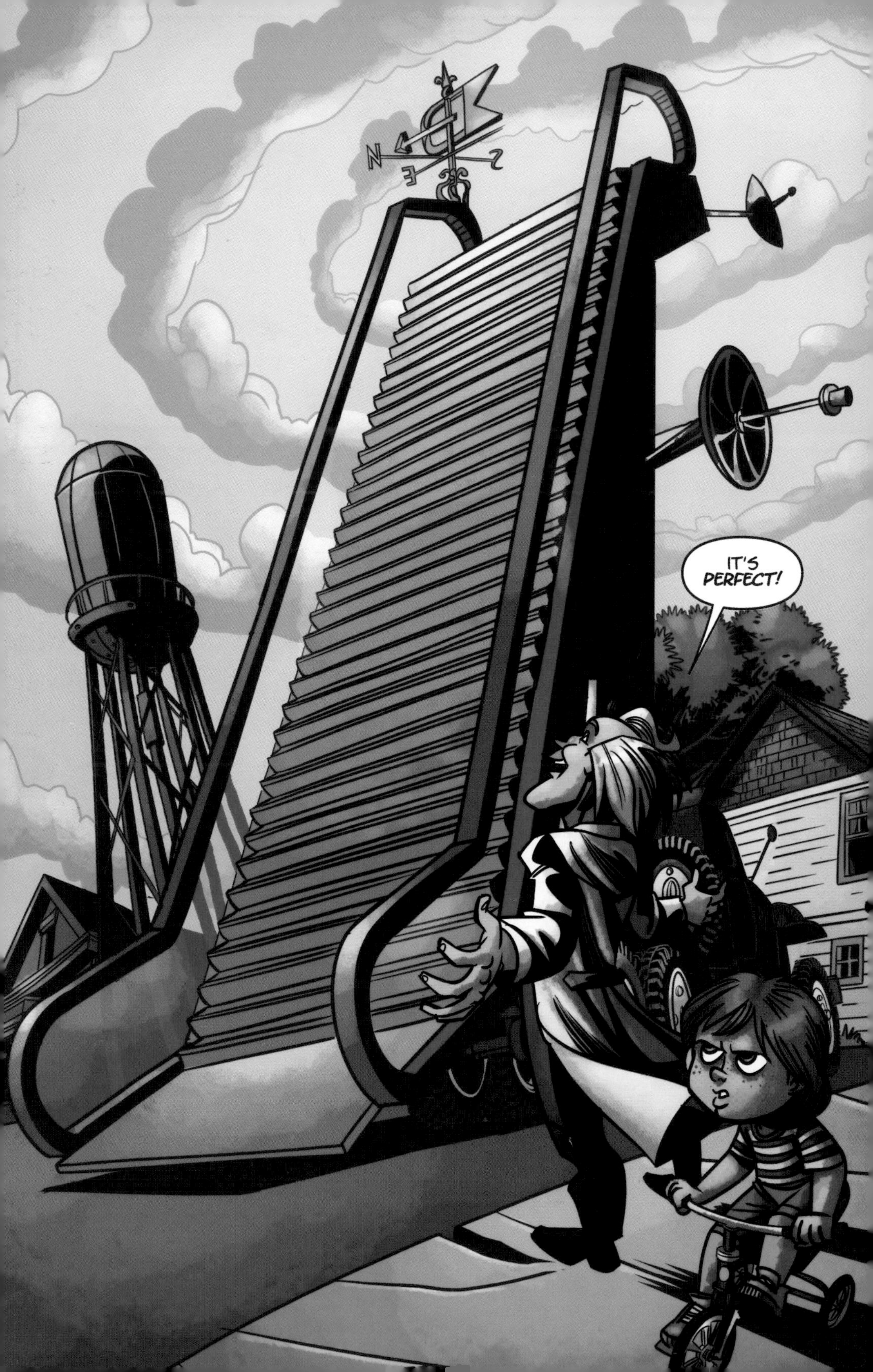
IT'S PERFECT!

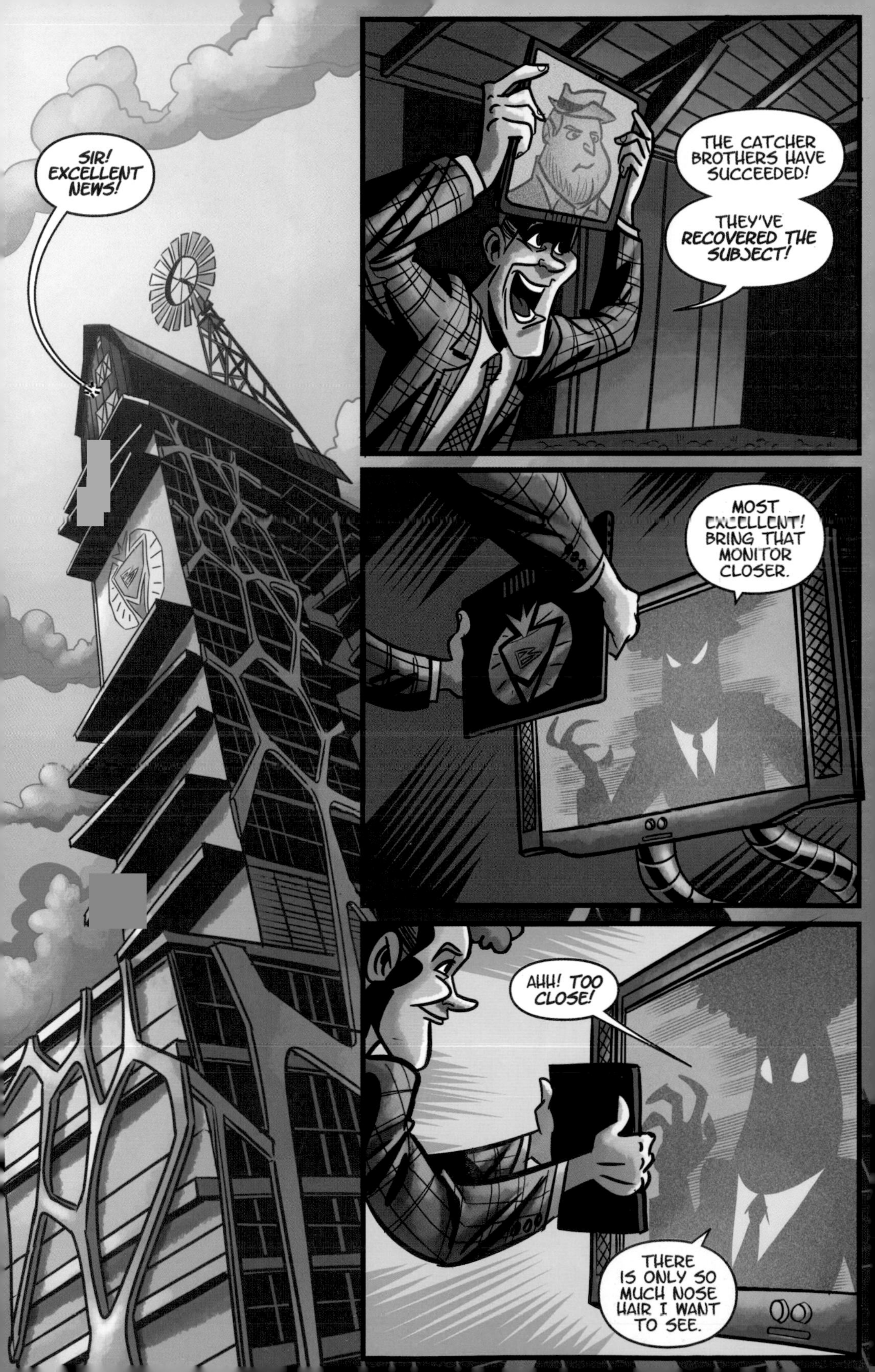
SIR! EXCELLENT NEWS!
THE CATCHER BROTHERS HAVE SUCCEEDED!
THEY'VE RECOVERED THE SUBJECT!
MOST EXCELLENT! BRING THAT MONITOR CLOSER.
AHH! TOO CLOSE!
THERE IS ONLY SO MUCH NOSE HAIR I WANT TO SEE.

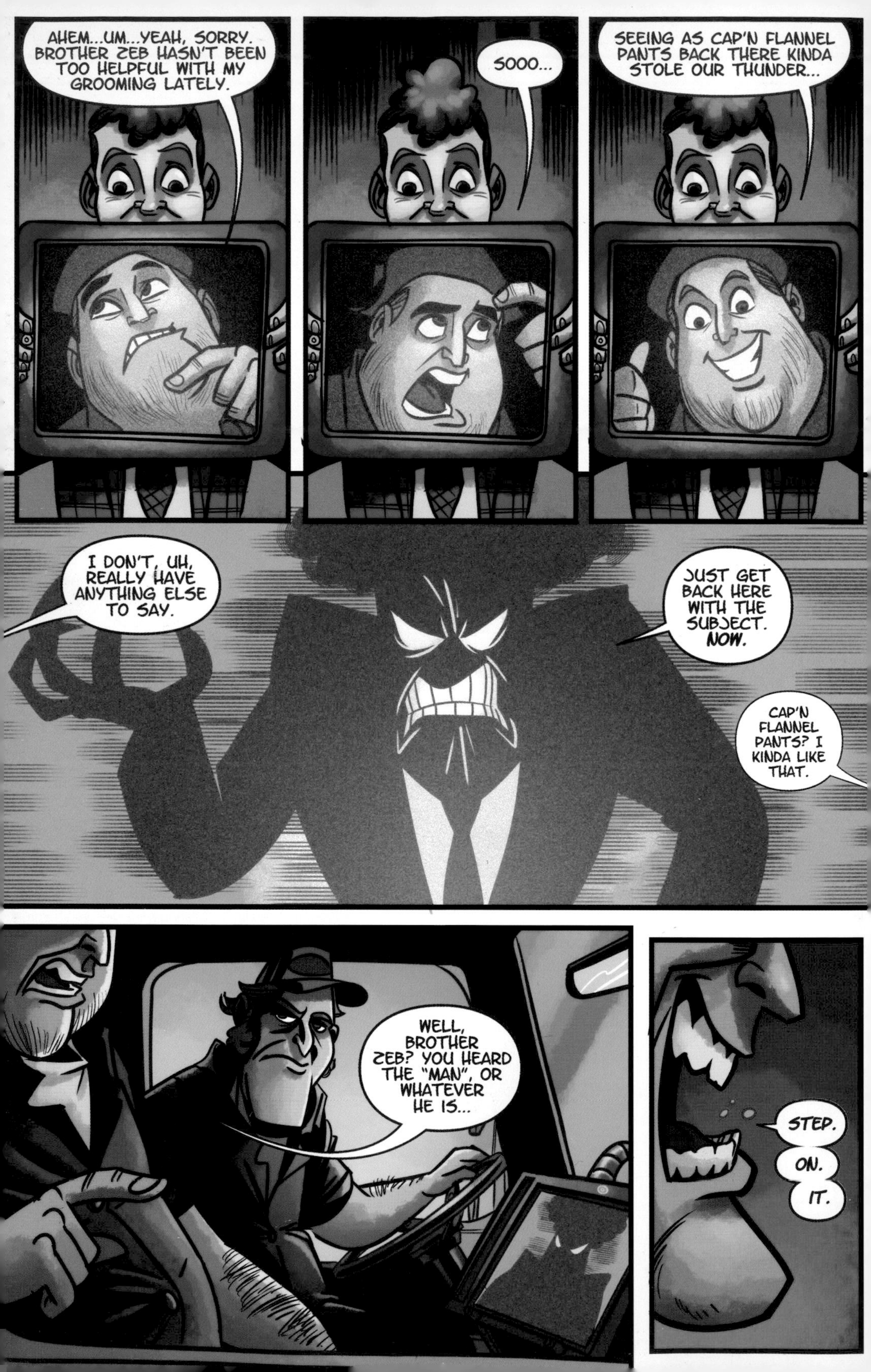
AHEM...UM...YEAH, SORRY. BROTHER ZEB HASN'T BEEN TOO HELPFUL WITH MY GROOMING LATELY.
SOOO...
SEEING AS CAP'N FLANNEL PANTS BACK THERE KINDA STOLE OUR THUNDER...
I DON'T, UH, REALLY HAVE ANYTHING ELSE TO SAY.
JUST GET BACK HERE WITH THE SUBJECT. NOW.
CAP'N FLANNEL PANTS? I KINDA LIKE THAT.
WELL, BROTHER ZEB? YOU HEARD THE "MAN", OR WHATEVER HE IS...
STEP.
ON.
IT.

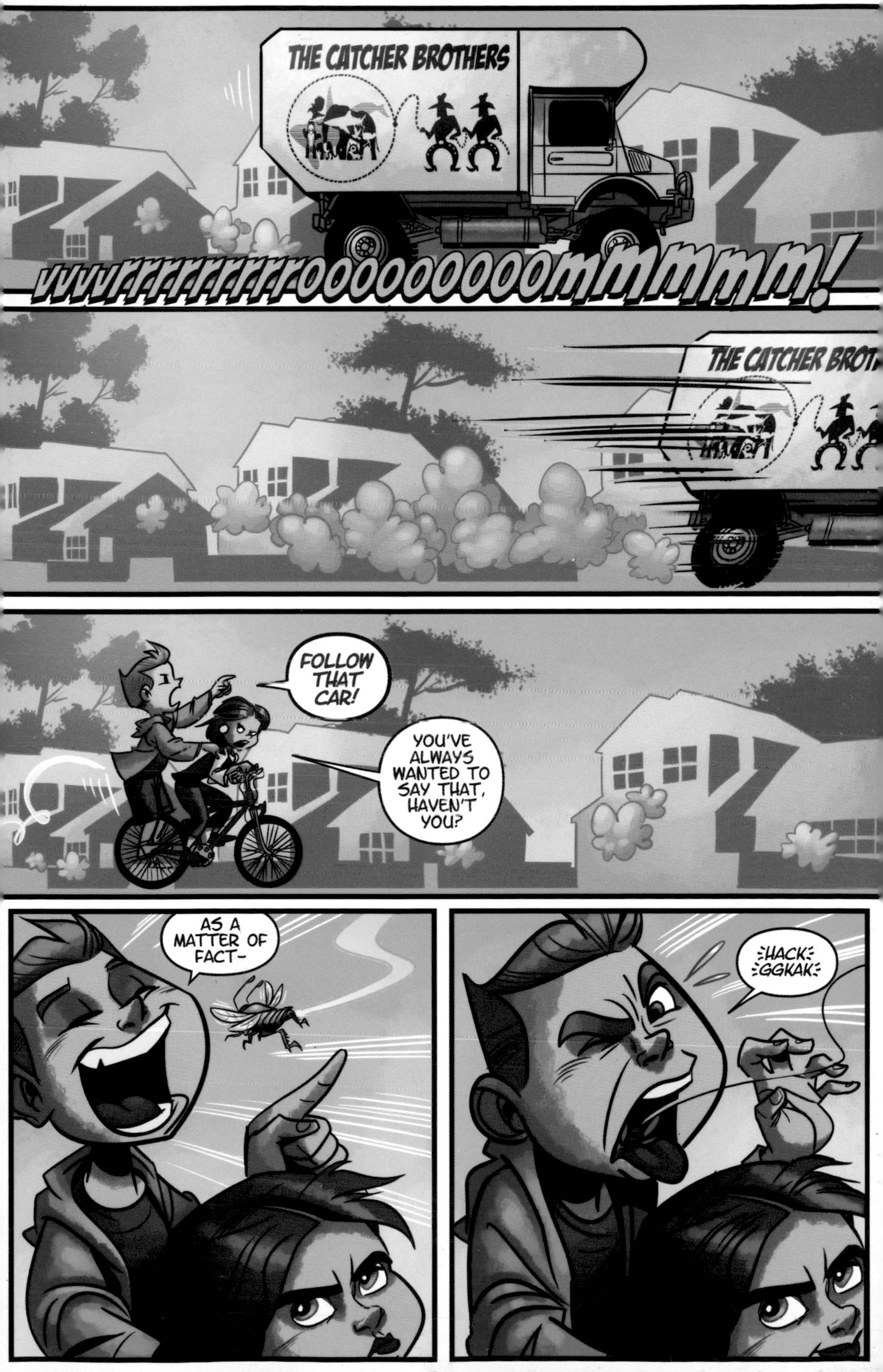
THE CATCHER BROTHERS
VVVVRRRRRRRRROOOOOOOOOOMMMMMMM!
THE CATCHER BROT
FOLLOW THAT CAR!
YOU'VE ALWAYS WANTED TO SAY THAT, HAVEN'T YOU?
AS A MATTER OF FACT-
HACK GGKAK

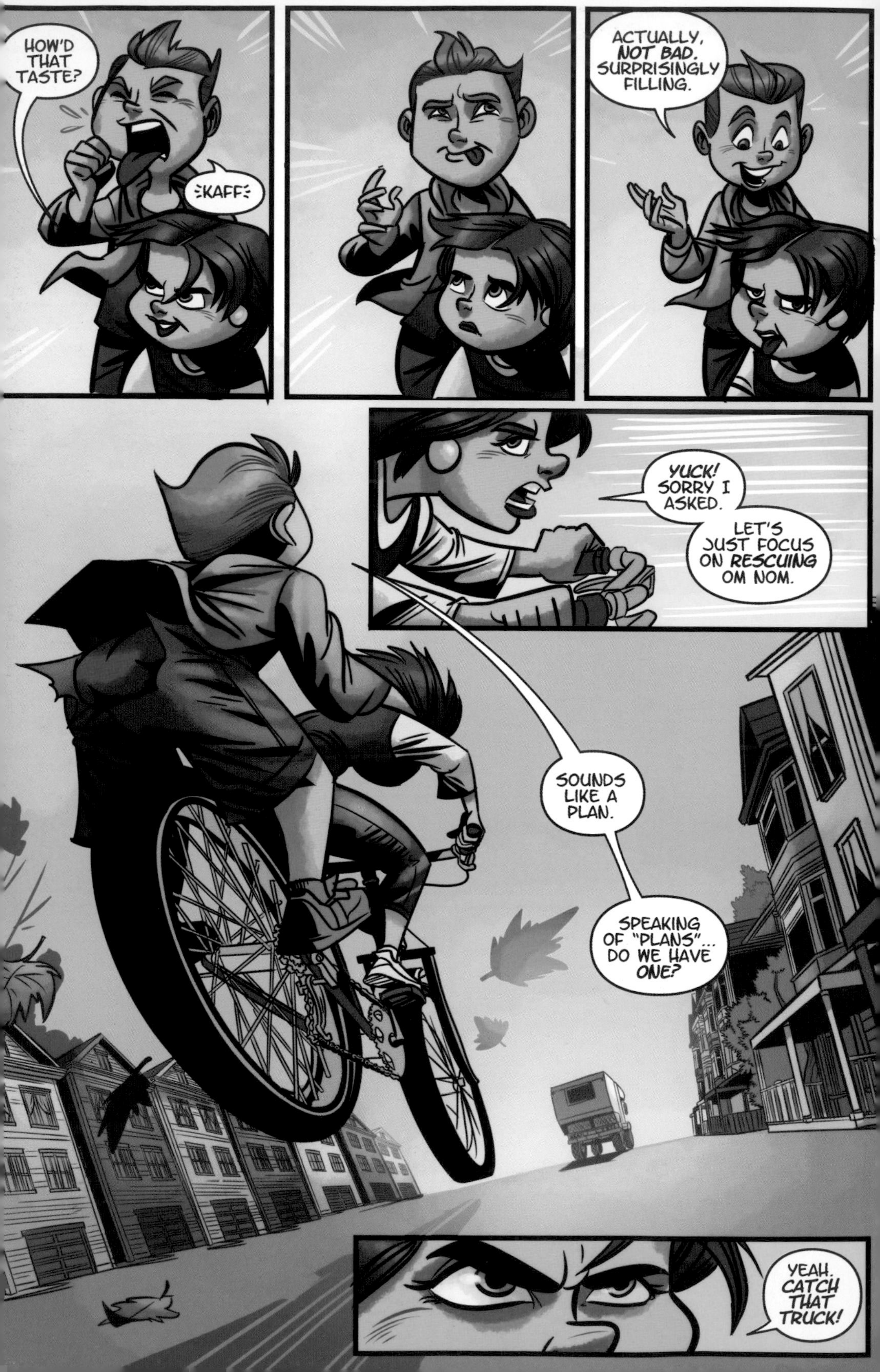
HOW'D THAT TASTE?
KAFF
ACTUALLY, NOT BAD. SURPRISINGLY FILLING.
YUCK! SORRY I ASKED.
LET'S JUST FOCUS ON RESCUING OM NOM.
SOUNDS LIKE A PLAN.
SPEAKING OF "PLANS"... DO WE HAVE ONE?
YEAH. CATCH THAT TRUCK!

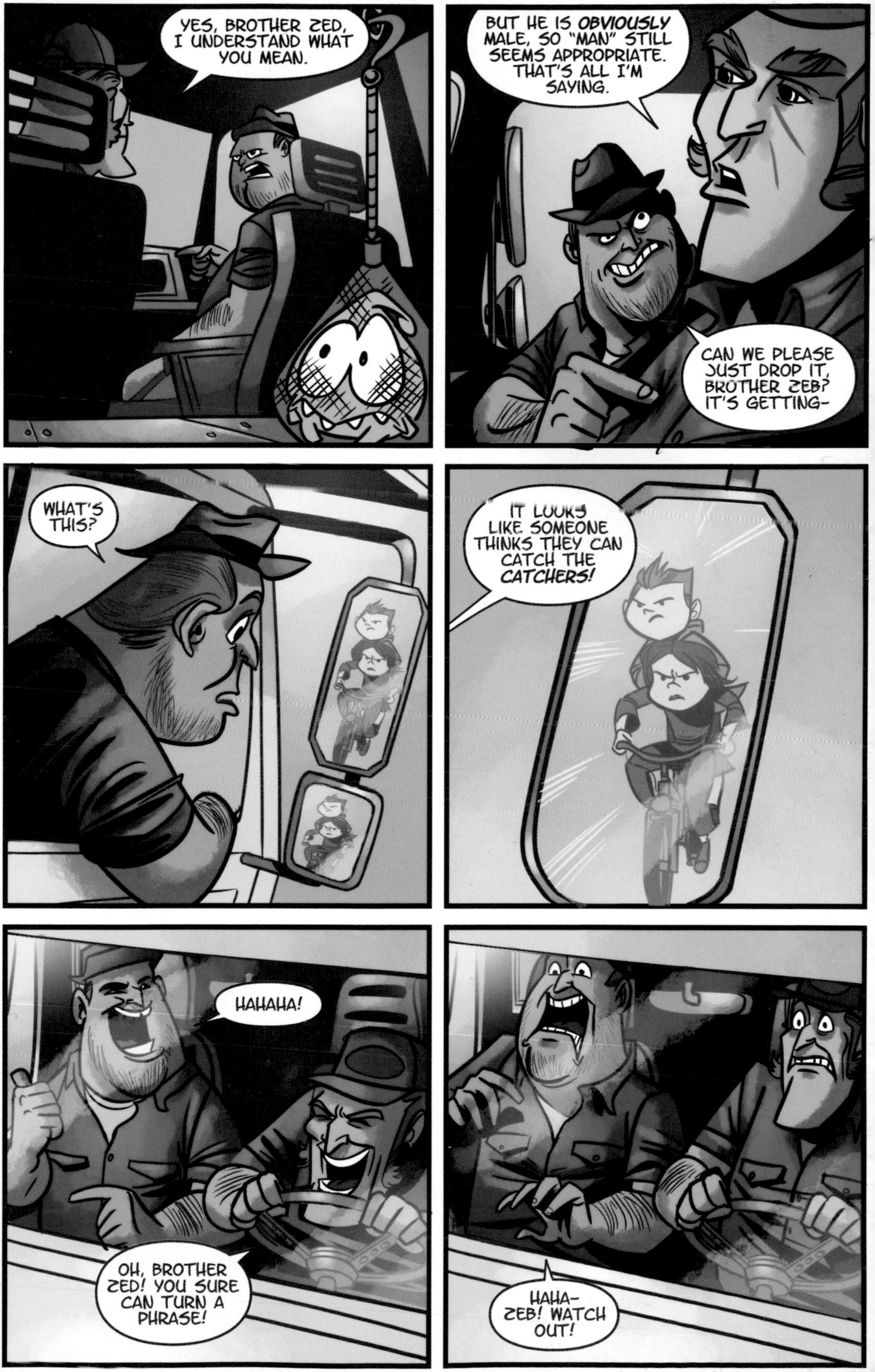
YES, BROTHER ZED, I UNDERSTAND WHAT YOU MEAN.
BUT HE IS OBVIOUSLY MALE, SO "MAN" STILL SEEMS APPROPRIATE. THAT'S ALL I'M SAYING.
CAN WE PLEASE JUST DROP IT, BROTHER ZEB? IT'S GETTING-
WHAT'S THIS?
IT LOOKS LIKE SOMEONE THINKS THEY CAN CATCH THE CATCHERS!
HAHAHA!
OH, BROTHER ZED! YOU SURE CAN TURN A PHRASE!
HAHA- ZEB! WATCH OUT!

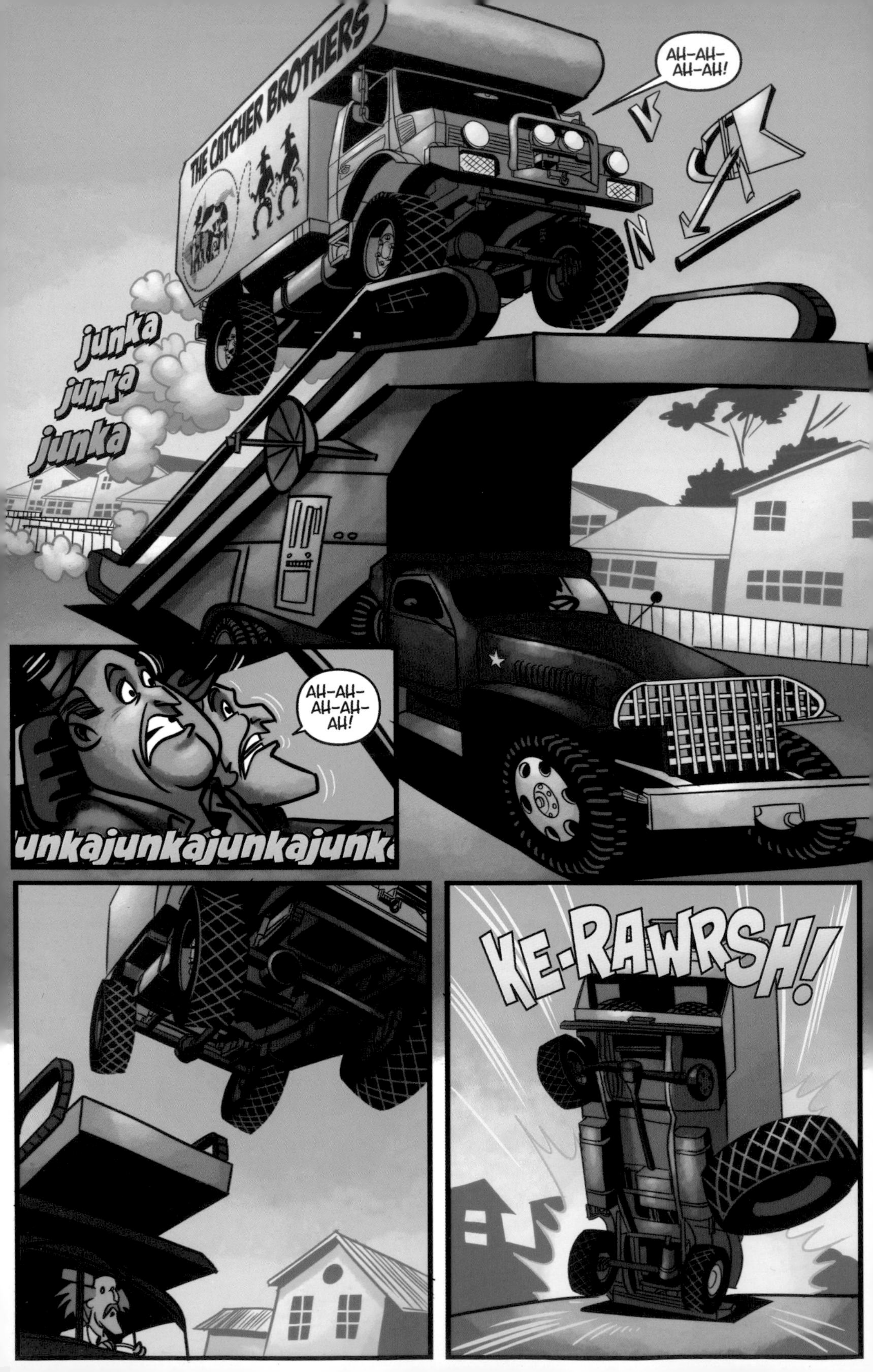
THE CATCHER BROTHERS
AH-AH-
AH-AH!
VNNRAK
junka
junka
junka
AH-AH-
AH-AH-
AH!
junkajunkajunkajunka
KE-RAWRSH!

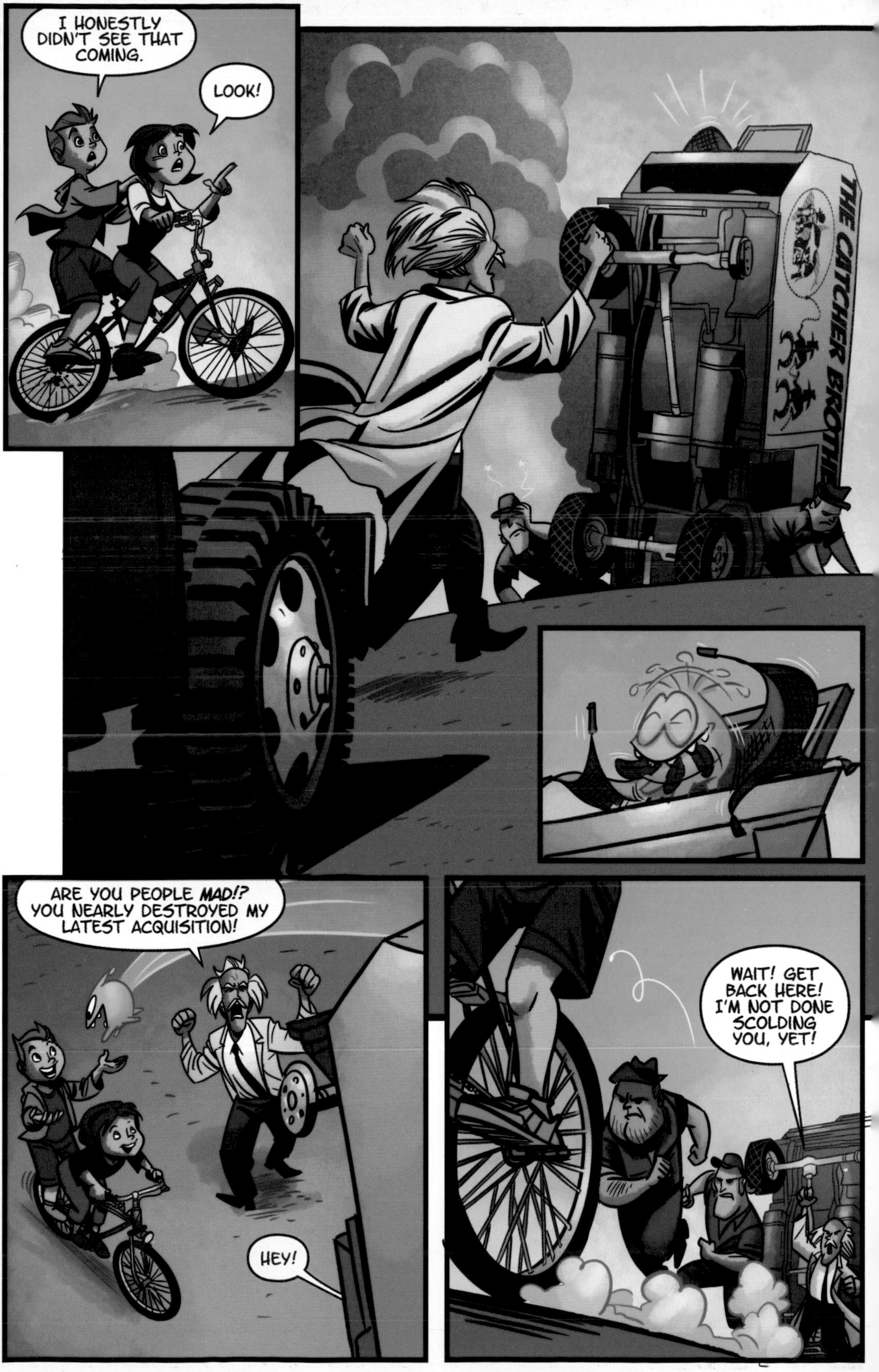
I HONESTLY DIDN'T SEE THAT COMING.
LOOK!
THE CATCHER BROTHE
ARE YOU PEOPLE MAD!? YOU NEARLY DESTROYED MY LATEST ACQUISITION!
HEY!
WAIT! GET BACK HERE! I'M NOT DONE SCOLDING YOU, YET!

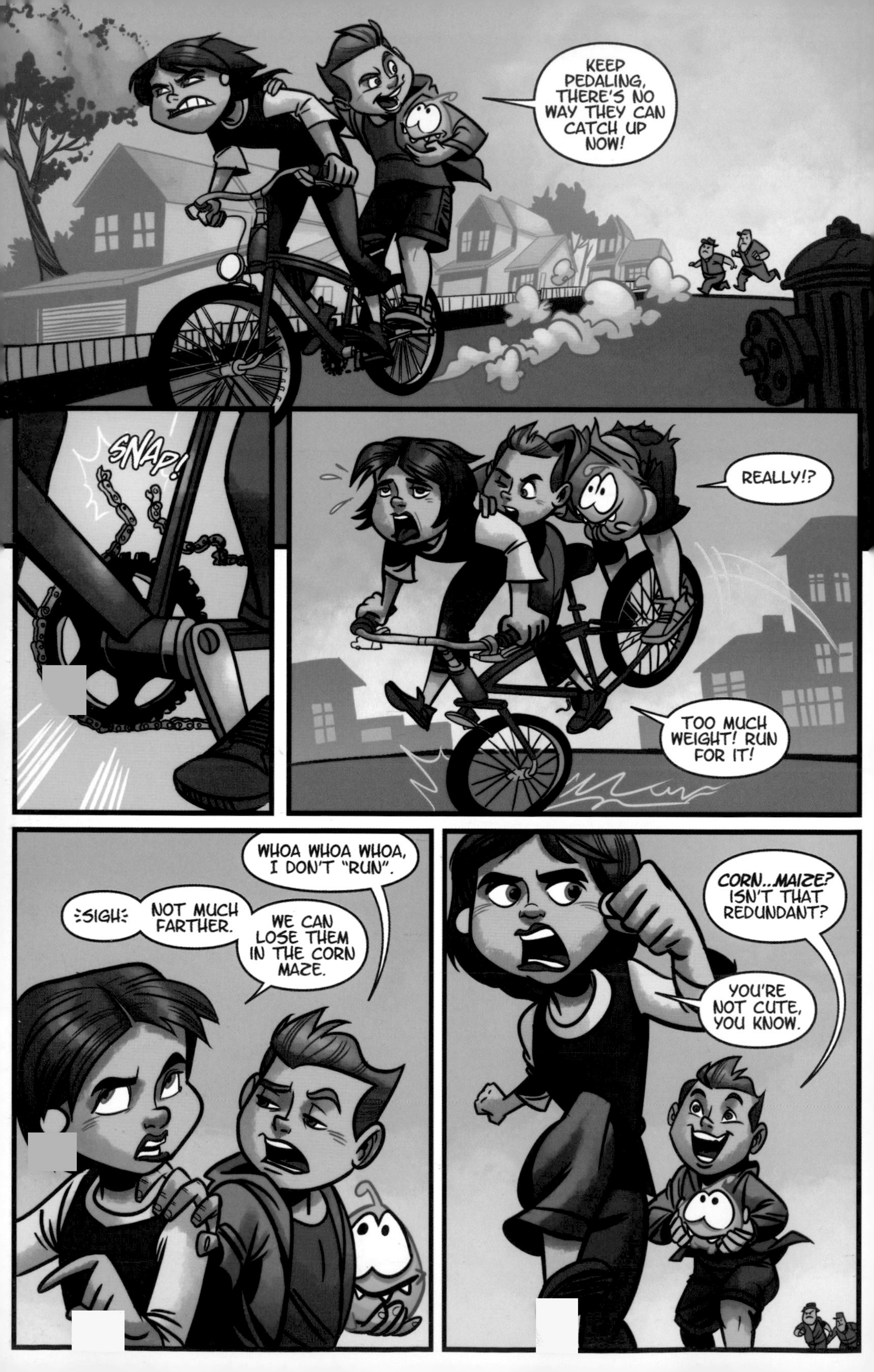
KEEP PEDALING, THERE'S NO WAY THEY CAN CATCH UP NOW!
SNAP!
REALLY!?
TOO MUCH WEIGHT! RUN FOR IT!
SIGH
NOT MUCH FARTHER.
WE CAN LOSE THEM IN THE CORN MAZE.
WHOA WHOA WHOA, I DON'T "RUN".
CORN...MAIZE? ISN'T THAT REDUNDANT?
YOU'RE NOT CUTE, YOU KNOW.

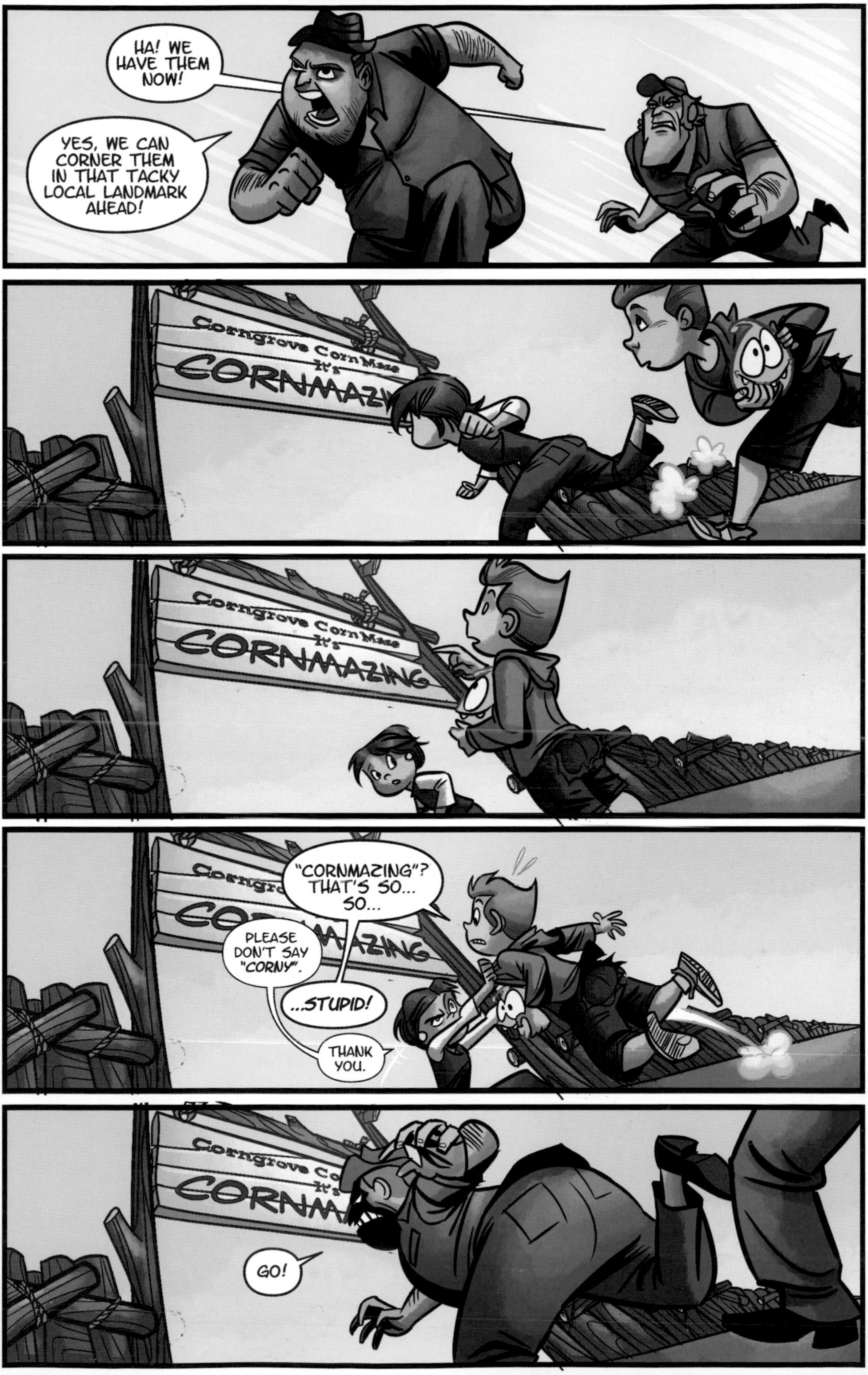
HA! WE HAVE THEM NOW!
YES, WE CAN CORNER THEM IN THAT TACKY LOCAL LANDMARK AHEAD!
Corngrove Corn Maze
It's
CORNMAZING
"CORNMAZING"? THAT'S SO... SO...
PLEASE DON'T SAY "CORNY".
...STUPID!
THANK YOU.
GO!

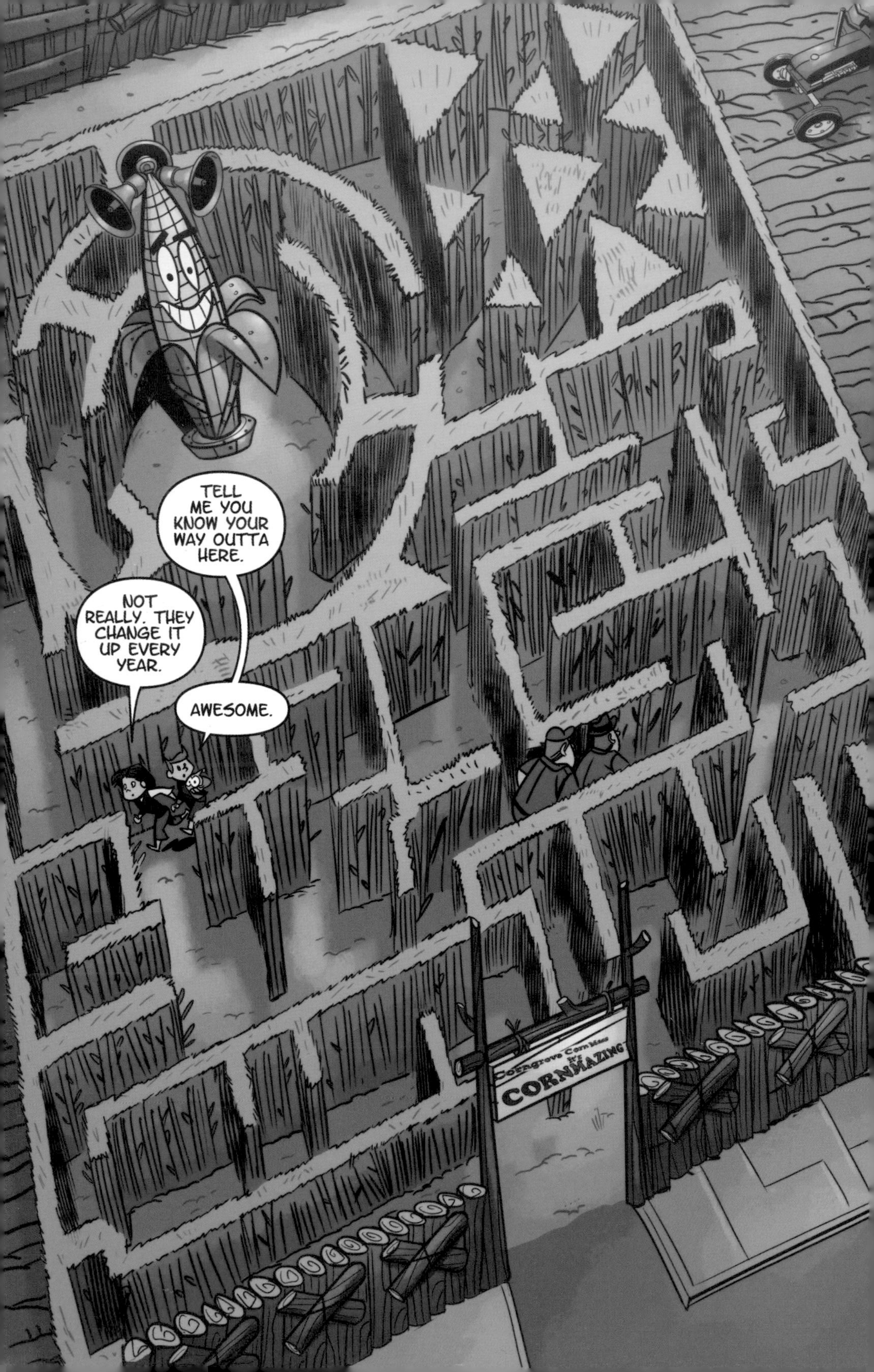
TELL ME YOU KNOW YOUR WAY OUTTA HERE.
NOT REALLY. THEY CHANGE IT UP EVERY YEAR.
AWESOME.
CORNMAZING

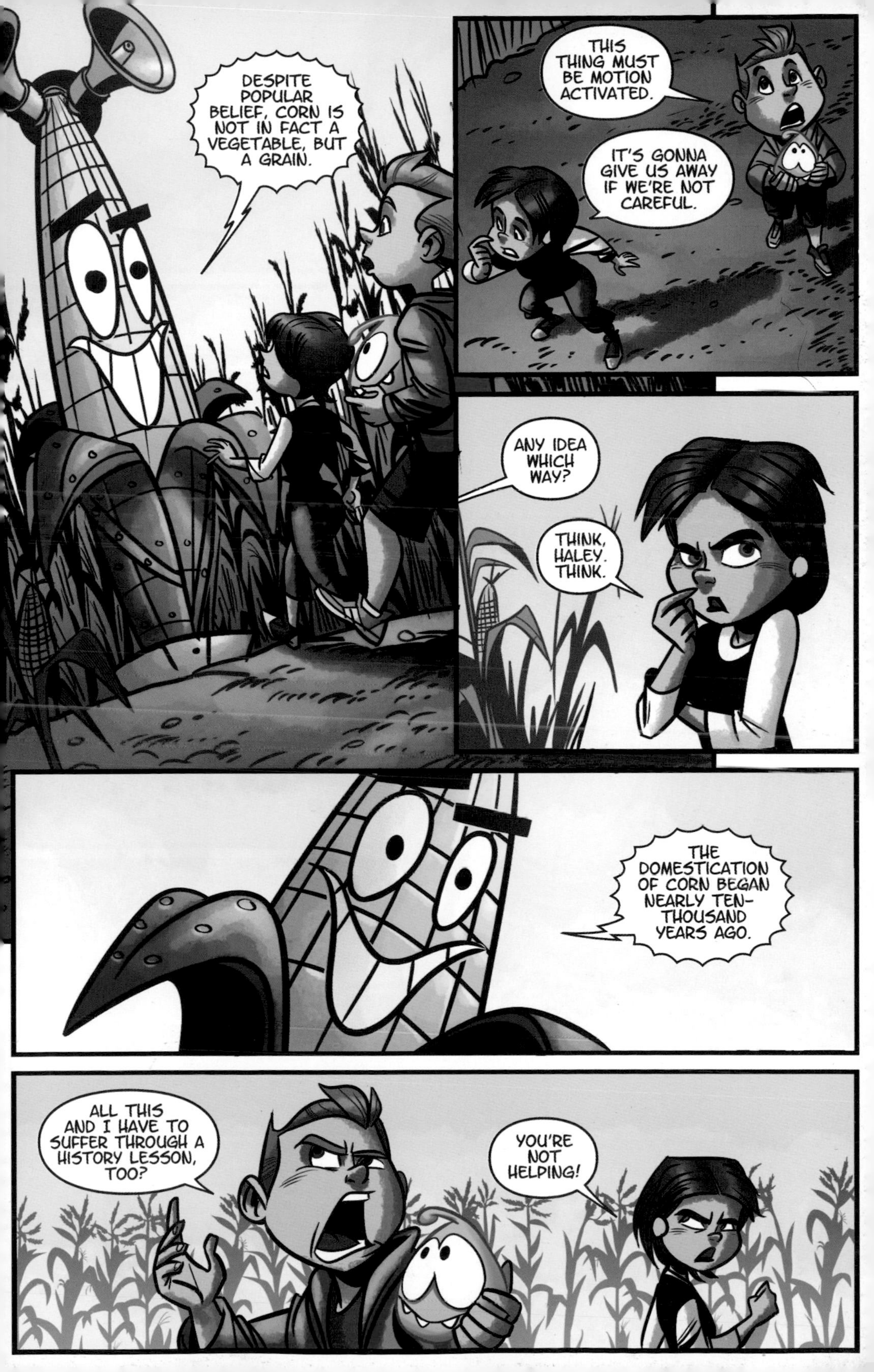
DESPITE POPULAR BELIEF, CORN IS NOT IN FACT A VEGETABLE, BUT A GRAIN.
THIS THING MUST BE MOTION ACTIVATED.
IT'S GONNA GIVE US AWAY IF WE'RE NOT CAREFUL.
ANY IDEA WHICH WAY?
THINK, HALEY. THINK.
THE DOMESTICATION OF CORN BEGAN NEARLY TEN-THOUSAND YEARS AGO.
ALL THIS AND I HAVE TO SUFFER THROUGH A HISTORY LESSON, TOO?
YOU'RE NOT HELPING!

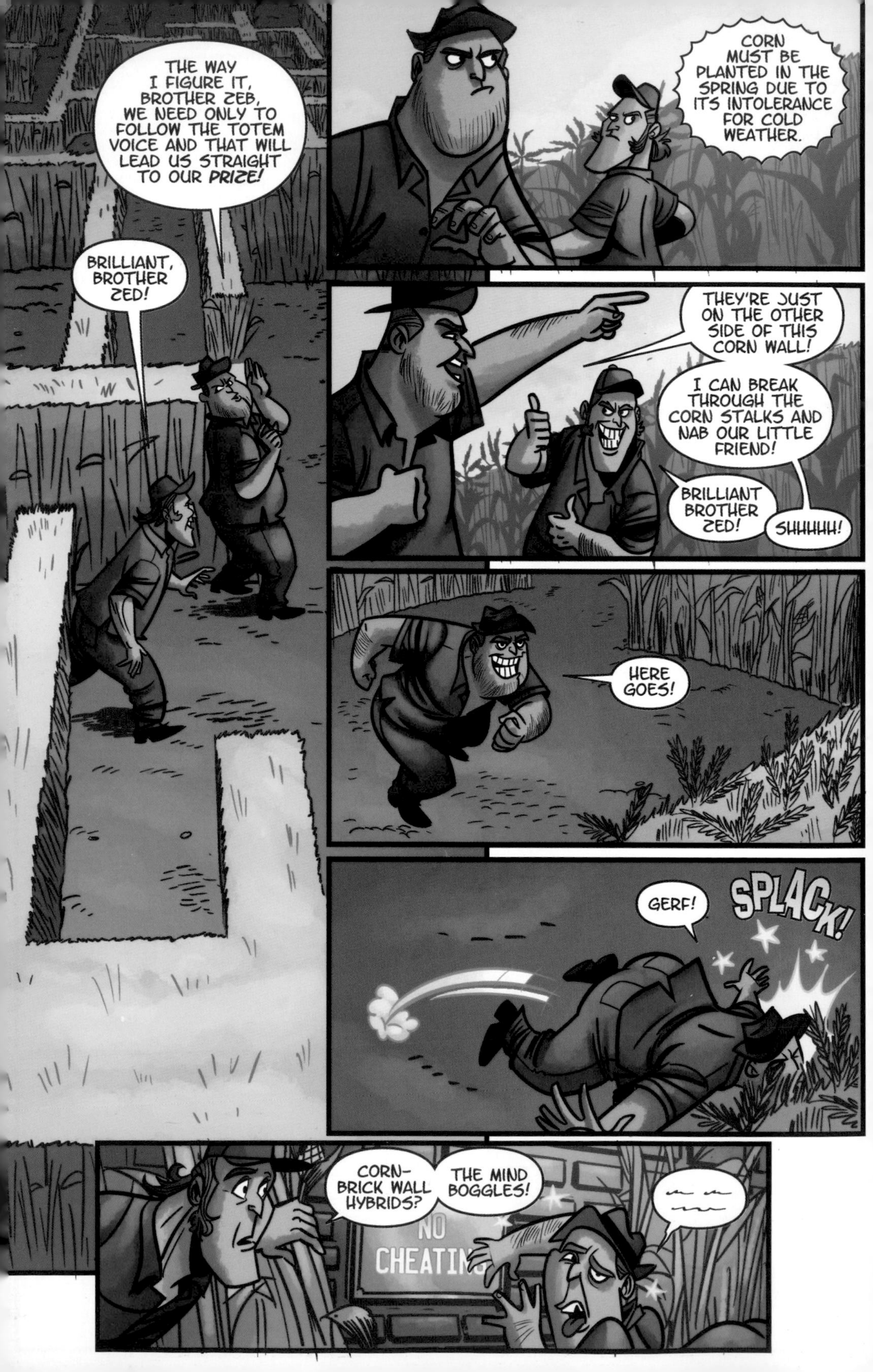
THE WAY I FIGURE IT, BROTHER ZEB, WE NEED ONLY TO FOLLOW THE TOTEM VOICE AND THAT WILL LEAD US STRAIGHT TO OUR PRIZE!
BRILLIANT, BROTHER ZED!
CORN MUST BE PLANTED IN THE SPRING DUE TO ITS INTOLERANCE FOR COLD WEATHER.
THEY'RE JUST ON THE OTHER SIDE OF THIS CORN WALL!
I CAN BREAK THROUGH THE CORN STALKS AND NAB OUR LITTLE FRIEND!
BRILLIANT BROTHER ZED!
SHHHHH!
HERE GOES!
GERF!
SPLACK!
CORN-BRICK WALL HYBRIDS?
THE MIND BOGGLES!
NO CHEATIN

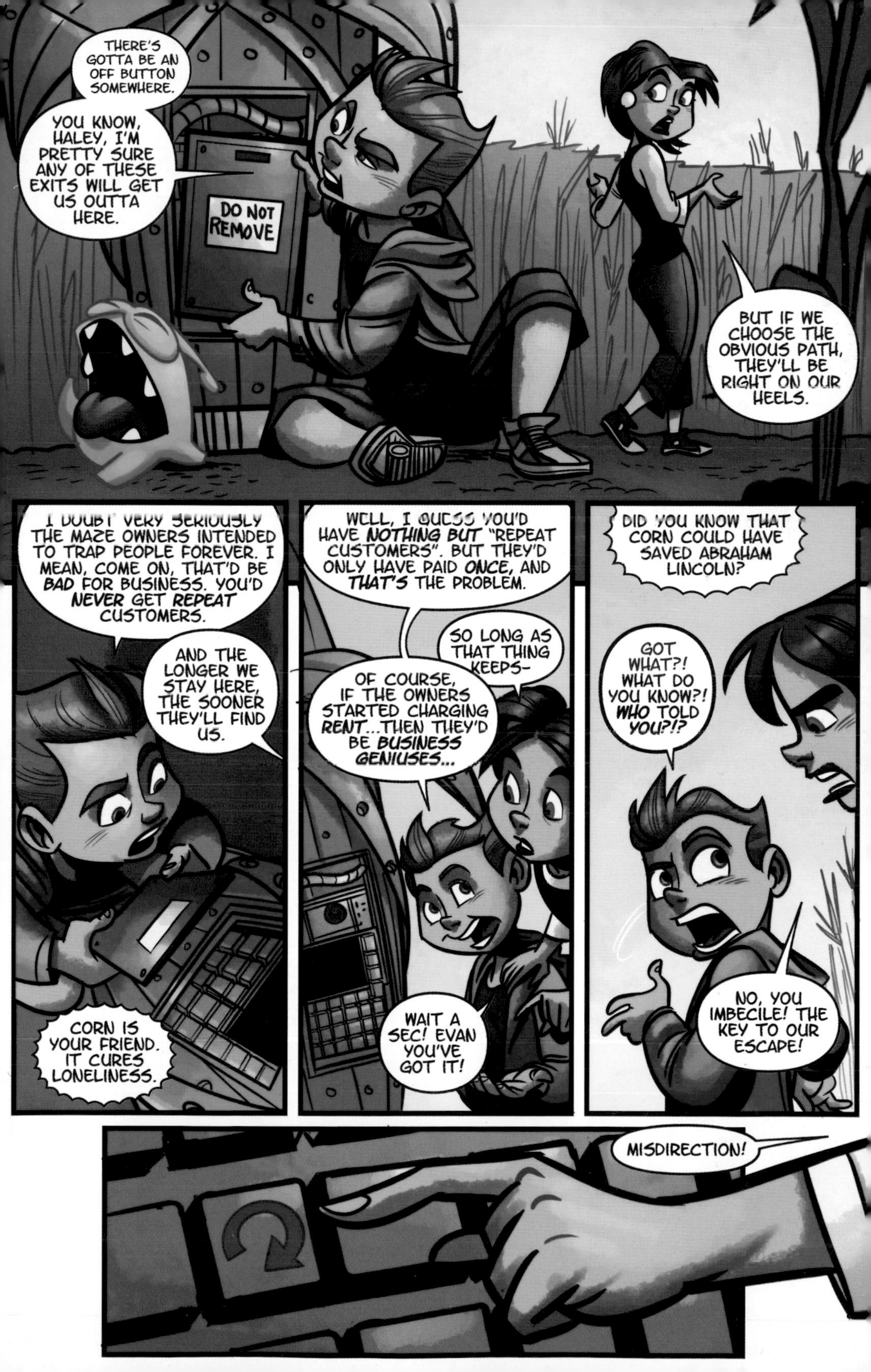
THERE'S GOTTA BE AN OFF BUTTON SOMEWHERE.
YOU KNOW, HALEY, I'M PRETTY SURE ANY OF THESE EXITS WILL GET US OUTTA HERE.
DO NOT REMOVE
BUT IF WE CHOOSE THE OBVIOUS PATH, THEY'LL BE RIGHT ON OUR HEELS.
I DOUBT VERY SERIOUSLY THE MAZE OWNERS INTENDED TO TRAP PEOPLE FOREVER. I MEAN, COME ON, THAT'D BE BAD FOR BUSINESS. YOU'D NEVER GET REPEAT CUSTOMERS.
AND THE LONGER WE STAY HERE, THE SOONER THEY'LL FIND US.
CORN IS YOUR FRIEND. IT CURES LONELINESS.
WELL, I GUESS YOU'D HAVE NOTHING BUT "REPEAT CUSTOMERS". BUT THEY'D ONLY HAVE PAID ONCE, AND THAT'S THE PROBLEM.
SO LONG AS THAT THING KEEPS-
OF COURSE, IF THE OWNERS STARTED CHARGING RENT...THEN THEY'D BE BUSINESS GENIUSES...
WAIT A SEC! EVAN YOU'VE GOT IT!
DID YOU KNOW THAT CORN COULD HAVE SAVED ABRAHAM LINCOLN?
GOT WHAT?! WHAT DO YOU KNOW?! WHO TOLD YOU?!?
NO, YOU IMBECILE! THE KEY TO OUR ESCAPE!
MISDIRECTION!

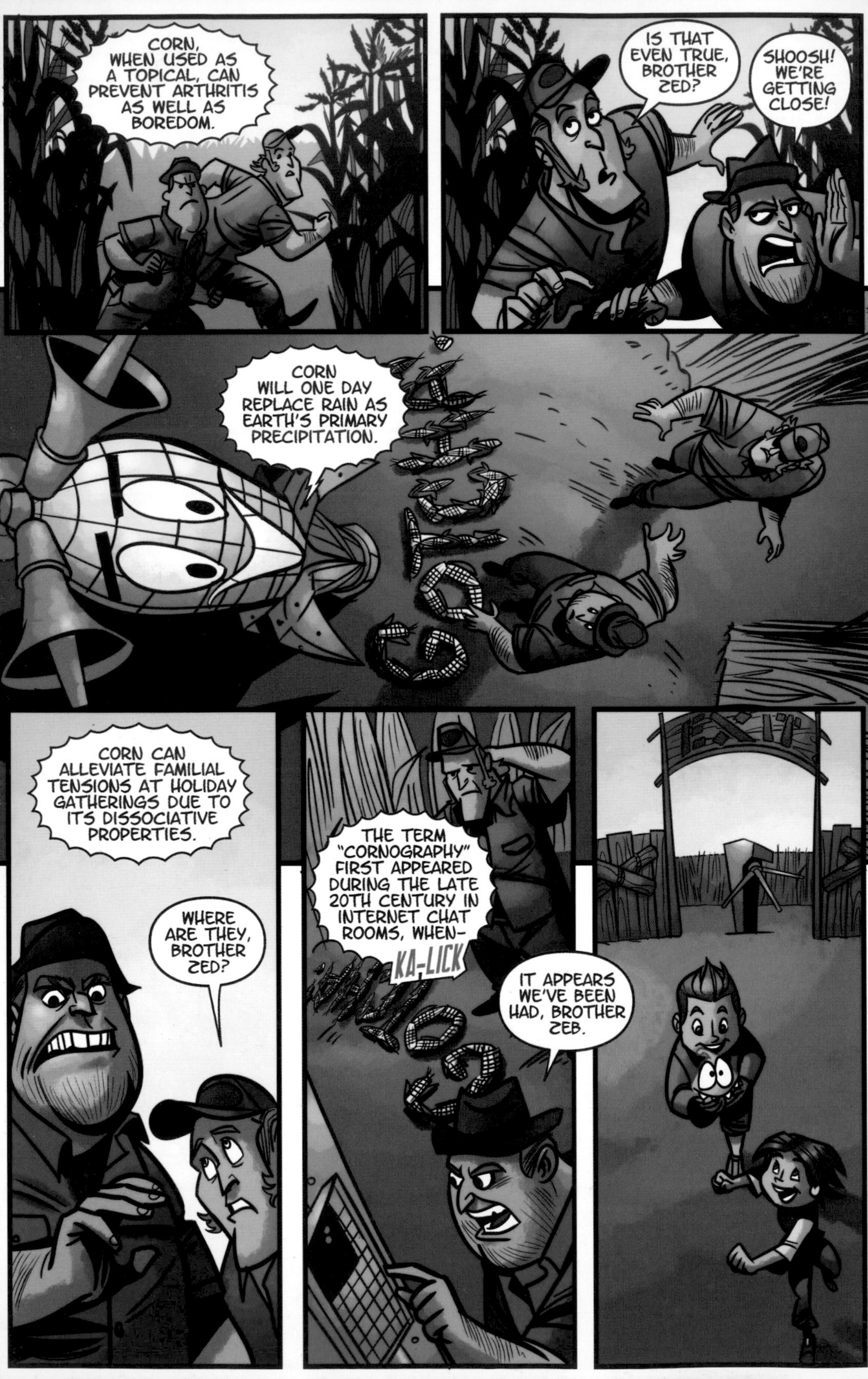
CORN, WHEN USED AS A TOPICAL, CAN PREVENT ARTHRITIS AS WELL AS BOREDOM.
IS THAT EVEN TRUE, BROTHER ZED?
SHOOSH! WE'RE GETTING CLOSE!
CORN WILL ONE DAY REPLACE RAIN AS EARTH'S PRIMARY PRECIPITATION.
CORN CAN ALLEVIATE FAMILIAL TENSIONS AT HOLIDAY GATHERINGS DUE TO ITS DISSOCIATIVE PROPERTIES.
WHERE ARE THEY, BROTHER ZED?
THE TERM "CORNOGRAPHY" FIRST APPEARED DURING THE LATE 20TH CENTURY IN INTERNET CHAT ROOMS, WHEN-
KA-LICK
IT APPEARS WE'VE BEEN HAD, BROTHER ZEB.

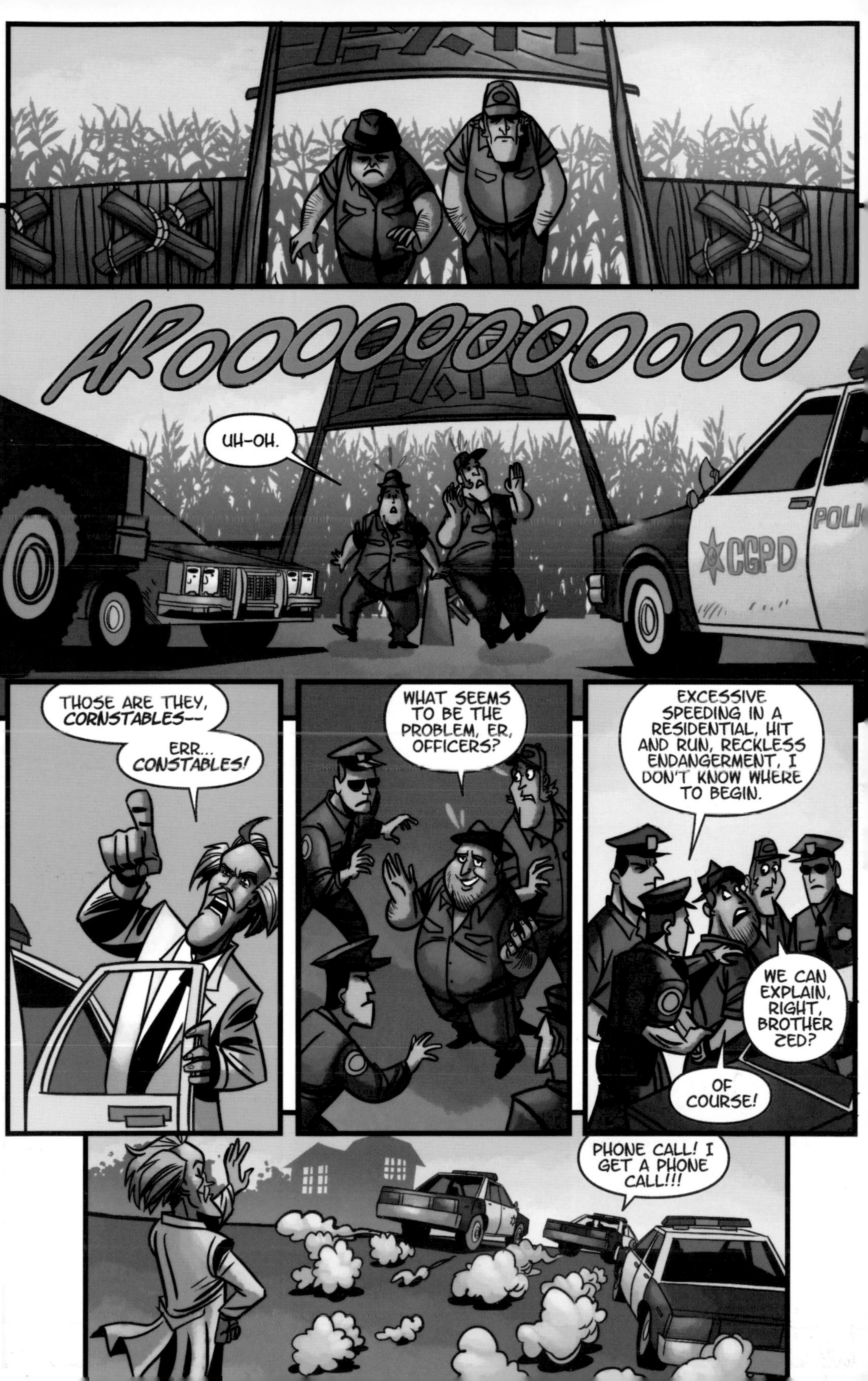
AROOOOOOOOOO
UH-OH.
POLICE
CGPD
THOSE ARE THEY, CORNSTABLES--
ERR... CONSTABLES!
WHAT SEEMS TO BE THE PROBLEM, ER, OFFICERS?
EXCESSIVE SPEEDING IN A RESIDENTIAL, HIT AND RUN, RECKLESS ENDANGERMENT, I DON'T KNOW WHERE TO BEGIN.
WE CAN EXPLAIN, RIGHT, BROTHER ZED?
OF COURSE!
PHONE CALL! I GET A PHONE CALL!!!

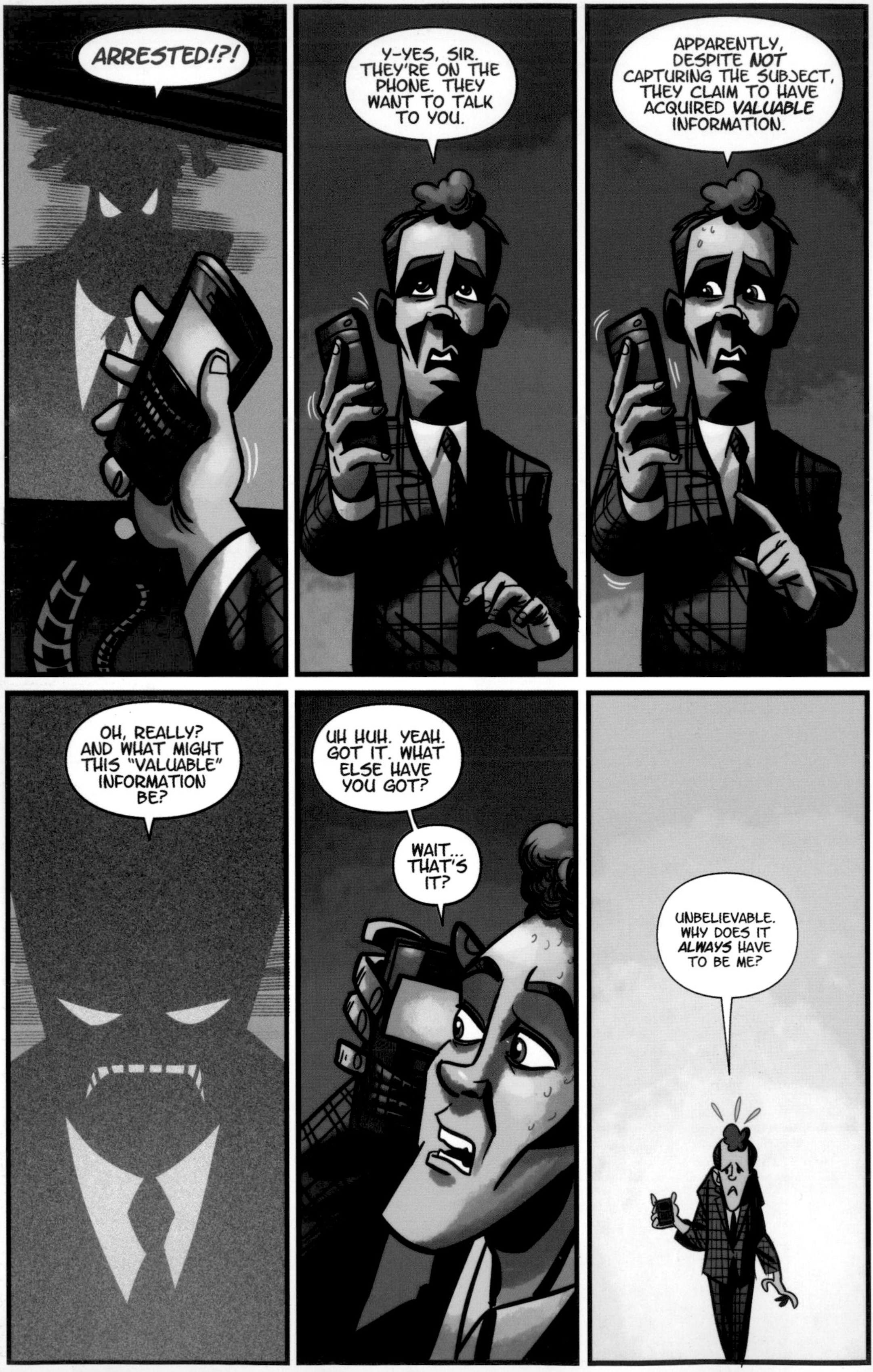
ARRESTED!?!
Y-YES, SIR. THEY'RE ON THE PHONE. THEY WANT TO TALK TO YOU.
APPARENTLY, DESPITE NOT CAPTURING THE SUBJECT, THEY CLAIM TO HAVE ACQUIRED VALUABLE INFORMATION.
OH, REALLY? AND WHAT MIGHT THIS "VALUABLE" INFORMATION BE?
UH HUH. YEAH. GOT IT. WHAT ELSE HAVE YOU GOT?
WAIT... THAT'S IT?
UNBELIEVABLE. WHY DOES IT ALWAYS HAVE TO BE ME?

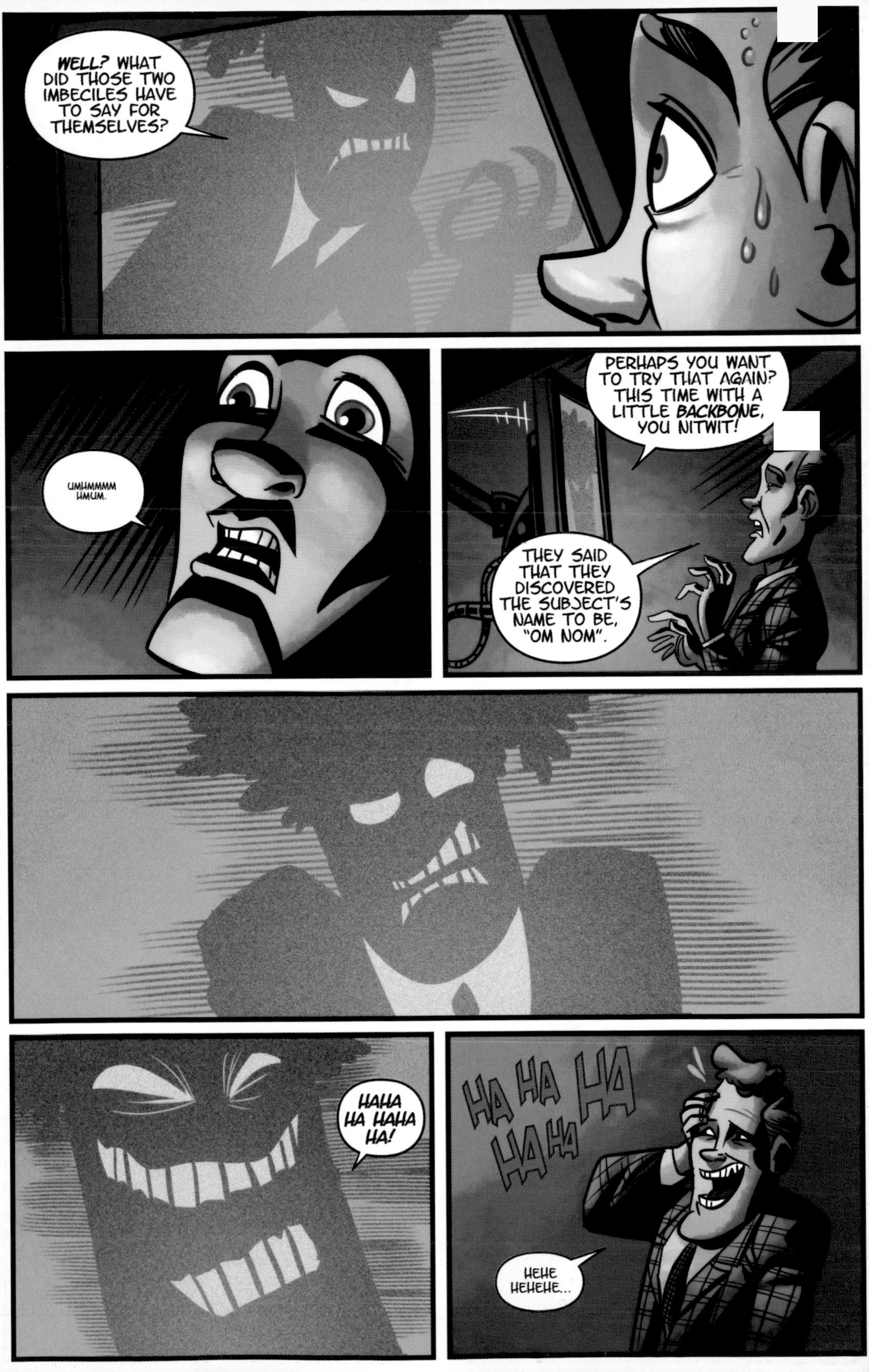
WELL? WHAT DID THOSE TWO IMBECILES HAVE TO SAY FOR THEMSELVES?
UMHMMMM HMUM.
PERHAPS YOU WANT TO TRY THAT AGAIN? THIS TIME WITH A LITTLE BACKBONE, YOU NITWIT!
THEY SAID THAT THEY DISCOVERED THE SUBJECT'S NAME TO BE, "OM NOM".
HAHA HA HAHA HA!
HA HA HA HA HA
HEHE HEHEHE...

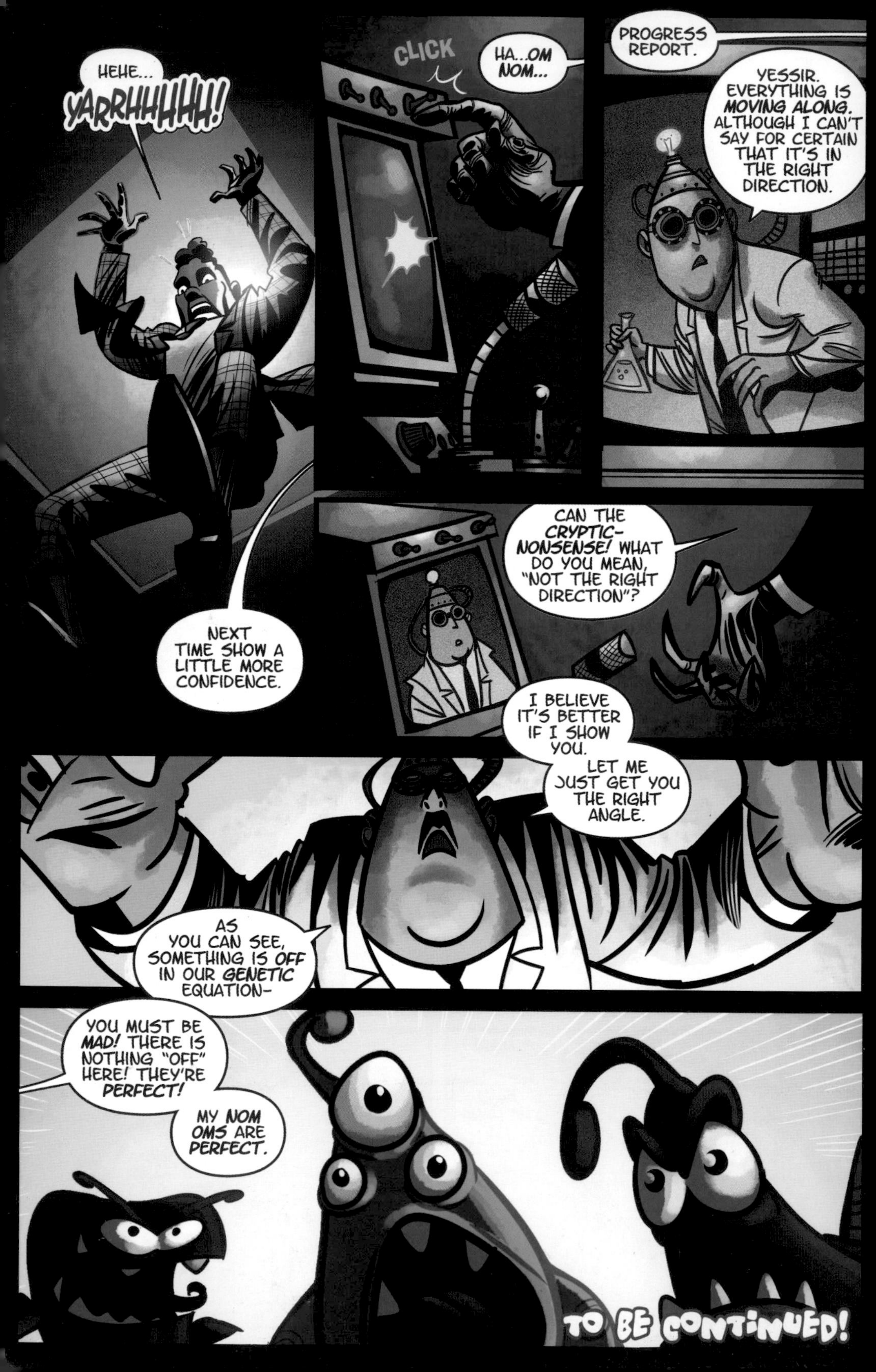
HEHE... YARRHHHHH!
CLICK
HA...OM NOM...
PROGRESS REPORT.
YESSIR. EVERYTHING IS MOVING ALONG. ALTHOUGH I CAN'T SAY FOR CERTAIN THAT IT'S IN THE RIGHT DIRECTION.
NEXT TIME SHOW A LITTLE MORE CONFIDENCE.
CAN THE CRYPTIC-NONSENSE! WHAT DO YOU MEAN, "NOT THE RIGHT DIRECTION"?
I BELIEVE IT'S BETTER IF I SHOW YOU.
LET ME JUST GET YOU THE RIGHT ANGLE.
AS YOU CAN SEE, SOMETHING IS OFF IN OUR GENETIC EQUATION-
YOU MUST BE MAD! THERE IS NOTHING "OFF" HERE! THEY'RE PERFECT!
MY NOM OMS ARE PERFECT.
TO BE CONTINUED!

POCKET GOD

COMICS ARE HERE, ORDER TODAY!
AVAILABLE AT APECOMICS.COM

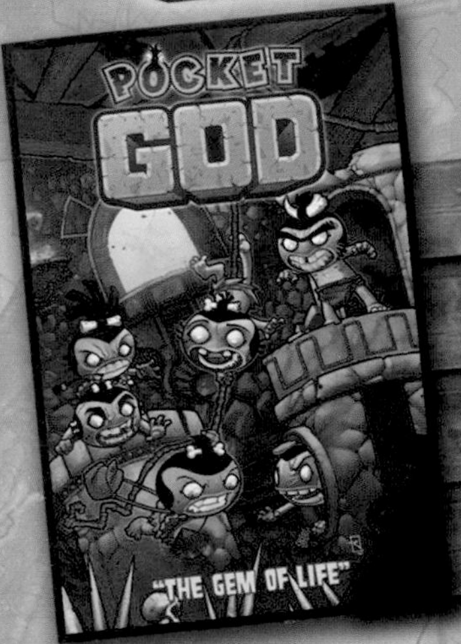
POCKET GOD
"THE GEM OF LIFE"

DIGEST #1 "THE GEM OF LIFE"

$9.99 FULL COLOR, DIGEST, 96 PG

"IF YOU'RE LOOKING FOR A BOOK THAT WILL PROVIDE YOU WITH SOME GOOD LAUGHS, THEN CHECK THIS ONE OUT!" -COMICNEWS.INFO

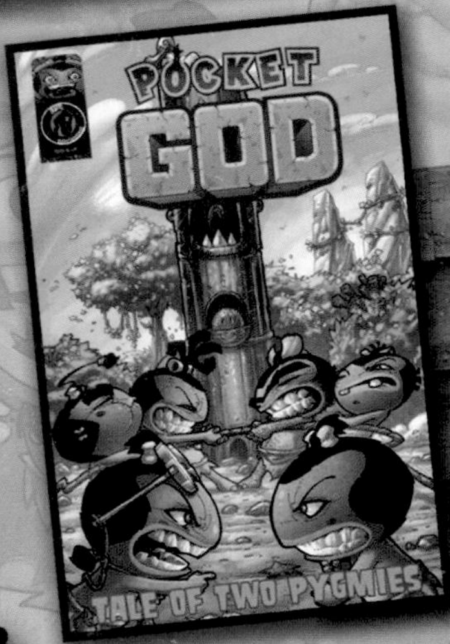
POCKET GOD
TALE OF TWO PYGMIES

DIGEST #2 "TALE OF TWO PYGMIES"

$12.99 FULL COLOR, DIGEST, 88 PG

"IF YOU'RE A FAN OF THE GAME, JUST LOOKING FOR A BREAK FROM THE HERO GENRE, OR IN SEARCH OF A BOOK TO RECOMMEND TO YOUNGSTERS, POCKET GOD SHOULD BE TOWARD THE TOP OF YOUR LIST."

-NEWSARAMA

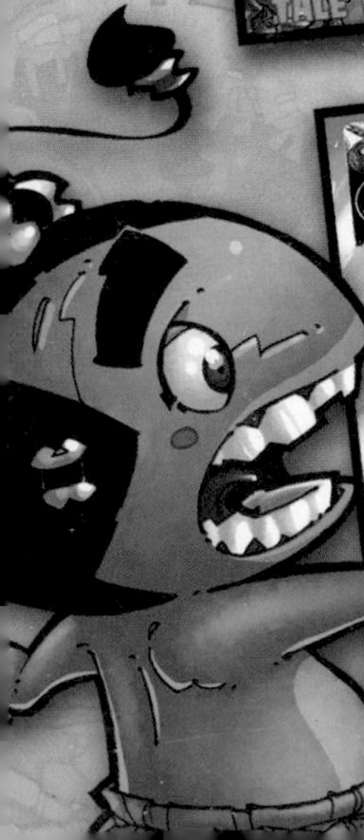

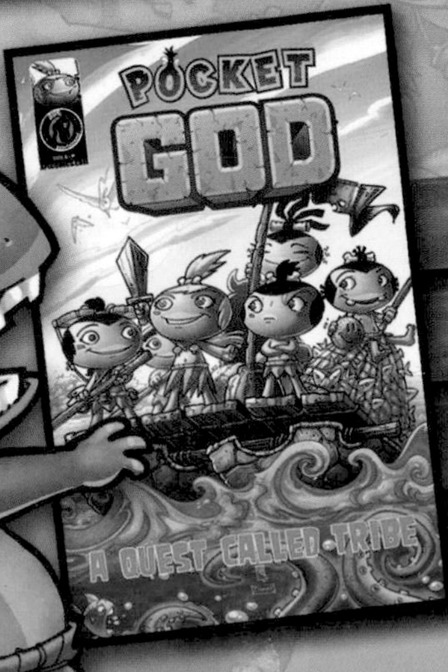
POCKET GOD
A QUEST CALLED TRIBE

DIGEST #3 "QUEST CALLED TRIBE"

$12.99 FULL COLOR, DIGEST, 104 PG

"THIS BOOK IS WAY BETTER THAN I WOULD HAVE EXPECTED IT TO BE. IT'S FUNNY, IT'S CUTE, AND IT'S JUST MORBID ENOUGH TO BE ENTERTAINING. EVEN IF YOU'RE NOT INTO THE GAME, THIS IS A BOOK THAT WILL GIVE YOU A GOOD CHUCKLE."

-COMIXTREME

Available on the App Store